1990

WOMEN
POETS
AND
THE
AMERICAN
SUBLIME

EVERYWOMAN: Studies in History,
Literature, and Culture

Susan Gubar, General Editor

WOMEN
POETS
AND
THE

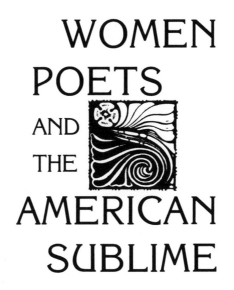

AMERICAN
SUBLIME

Joanne Feit Diehl

INDIANA
UNIVERSITY
PRESS

Bloomington & Indianapolis

Manufactured in the United States of America

Library of Congress Cataloging-in-Publication Data

Diehl, Joanne Feit.
Women poets and the American sublime / Joanne Feit Diehl.
p.   cm. — (Everywoman)
Includes bibliographical references.
ISBN 0-253-31741-X
1. American poetry—Women authors—History and criticism.
2. Women and literature—United States—History.   3. Sublime, The, in literature.   4. Sex role in literature.   I. Title.   II. Series.
PS310.S87E54   1990
811.009'9287—dc20   89-45859

1 2 3 4 5   94 93 92 91 90

With love for my daughter,
Catharine Elizabeth

. . . Then we,
As we beheld her striding there alone,
Knew that there never was a world for her
Except the one she sang and, singing, made.

—Wallace Stevens

With Midnight to the North of Her—
And Midnight to the South of Her—
And Maelstrom—in the Sky—

—Emily Dickinson, poem 721

It is like what we imagine knowledge to be:
dark, salt, clear, moving, utterly free,
drawn from the cold hard mouth
of the world, derived from the rocky breasts
forever, flowing and drawn, and since
our knowledge is historical, flowing, and flown.

—Elizabeth Bishop

CONTENTS

PREFACE

American women poets face both a burden and a challenge as they confront the magisterial tradition of the American Sublime. This book attempts first to clarify that tradition and second to study those women poets who inherit and, in various ways, revise it. I have chosen to focus on Dickinson, Moore, Bishop, Plath, and Rich because of their acknowledged eminence and my conviction that their work is essential to those of us who care about poetry. I have tried in my readings to attend to subtleties of style and modulations in sensibility; I have attempted to balance argumentation with textual interpretation. My project involves, therefore, not only the delineation of a gender-identified poetics, but also the close textual analysis that must guide literary study if generalizations, however theoretical, are to acquire meaning.

Initially, this book explores the ways in which major women poets respond to the Emersonian and Whitmanian identification of the poet as the central man and their vision of the poetic Sublime as a male-identified experience. If, as my opening chapter suggests, Emerson and Whitman define the power of the poet as exclusively male, if the poet at the center of the drama of inspiration is known by his gender, then women poets who would assert their own power must confront that conception and redefine the experiential Sublime in light of their identity as women. Each of the poets I discuss achieves her individuating approach to the Sublime as she simultaneously participates in the evolution of an alternative tradition. The aim of this book is to attend to these distinctive styles and, by bringing them to light, to trace the continuities and discontinuities among often apparently divergent voices. There are, of course, various intertextual links among the women poets treated here. Of these, the Moore-Bishop relationship is certainly the most intense and the most significant for any study of female poetic influence. But I reserve an extended investigation of the influence relations between these poets for a later project. In this book, I have chosen to incorporate recent critical work in gender studies, psychoanalytic insights, and techniques of literary interpretation to elucidate the ways in which women poets revise the Sublime in order to grant themselves access to its power. I ask that we consider how, in response to this revisionist poetics, we might reconceptualize the terms in which we view the American poetic canon and the work of those who stand in complex relation to it.

A note about method. In the opening chapter, I provide a working definition of the Sublime that is based more on contemporary psychoanalytic interpretations than upon Longinian and Kantian descriptions, although these, too, inform my thought. Working with this psychoanalytically inflected model, I evaluate Emerson's identification of the poet as central man and the Sublime as a gender-linked experience. I proceed to show how Whitman, with his passion for embodying Emersonian abstraction, re-creates a Sublime that is deeply implicated in the life of the body, in sensation, and, more specifically, in sexual feeling. I suggest, moreover, that Whitman's vision of women threatens to deprive individual women poets of their imaginative autonomy as it extols the preeminence of maternal power.

C.2.

I then turn to Dickinson, who offers an alternative version of the Sublime that disrupts Emerson's and Whitman's identifications of the poet with the natural world, the central man with the life of the imagination. The Dickinsonian Sublime, as I define it, repudiates the Whitmanian continuities between self and nature; instead, Dickinson designs an austere, conflictual poetics that counters all authority beyond her consciousness. Furthermore, Dickinson explicitly identifies the male (be he God, lover, or stranger) as benefactor and destroyer whose power endangers her literary authority. Responding to this intimidating benefactor, Dickinson asserts her own forbidding imaginative powers, creating poems that employ encoded linguistic forms and suppressed verbal aggression to wrest the Sublime away from the external and restore it to the self.

Subsequent chapters follow the trajectory outlined in the opening pages, focusing on the interrelations of sexual identity and poetic praxis in the work of twentieth-century American women poets. I devote a chapter to each poet, and my readings of individual poems, indeed, the choice of texts itself, reflect my interest in how a poem might reveal its values to further our understanding of the interactions between voice and word. What unites these discrete readings is my desire to identify the lineaments of a poetics related to the engendered imagination and to observe the ways in which self-conscious recognition of gender influences poetics. There are, of course, other women poets (one thinks especially of "H. D.") who could be read within this context. I have chosen, however, to limit the number of poets in order to elaborate upon their often ambivalent reactions to the burdensome yet potentially liberating legacy of the American Sublime.

A word, too, regarding the absence of a more overt, historicist approach. Although, like so many critics writing on women, I am deeply indebted to the literary historical work of Sandra Gilbert and Susan Gubar, I leave to them, with their powerful metaphoric and conceptual capacities, the delineation of a female literary tradition. One writes according to one's temperament, and in this regard, I recall Emerson's lament, "But I am not wise enough for a national criticism. . . ."

In addition to the work of Gilbert and Gubar, I am indebted to Margaret Homans, who so persuasively articulates the distinctive attributes of women's writing. Recent work in French feminist and linguistic theory, most notably the essays of Julia Kristeva, have changed the way I perceive issues of gender and language. The sociological and psychoanalytic work of Melanie Klein, Nancy Chodorow, and Juliet Mitchell, while not frequently alluded to in this study, has provided an important context in which to formulate my ideas. The revisionist work of those writing about the poetics of gender has necessarily influenced my own. Yet I am committed to writing about women poets from a pluralistic point of view; thus, this book is indebted to interpreters of lyric poetry as well as literary theorists. To elaborate my ideas, I have used what seemed most helpful, drawing upon critics of avowedly differing and often opposing schools of thought. I am especially grateful for the work of Harold Bloom, Marie Borroff, and Geoffrey Hartman, whose ideas I engage in various moments throughout this book. Finally, it is my hope that by participating in the continuing critical process of de-idealizing literary study, *Women Poets and the American Sublime* will not only contribute to our understanding of the women and men who write poetry, but also allow us to gauge with greater accuracy the work of women poets and so enable us to listen with a finer ear to the formidable eloquence of the American Counter-Sublime.

ACKNOWLEDGMENTS

I wish to take this opportunity to thank the individuals and institutions whose support and encouragement have enabled me to complete this book. I am grateful to the University of California, Davis, for Faculty Research Awards that have funded my work and to Bowdoin College for its research support. The librarians at the Houghton Library, Harvard University; the Humanities Research Center, the University of Texas at Austin; the Vassar College Library; and the Rosenbach Museum in Philadelphia have generously assisted me in my archival work.

I wish to thank as well those colleagues and friends who have contributed significantly to this project. My especial thanks to Sandra Gilbert, Susan Gubar, Alan Williamson, David Van Leer, Sandra McPherson, and Lee Edelman. To these and other friends, both within and beyond the scholarly community, I express my gratitude.

copyright © 1963 by Ted Hughes; "Nick and the Candlestick" copyright © 1966 by Ted Hughes; "Stings" copyright © 1963 by Ted Hughes; "The Jailer" copyright © 1962 by Ted Hughes; "Morning Song" copyright © 1961 by Ted Hughes; "Fever 103" copyright © 1963 by Ted Hughes; "Ariel" copyright © 1965 by Ted Hughes, reprinted by permission of Harper & Row, Publishers, Inc.

Excerpts from the following poems by Sylvia Plath: "Ode for Ted," "Virgin in a Tree," "Three Women," "Elm," "You're," "Crossing the Water," "Poppies in July," "Poppies in October," "Totem," "Berck-Plage," "Contusion," "Poems, Potatoes," "Barren Woman," "Gulliver," "Getting There," "Amnesiac," reprinted by permission of Harper & Row, Publishers, Inc.

Excerpts from the following prose and poems by Adrienne Rich, reprinted by permission of W. W. Norton & Company, Inc. and Virago Press, Ltd.: "Women and Honor: Some Notes on Lying"; "When We Dead Awaken: Writing as Re-Vision"; and "Power and Danger: Works of a Common Woman," in *On Lies, Secrets, and Silence: Selected Prose (1966–78)*. Lines from "Power"; "Phantasia for Elvira Shatayev"; "Splittings"; "Twenty-One Love Poems," I, V, VII, XIII, XXI; "Cartographies of Silence"; "Natural Resources"; "Toward the Solstice"; "Transcendental Etude"; "Contradictions: Tracking Poems," 29, 15, 11, 24; "Sources," II, IV, V, VI, VII, XV, XVII, XXII, XXIII; "Emily Carr"; "Poetry III"; "Blue Rock"; "The Blue Ghazals."

The following poems by Wallace Stevens are reprinted with the permission of Alfred A. Knopf, Inc.: "The American Sublime"; "The Auroras of Autumn"; "Idea of Order at Key West"; and "The Owl in the Sarcophagus."

WOMEN
POETS
AND
THE
AMERICAN
SUBLIME

1

FROM EMERSON TO WHITMAN

Engendering the Sublime

Emerson, the father of the American Sublime, writing in 1837, revels in the possibilities of the power that emanates from new men in a new land, a power that has its source in abandonment to "the nature of things," in an ecstasy of release:

> It is a secret which every intellectual man quickly learns, that beyond the energy of his possessed and conscious intellect he is capable of a new energy (as of an intellect doubled on itself), by abandonment to the nature of things; that beside his privacy of power as an individual man, there is a great public power on which he can draw, by unlocking, at all risks, his human doors, and suffering the ethereal tides to roll and circulate through him; then he is caught up into the life of the Universe, his speech is thunder, his thought is law, and his words are universally intelligible as the plants and animals.[1]

Transformed by the universe flowing through him, the new man experiences the apotheosis of the Emersonian Sublime—one with the world, he assumes its authority, his speech achieving the clarity of cosmic law. Implicit in this wondrous transformation is Emerson's faith in the self's ability to open doors, experience the flood, and speak with a voice of thunder in language bold as it is clear, a language where sign and signification are one. Yet Emerson's assertion presents difficulties not easily overcome by poets of lesser confidence or by those who lack the support of a tradition, even if it be one Emerson himself would advise the new man to discard.[2] Women poets experience the burden of these difficulties in ways that bar their free access to the Sublime, for gender blocks the identifications Emerson so fluently assumes. If the principle of desire governs the subject's reaching for fulfillment in the Sublime, then the Sublime finds its origins in the realm of eros. Thus, the relation of sexual identity to the quest for the Sublime reveals the woman poet's provisional status within the Romantic literary tradition.

Translated into psychosexual terms, the tensions of the experiential Sublime have been most clearly articulated by Bruce Clarke:

Sublimity is psychologically cognate with the structure of desire and its repression: it is the mark of the momentary intense experience of a discontinuity between desire and the possibility of its fulfillment. Sublimation occurs on either side of this moment: it pertains to the status quo disrupted by the sublime encounter, and consequent upon this disruption works towards the reinstatement of a renewed, although possibly altered, equilibrium. . . . The sublime tends to accentuate disparities, or to create them; it tends to break continuities and open epistemological gaps—it is the creature of duality . . . sublimity is generally the preferred term for great poetry or great experience; it is the attribute of those moments of confrontation, risk, trial, or terror, at which point one's great lessons are learned. Yet efficacy of sublimation will determine our relative ability to convert the experience of sublimity into daily use.[3]

In the play of desire and its repression, in the currents between sublimation and the Sublime, Clarke finds the strength of the Wordsworthian imagination and, I would venture, the tradition of a naturalizing Romanticism. Women poets, however, experience difficulty in achieving access to this version of the Sublime because in order to withstand the accentuated disparities, the breaking up of continuities, and the re-creation of an experiential duality, the poet must have faith that he/she retains the capacity to survive such an upheaval intact—either that the self will reassert its power after the tide of Spirit has ebbed, or that the external power is experienced as being related to the self, and so possession, in some hidden way, becomes a repossession of uncharted regions of the self.[4] The poet, furthermore, must believe that he can find within not only the restitutive capacity for survival, but also the ability to call forth language adequate to the experience he has undergone. As Emerson assures us, the poet thus speaks for all men, although paradoxically (and such paradoxes lie at the heart of the experiential Sublime), the internal power he discovers depends upon the energies of the world.

But the woman poet does not, in the nineteenth century, or for that matter in the early twentieth century, perceive herself as speaking for commonal experience, as "representative." Instead, women poets more often perceive themselves as exceptions, as isolates, departing from, rather than building upon, a tradition. Thus, when the external power floods into the self, so that the self must momentarily fall away, the subject experiences no assurance either that this influx of power shares her identity or that the Sublime encounter, once undergone, will prove emblematic for a whole company of poets, prove true for womankind as a recognizable, emergent tradition. Thus, the woman poet is particularly susceptible to the dangers of a momentary discontinuity such as Clarke describes, for it severs her from the origins as well as the fulfillment of her desire by rendering her passive in literary as well as in biographical terms. The woman poet who possesses an independent, heterodox intellect would be wary of such experience, dreading its power to usurp her energies as she acknowledges the crucial nature of the Sublime encounter itself.

In more explicitly Freudian terms, Thomas Weiskel describes the oedipal interactions at the heart of the Romantic Sublime, an experience that threatens to vanquish the poet as it challenges the autonomous imagination. This sense of threat fades, Weiskel notes, when the poet can recognize the identity between himself and the engulfing Other (an identity, I would add, that women poets cannot simply assume): "The fantasy of injury ends in the simultaneous perception of defeat and the realization that the threat is not, after all, a real one. This makes possible a positive resolution of the anxiety in the delight of the third phase, which is psychologically an identification with the superior power."[5] This reconciliation won by poets who survive to write of the Sublime presents the crux of the difficulty for women. Traditionally the superior power can be either the image of patriarchal authority whose spirit in Freudian terms would merge with the father's or, for the poets of a naturalizing Romanticism, a feminine image, Mother Nature who weds as she nurtures her son. Indeed, this second pattern, with its carefully modulated violation of the incest taboo, defends against a too literal psychosexual examination of the workings of the Romantic Sublime. Yet it is just here that women poets encounter their major conflict with the traditional manifestations of the Sublime experience, a difficulty that threatens to cut them off from the rest of Sublimity—from achieving the poetry of grandeur and consummation that draws on a power greater than that found in the conscious self alone. If this vision of power describes the imagination's experience of unconscious forces, then the question becomes how women's experience of the unconscious redefines rhetorical forms. But I wish for the moment to stay within the realm of an idealizing poetics and speculate that women poets must redefine their relationship to this authority as they have had to reimagine their relationships with their poetic precursors. As Weiskel shows us, the workings of poetic influence and the experience of the Sublime are intimately related and often merge into a single phenomenon when that external presence finds its authority in an earlier poet.[6]

Consider the possibilities—if authority is associated with the patriarch, then the woman poet cannot so easily experience the identity between self and all-powerful other; instead, his presence may seem so "ravishing" (a term long associated with the workings of the Sublime), that she is vanquished. As avatar of the patriarch, his power remains external to hers, for she is not the son who joins that male company of descendental poets known as poetic tradition. If, on the other hand, the woman poet experiences this external power as feminine, as the mother, her "inspiration" does not impart the gift of tradition. Instead, the woman poet develops an alternative line of descent where the maternal image coincides with poetic identity. This matriarchal genealogy—although promising future power—remains largely nascent in the nineteenth century, the power of the poet/mother yet to be freed. Consequently, verbal inspiration may tentatively be identified by the woman poet with maternal/natural forces, an identification that carries with it an aura of the heterodox and a quality of subversion, resulting from the disrupted canonical relations of poet to muse. The male poet resolves his difficulties—the terrifying discontinuity in his selfhood—by aligning himself with the culturally assumed identity of the patriarchal voices of authority, at once reclaiming his own superiority without denying access to the reciprocal relationship between the imagination and the natural world. Not so, the woman poet. Faced with an overdeterminacy born of a relationship where her position as passive, receptive self mirrors her culturally assumed identity, a relationship where the authoritative power *is* the masculine other, she is either silenced by the incursions of the Sublime or radicalized by the process. But before investigating the relations of women poets to the American Sublime, I return to the tradition's origins, to the conditions of the soil that create the spirit of poetry in the wilderness.

EM.

The imagination whose power initially shapes the tradition of the American Sublime is, of course, Emerson's, and it is to his conception of the Sublime that I return. Critics have rightly emphasized the orphic power of the Emersonian Sublime, its regenerative and liberating aspects. If one views the American Sublime from an antithetical vantage point, however, other, more disturbing qualities appear that illuminate the severely exclusionary character of this tradition for women poets, exiled by definition from apprehensions of the native Sublime and banished from their traditional social sphere of domesticity. Emerson's sweeping gesture of inclusiveness, his great incursion of power into the Me, incorporates both male and female identities and appropriates the language of the home to describe male consciousness. Emerson's vision of the Poet does more, however, than simply relegate the domestic world to the province of men. Following his Romantic fathers, Emerson claims the domestic sphere for the poet and finds in the ordinary, in household implements and daily physical experience, the groundwork of the Sublime.[7]

> . . . I embrace the common, I explore and sit at the feet of the familiar, the low. Give me insight into today, and you may have the antique and future worlds. What would we really know the meaning of? The meal in the firkin; the milk in the pan; the ballad in the street; the news of the boat; the glance of the eye; the form and the gait of the body;—show me the ultimate reason of these matters; show me the sublime presence of the highest spiritual cause lurking, as always it does lurk, in these suburbs and extremities of nature . . .[8]

"The Am." Scholar

Such an assertion apparently offers both men and women renewed access to the origins of the experiential Sublime, divorcing Sublimity from the exotic, the terrifying, the strange, and severing its ties from the Gothic imagination to which it had historically been so closely allied. This advantageous revision (particularly for women both as victims in the Gothic and as dominant presence in the house) becomes starkly modified, however, when Emerson moves from the world of things to a landscape of persons. For here the domestic world of dailiness quickly becomes an enemy of the single soul's quest for the Sublime as the knot of family affections threatens to shatter the requisite solitude of the individual, thus disrupting the possibility of apprehending the Oversoul.

If Emerson laments the ruins of the affective life, he cannot satisfactorily resolve this conflict, for it remains to haunt him through his last years. When they stand in the way of the "great and crescive self," the soul rejects family ties, turning its attentions exclusively within. "I shun father and mother and wife and brother when my genius calls me" (Emerson in *Self-Reliance*).[9] Such whim is not, of course, without its human implications, implications that force a choice between the mediating aspects of personal relationships and the Sublime experience of the Self's union with the Oversoul, unencumbered by any other human presence.[10] Incorporating domesticity within the Self as subject, the Me further severs the possibility of family ties and the discrete balancings of friendship to attend to the solitary imagination's enterprise. Thus women are doubly excluded from Emerson's poetic program—they are neither required for the domestic sphere (recall *Walden,* Thoreau's project of celibate domesticity) nor needed to fulfill a man's desire in the realm of the imagination. When Emerson identifies the Poet with Christ or ancient bard, his ancestors as well as origins assert their patriarchal associations. Although this identification is certainly not new in Emerson, its force renders his poetic vision intensely exclusionary and dominated by male presence.

Even more severely than in British Romanticism, consequently, American Romanticism displaces the woman from poetic identity. Marriage between mind and nature no longer serves as the primary model for imaginative celebration; instead, the Wordsworthian epithalamion fades before the acquisitive demands of the Intellect ("marriage [in what is called the spiritual world] is impossible, because of the inequality between every subject and every object").[11] If such a vision leads Emerson to the brink of despair before a universe which contains only "I and the abyss," he can still potentially revive the powers of the single soul. But woman, apparently barred from identification with the Poet as the new Christ, removed from the plane of domestic activity appropriated by men, and denied access to the speaking Soul's affective life, finds herself virtually stripped both of her province and her power. When Emerson searches for an analogic language in which to describe the psychic process of poetic activity to delineate the poet's power, he chooses a myth that entwines heterosexual and vegetative modes of reproduction. The engendering muse (product of heterosexual fantasy) no longer signifies the external force that bestows her blessing on the aspiring poet. Instead, Emerson picks, for his analog, the agaric (the mushroom), which does, of course, shed its seeds but requires no feminine body in which to nurture growth. As Thoreau supplants heterosexual activity with the workings of metamorphosis as a way to abrogate the feminine, so in his use of the fungus metaphor Emerson bypasses human sexuality as a trope for poetic fertility. Here is Emerson:

> Genius is the activity which repairs the decays of things, whether wholly or partly of a material and finite kind. Nature, through all her kingdoms, insures herself. Nobody cares for planting the poor fungus; so she shakes down from the gills of one agaric countless spores, any one of which, being preserved, transmits new billions of spores tomorrow or next day. The new agaric of this hour has a chance which the old one had not. This atom of seed is thrown into a new place, not subject to the accidents which destroyed its parent two rods off. She makes a man; and having brought him to ripe age, she will no longer run the risk of losing this wonder

at a blow, but she detaches from him a new self, that the kind may be safe from accidents to which the individual is exposed. So when the soul of the poet has come to ripeness of thought, she detaches and sends away from it its poems or songs,—a fearless, sleepless, deathless progeny, which is not exposed to the accidents of the weary kingdom of time; a fearless, vivacious offspring, clad with wings (such was the virtue of the soul out of which they came) which carry them fast and far, and infix them irrecoverably into the hearts of men. . . .[12]

Although the obvious emphasis in Emerson's passage is on the power of the poet's genius to survive the ravages of time, this description of poetic production as a form of natural survival carries within it, like the seeds of the agaric itself, its own subtext—that of sexual politics, which has significant implications for the woman who seeks a place for herself as creator. Although originally the agaric is identified with the feminine principle of nature, sexual identification changes as the seed drops to form new life: "She makes a man." Nature limits her role to a maternal function by paradoxically ensuring *asexual* reproduction—she creates the agaric (as male poet), which goes on to reproduce without the necessity of a female partner. Thus, in the preservation of the initiatory maternal form, Emerson discovers a reassuring means for accommodating the principle of sexuality in a world he determinedly seeks to defeminize; the feminine plays the role of functionary in the latter stages of the agaric's creation, detaching from him a new self. Here, Mother Nature's active introduction into the agaric's life cycle is to remove and plant again, activities that demand no reciprocal participation on the part of the agaric (this circumstance itself perhaps a cause of male anxiety). In this extended description of poetic immortality, Emerson conjoins the asexual pattern of agaric regeneration and a human, albeit remarkably dephysicalized, myth of procreation. Emerson invokes human regeneration as he evades it, keeping before us the image of maternity while developing a paradigm that eschews mature heterosexuality.[13]

Marriage not only fails as a model for poetic propagation but also as a symbol for the mind's relations with other selves. The consequences of such disparity are to render affective relationships tenuous. "All private sympathy is partial. Two human beings are like globes, which can touch only in a point, and whilst they remain in contact all other points of each of the spheres are inert; their turn must also come, and the longer a particular union lasts the more energy of appetency the parts not in union acquire."[14] So we are drawn away from each other, thrust back upon our original confrontation between the Me and the Not Me. When Self communes with the powers outside it, nature alone can be our bride. But even this attenuated marriage metaphor is, throughout Emerson, further qualified, for he distrusts to the point of denying the power of anything beyond the great and crescive Self.[15] This tenuous marriage with nature, caged in by doubts and often denied in principle, serves to erase the possibility of any explicitly human mutuality that can survive the incursions of the acquisitive imagination. Instead of denying the process of physical regeneration, Emerson recurrently alters the patterns of relationships so that propagation can occur without recourse to heterosexual activity. So complete is Emerson's usurpation of sexuality by the intellect that it is easy to overlook its implications for a woman poet as reader of Emerson's text, the reader who finds herself not only excised from his vision of home, family, or sexual intimacy, but also severed from the very powers associated with her gender, for "mother" nature is more a benign, elderly godmother than an active mate. Sensing the implications of such a dismissal, the woman committed to poetry would struggle to retrieve from the Emersonian conception of the poet fragments applicable to herself.

Speaking before a meeting of the Woman's Rights Convention in Boston on 20 September 1855, Emerson combines a vision of the possibilities opening to women and a firm sense of the individuating qualities, talents, and limitations of her sex. Making the by-now-familiar argument that women possess a greater sensibility, "are more delicate than men," and hence are "more impression-able," Emerson asserts that they are "the best index of the coming hour."[16] But in this very locution, he renders woman a phenomenon to be observed, reifying her into a text (no matter how prophetic) to be read. Drawing upon Plato, Emerson states, "Women are the same as men in faculty, only less in degree. But the general voice of mankind has agreed that they have their own strength; that women are strong by sentiment; that the same mental height which their husbands attain by toil, they attain by sympathy with their husbands. Man is the will, and Women the sentiment." Because "the life of the affections is primary to them" ("Woman," 407) women are best suited to "making that civilization which they require; that state of art, of decoration, that ornamental life in which they best appear." Due to their sensibility, "women," in Emerson's eyes, are more vulnerable than men.

> More vulnerable, more infirm, more mortal than men, they could not be such excellent artists in this element of fancy if they did not lend and give themselves to it. They are poets who believe their own poetry. They emit from their pores a colored atmosphere, one would say, wave upon wave of rosy light, in which they walk evermore, and see all objects through this warm-tinted mist that envelops them.

But this rose-tinted description itself converts woman into a poem, reifying her by depriving her of the necessary distance Emerson believes essential to the active intellect. All is sensibility; there is no backbone. If she is deprived of action through excess of praise, "woman," in Emerson's view, achieves mastery through humility: "We men have no right to say it, but the omnipotence of Eve is in humility. The instincts of mankind have drawn the Virgin Mother—'created beings all in loveliness/Surpassing, as in height above them all.' " Thus the process of idealization has done its work, the conventionally Victorian strategy of so praising woman as to render her powerless in any meaningful way is complete. Witnessing the cultural ramifications of change, Emerson responds by suggesting that "woman should find in man her guardian," reassuring his audience that "the new movement is only a tide shared by the spirits of man and woman; and you may proceed in the faith that whatever the woman's heart is prompted to desire, the man's mind is simultaneously prompted to accomplish."[17] Ready to do her bidding, man has become essential to her own fulfillment. With his consummate authority and intellectual economy, Emerson courts as he undercuts his audience of women.[18]

There is, however, another woman who emerges from Emerson's imagination, one who transcends the platitudes of his Convention speech. In the essay "Heroism," the visionary power Emerson has so often bestowed upon the American scholar he ascribes to the new woman herself.

> Or why should a woman liken herself to any historical woman, and think, because Sappho, or Sevigne, or De Stael, or the cloistered souls who have had genius and cultivation do not satisfy the imagination and the serene Themis, none can— certainly not she? Why not? She has a new and unattempted problem to solve, perchance that of the happiest nature that ever bloomed. Let the maiden, with erect soul, walk serenely on her way, accept the hint of each new experience, search in turn all the objects that solicit her eye, that she may learn the power and the charm of her newborn being, which is the kindling of a new dawn in the recesses of space. The fair girl who repels interference by a decided and proud choice of influences, so careless of pleasing, so wilful and lofty, inspires every beholder with somewhat of her own nobleness. The silent heart encourages her; O friend, never strike sail to a fear! Come into port gently, or sail with God the seas. Not in vain you live, for every passing eye is cheered and refined by the vision.[19]

Intriguingly, the maiden wins admiration if she can choose among her influences, thus preserving a serenity and independence that could seem admirable only to someone who shunned any appearance of influence—Emerson himself. By the paragraph's close, this stoic Diana of the intellect has metamorphosed into a ship that, when sighted, "cheers" and "refines" others' vision. This description, while emphasizing the processual journey of the "fair girl" into knowledge of the self, simultaneously usurps her power of action as she becomes an object intended to enlighten the eye of the observer. Her statuesque calm is a far cry from Emerson's impassioned description of the American Poet seized by the demonic Sublime:

> Doubt not, O poet, but persist. Say "It is in me, and shall out." Stand there, balked and dumb, stuttering and stammering, hissed and hooted, stand and strive, until at last rage draw out of thee that *dream*-power which every night shows thee is thine own; a power transcending all limit and privacy, and by virtue of which a man is the conductor of the whole river of electricity. Nothing walks, or creeps, or grows, or exists, which must not in turn arise and walk before him as exponent of his meaning. Comes he to that power, his genius is no longer exhaustible. All the creatures by pairs and by tribes pour into his mind as into a Noah's ark, to come forth again to people a new world.[20]

Generative, life-giving, powerfully irresistible, the poet becomes the "true landlord! sea-lord! air-lord!"[21] Could this poet, as Emerson envisions him, be a woman? If she stood "balked and dumb, stuttering and stammering, hissed and hooted," would she not be labeled mad? Or, in an earlier time, declared a witch? Surely, this recuperative, wildly impassioned, utterly free Emersonian moment of the poetic Sublime belongs only to the man. Note, by contrast, how severely Emerson controls his vision of the "heroic" woman walking alone. She is virginal, silent, an isolated object of observation, whereas a vast attractant power emanates from the male poet, and all life serves him as "exponent of his meaning." Herein lies the fundamental distinction, as defined by Emerson, between the possibilities of heroism for men and for women.

II

If Emerson offered the woman poet a sense of the imagination's possibilities while simultaneously according her an inherently secondary and passive position in terms of those possibilities, it is Walt Whitman, with his assertions of power, aggressive amativeness, and supremely iconoclastic poetics, who defines the American Sublime. As Whitman himself was quick to recognize, the poetic identity toward which he aspired is innately associated with corporeal presence. The elision of body and text, the insistence that the reader experience the poem as body, informs a poetics that underscores the imagination's coupling of poetic and sexual powers. Such an identification, based upon the presence of the imminent Self, serves to restrict (as the text overtly invites) other persons' involvement in poetic activity. So insistent is the Whitmanian voice on its own presence that it leaves little or no room, despite repeated democratic avowals, for the voices of others. Whitman's assertion of his priority, inclusiveness, and ability to triumph over restrictions of time and place implies a controlling authority that challenges the independence of all persons and experiences beyond himself.[22]

Such a poetics, at once prescriptive and oracular (with its assertion that Walt Whitman is both "one of the roughs" and a prophetic sage), has a long-recognized, undeniably powerful impact upon the history of American poetry. That the form of Whitman's poetic embodiment is male, that he takes upon himself the task of reenvisioning and so remaking the character of all experience beyond the self, intensifies women poets' sense of their exclusion from the possibilities of the Emersonian imagination and the Whitmanian or American Sublime.[23] Burdensome though this influence may be, the centrality of Whitman for women poets in America should not be ignored, having much to tell us not simply about individual influences, but also about larger questions concerning the imagination and gender. Although Whitman explicitly emphasizes the need for women to achieve a position of equality in American life, his vision is an inherently mythologizing one. For the woman reader, therefore, Whitman's poetics presents an especially frustrating double bind: at once offering the woman of imagination a potential equality while committing her, within his own work, to an archetypal, hence restrictive role as a procreative force. Whether it would be possible in Whitman's conceptual universe for the woman to achieve a poetic independence apart from her biological identification as maternal muse remains an open question, one that troubles future women poets who

seek access to Whitmanian authority while being forced by his conceptualiza-
tion of the feminine to renounce the position he would assign them.

If Whitman envisions the maternal presence at the beginning and the end of
things, his poetry enacts a desire for such a union, for contact, for words that will
touch the Mother. Fearing as he desires her, Whitman is compelled to invent a
language adequate to these desires. In Whitman's omnivorous, expansive poem
"By Blue Ontario's Shore," the Mother's image functions as a refrain, calling the
poet back from his far-flung imaginative journeys. Even during the moment of
Sublime election, when Whitman summons the "loftiest bards of past ages"
(the preeminent motive for his poems), the dread Mother does not evade but
rather supplants the entire male poetic tradition. As if the principle of the Mother
were to remain the only true idea, it resides in the poem as a test against the
accretions of geography, of travel, and of life. Here, in the Sublime Whitmanian
moment, the Mother appears at the heart of the heart of things:

> Thus by blue Ontario's shore,
> While the winds fann'd me and the waves came trooping toward
>   me,
> I thrill'd with the power's pulsations, and the charm of my theme
>   was upon me,
> Till the tissues that held me parted their ties upon me.
>
> And I saw the free souls of poets,
> The loftiest bards of past ages strode before me,
> Strange large men, long unwaked, undisclosed, were disclosed to
>   me.[24]

If earlier, Whitman had turned to the Mother for the blessing of understanding, a
primal word equivalent to her nurturant milk, now he discovers what he already
knows, that his words' origins reside less with the male poetic tradition than with
that maternal principle: "Not for bards of the past," he chants, but "to cheer O
Mother your boundless expectant soul" (section 20).[25] He begs to be succored
for life, to find the sustenance that will quench the imagination's need as it once
fed the "infant self."

> (Mother, bend down, bend close to me your face,
> I know not what these plots and wars and deferments are for,
> I know not fruition's success, but I know that through war and
>   crime your work goes on, and must yet go on.)
>   (18.313–15, p. 355)

Surely the Mother is both justification and answer to the otherwise unfathom-
able logic of war and human suffering.[26] Whitman had earlier elided the
maternal with the democratic into a politics of the family that becomes a
national identity:

(Democracy, while weapons were everywhere aim'd at your breast,
I saw you serenely give birth to immortal children, saw in dreams
    your dilating form,
Saw you with spreading mantle covering the world.)
                                             (17.297–99, p. 354)

Although here Whitman draws upon the popular association of the democratic nation with the matronly ideal, the Whitmanian Mother is easily distinguished from her stereotypic sisters.

Yet, essential as the Whitmanian Mother may be, she remains an instrument, as through her, the poet reaffirms *his* own priority. Despite the mother's powers, without the poet she would remain barren. Just as Whitman asserts that he bestows power upon woman by speaking for her, so he reclaims her fertility through his verbal as well as physical presence.

(Soul of love and tongue of fire!
Eye to pierce the deepest deeps and sweep the world!
Ah Mother, prolific and full in all besides, yet how long barren,
    barren?)
                                             (9.134–36, p. 347)

Gazing past Ontario's shores, the poem turns ever inward, testifying to its own faithfulness toward maternal origins.

(Say O Mother, have I not to your thought been faithful?
Have I not through life kept you and yours before me?)
                                             (14.248–49, p. 352)

Each parenthetical appeal to the Mother after a foray into visionary and expansive geography returns us to the groundtone of meaning, the plaintive dialogue between the pleading bard and his otherwise inarticulate female origins.

As if fearing abandonment by the Mother because he himself has and will travel from her, the poet returns to plead his case in her presence. The fear is always there, lurking under the surface of Whitman's textual plenitude, the fear of not having enough, of a deprivation at once maternal and cosmic, a fear that for all the journeyings of the imagination, he may discover, at their end, that he has lost what he most longed for—the *maternal* motive for the voyage itself.

Facing west from California's shores,
Inquiring, tireless, seeking what is yet unfound,
I, a child, very old, over waves, towards the house of maternity,
    the land of migrations, look afar, . . .

> Now I face home again, very pleas'd and joyous,
> (But where is what I started for so long ago?
> And why is it yet unfound?)
>   (no. 10, *Enfans d'Adam*, 1860 ed. "Facing West from
>   California's Shores")

At the edge of the continent, a boundary to which, in actuality, he never traveled, Whitman gazes over the threshold; and (as so often in the poems) Whitman merges the child he was with the old man he would will himself into becoming. The burden of memory reminds him of the haunting motive for his quest begun "so long ago." Searching for the house of maternity, Whitman discovers that it is "yet unfound." This troubling absence acquires an obsessive force as Whitman searches for the original plenitude that constitutes, through its lack, the restorative motive for making poems.

In other moods and at other times, Whitman manages to evade the plangent limitations of the disillusioned heroic self by insisting that all he requires can be found within, that the ever-expanding boundaries of the Self encompass all. And by incorporating the Female into the Self, he obliterates, if only intermittently, his otherwise intensely experienced sense of longing.

> I am of old and young, of the foolish as much as the wise,
> Regardless of others, ever regardful of others,
> Maternal as well as paternal, a child as well as a man, . . .
>   ("Song of Myself," 16.330–32, p. 44)

He continues to attest to his role as speaker for the woman as much as for the man, for her equality as subject, for her incorporation into himself.

> I am the poet of the woman the same as the man,
> And I say it is as great to be a woman as to be a man,
> And I say there is nothing greater than the mother of men.
>   ("Song of Myself," 21.425–27, p. 48)

While at once proclaiming her importance, indeed, through the very act of asserting the woman's power, Whitman renders her dependent upon his incorporative, exuberant speech. Such exuberance spells danger for the woman who reads, among other reasons, to discover ways to identify her own divergent consciousness, a vision founded in her perceptions apart from what Whitman would assign her in his mythological formulations of sexual identity.

From the beginning of *Leaves of Grass*, Whitman had sounded his theme: "The Female equally with the Male I sing" ("Inscriptions.", "One's-Self I Sing.," 5, p. 1), and he continues to assert that he not only gives woman her voice, but that he also has long anticipated and will now celebrate his arrival: "Daughter of the lands did you wait for your poet?" The question is, however, doubly rhetorical, for Whitman supplies both the form of the question and its unvoiced answer by honoring the speech that creates its own demand. His role is at once verbal and procreative, as essential as it is sought after. Listen again as Whitman skillfully employs a biological trope to assert his maculine powers:

> On women fit for conception I start bigger and nimbler babies,
> (This day I am jetting the stuff of far more arrogant republics) . . .

Whatever the eugenic origins of such an assertion (and much has been written about these sources), the relationships delineated by the claims of the phallus attempt to secure Whitman's centrality for the survival of the republic and for the fulfillment of women themselves. When such a phallogocentric appropriation conjoins with Whitman's other assertions of preeminence (his bids for control over time, the reader, and death itself), they create a superstructure impenetrable except by the internal pressures of his self-doubt and the hesitations of an acutely self-reflexive imagination. By constructing the identity of Self as Witness ("I am the man, I suffer'd, I was there") and by asserting that his perceptions measure the passage of time ("I am the clock / myself"), Whitman ironically fabricates the kind of self-sufficiency that renders him his own worst enemy ("Song of Myself," section 33.832, p. 66; section 331.857, p. 67). Like Dickinson's "Battle fought between the Soul and No Man," Whitman's inner confrontations challenge the survival of the self he seeks to protect. "Whoever denies me it shall not trouble me," Whitman assures us; yet a derogatory glance from the arrogant, internalized father may arrest if not completely destroy him. Only through the repetitive gestures of appropriation can the poet recuperate his Adamic Self ("Song of the Open Road," 6.70, p. 152).

Although Whitman may attempt to protect himself from internal and external threats to his powers by expressing his good will toward others, by coercing approval from those who might otherwise desire to reject or disparage him, he preserves an awareness of the risks of such amative aggression, a sense that he may have been defeated long before he has begun. The gentleness and pathos of Whitman's most moving poems stem from this groundtone of omnipresent loss. The thrust toward futurity, the incessant urge forward into the past, becomes a circular return whose trajectory has already been charted secretly and the impossibility of its destination silently acknowledged. This loss as well as the object of longing is tied to Woman both as mythic being and maternal presence. To admit the existence of an autonomous, preexistent Female would necessarily provoke resentment in a consciousness that must insist upon its self-originating powers and its self-willed authority to preserve its integrity of voice. Such covert resentment takes the form, in Whitman's poetics, of envisioning the Female as dependent. Thus the dynamics of the infant-mother relationship are inverted by the poet who envisions his muse as pleading for his arrival to ensure *her* progenerative possibilities. Searching Blue Ontario's shore, once again Whitman addresses the family of woman:

> (O Mother—O Sisters dear!
> If we are lost, no victor else has destroy'd us,
> It is by ourselves we go down to eternal night.)
> (2, 22–24, p. 341)

Against the inevitable progression from "Noon to Starry Night," the pain of separation from the Mother, "The Lord advances, and yet advances, / Always the shadow in front, always the reach'd hand bringing up the laggards" ("From Noon to Starry Night," 4.46–47, p. 466). So intimately austere are Whitman's metaphysics, so deeply implicated in the Family Romance, only the most extreme marshaling of forces can stave off the assaults of a world whose origins lie beyond the self. Ambition is therefore fueled by the need to outdistance its sources. As Whitman's appreciation of the beautiful, specular powers of nature ordains his commensurate anxiety over its intrusive possibilities, so the natural world becomes a projection of the poet's conflictual life and the ground for poetic transformation.

In a related conflict that grows out of a historical rather than a purely ontological awareness, Whitman defends against the anxiety of literary belatedness by predicating an equally intense anxiety of earliness. Here women poets paradoxically discover a precursor in Whitman, for if the woman poet must suffer from her sense of exclusion, the discontinuity between herself and the descendental tradition from which her gender putatively excludes her, she finds a commensurate if not directly equivalent defense in the claim of originality. Unburdened, because imaginatively excluded from the increasingly debilitating tradition of male poets that weighs so heavily upon its heirs, the woman poet can celebrate her earliness because of the very absence of this incremental history. She can reconstitute her illusory lack of tradition as a point of origin, thus celebrating her originality as Whitman can only strive to do. In his anomolous, self-created position as inheritor of the new, Whitman constructs himself as the American original by insisting upon his own ignorance (feigned, if not actual), a disruption of the formal continuities of poetry, and an armamentarium of techniques that causes his poems to resemble a revolutionary antipoetry.[27] Thus Whitman sustains the iconoclastic assertion of fulfilling Emerson's prophecy, the Emersonian dream of the new American poet.

Referring to himself in the third person, with the curiously intimate distance that characterizes his more ostensibly subjective allusions as well, Whitman strives to convert this primary anxiety into a more tolerable one: "Walt Whitman stands to-day in the midst of the American people, a promise, a preface, an overture. . . . Will he justify the great prophecy of Emerson?" (Whitman's notebook, 1855–56)[28]

The "preface" cannot disguise the fact that a "giant" has preceded it, creating the fear that Emersonian expectation will yield to disappointment. By anointing himself, by proclaiming himself the fulfillment of Emerson's dream, Whitman at once seeks to invoke the Father's blessing as he attempts to wrest his power from him. Time waits; it does not irrevocably carry him into the past, at least not without the possibility of his emerging triumphant at some otherwise unattainable future. Such a self-bestowal becomes a means of preserving continuity with the empowering Emerson while making his forebear himself appear to be yielding to a greater manifestation of earliness. Emersonian prophecy is thereby relegated to a historical belatedness much as the Old Testament antetype may become theologically secondary in regard to the later story it foretells. Moreover, Whitman's stance of expectation is not unrelated to his consciousness of himself as a distinctly masculine poet. The Other, externally and specifically female, depends upon his arrival for her completion:

> "Daughter of the lands did you wait for your poet?"
> "Did you wait for one with a flowing mouth and indicative hand?"
> ("Starting from Paumanok," 14.190, p. 24)

That "indicative" hand gestures outward to the essential feminine and inward toward itself *(dictare),* speaking by and through its very presence. "The great women's land! the feminine!" (14.207, p. 25), potentially powerful as it might be, relies upon the male poet for fruition.

Such fulfillment is not free of danger either for the male poet, wary of his own aggression, or for the daughter who awaits him. This power must be reckoned with on its own terms before the land, the feminine, can wrest from him the gift of entitlement.

> No dainty dolce affettuoso I,
> Bearded, sun-burnt, gray-neck'd, forbidding, I have arrived,
> To be wrestled with as I pass for the solid prizes of the universe,
> For such I afford whoever can persevere to win them.
> ("Starting from Paumanok," 15.233–36, p. 26)

These lines recall Dickinson's poem, "A little East of Jordan—," where the poet, identified as Jacob, wrestles with the disguised angel only to discover that he has "worsted God." The negativity conveyed by "worsted," strange in the face of Jacob's apparent victory, suggests the ambivalence Dickinson felt toward her own powers; if the poet could prove "superior" to God's creation, then she inhabited a world made vulnerable by her potential power, a world that not even God could protect from the poet's awesome powers. Whitman expresses a related but not identical ambivalence toward the powers of his imagination, for his gestures of epistemological appropriation involve a coercive intensity that carries rapine associations. He, too, fears his own power, seeking protection by himself projecting that power upon the world. To wrest from the world the requirements of the self, to "know" the world, implies acting upon it, a transgressive activity that Whitman conceptualizes primarily in sexual terms.[29] "Lusty and phallic, with potent original loins, perfectly sweet, he comes" ("Children of Adam," "Ages and Ages Returning at Intervals"). And if the nation would discover its destiny, it must yield to his coming: "Submit to the most robust bard till he remedy your barrenness. Then you will not need to adopt the heirs of others; you will have true heirs, begotten of yourself, blooded with your own blood."[30]

Himself made anxious by the transgressive cast of such a deliverance, Whitman repeatedly seeks to reduce these anxieties by reassuring the woman who waits that he will treat her with requisite care. Always on the move, poetically speaking, Whitman's story is one of expectation, union, and departure, the punctuations of eros, the trope of writing as an act of copulation wherein language itself becomes the medium for sexual satisfaction as well as the expression of loss. In an assertion that fuses pen with phallus, Whitman states, "I have offer'd my style to every one" ("So Long," 1.12, p. 504). The "stylus" as pointed instrument for writing or incising letters on a wax tablet was still a current term in mid-nineteenth-century America; thus the phallic associations of such a sharp, pointed object, combined with the distribution of the literary definition of "style," suggests the identification of Whitman's conception of himself as masculine as well as prolific. The ability to offer his radical style to everyone depends therefore upon his sexual identity. What would be par for democratic poetics thus acquires an oddly transgressive character when read in the light of Whitman's habitual conflation of the sexual and the poetic. With such a sexually operative trope, issues of gentleness and violation assume renewed importance. Thus Whitman periodically feels impelled to assuage his own anxieties by testifying to his tenderness, insisting that he means no harm, assuring us that his aggression is under control. When he announces his own arrival, he guards against his aggressivity with overt guarantees of discretion and altruistic good will.

> It is I, you women, I make my way,
> I am stern, acrid, large, undissuadable, but I love you,
> I do not hurt you any more than is necesssary for you,
> I pour the stuff to start sons and daughters fit for these States, I
>   press with slow rude muscle,
> I brace myself effectually, I listen to no entreaties,
> I dare not withdraw till I deposit what has so long accumulated
>   within me.
>   ("A Woman Waits For Me," *Children of Adam*, 25–30, p. 102–3)

The suggestion that the infliction of pain may be "necessary" for "you women" underscores as it guards against the fundamentally rapine structure of Whitman's trope for creativity. He must act *upon* the woman, in a gesture that is at once violative and empowering. This requisite aggression, though requiring an apology, nonetheless constitutes the Whitmanian dynamic of Self and female Other. And it is this relationship, long established in the tradition of Western poetics, that he links to the conception of the American Adam. Yet the anxiety Whitman seeks to suppress both in himself and the Female Other is not restricted to an exclusively sexual trope, for Whitman aspires to an essentially eroticizing poetics wherein sexual interdynamics are fundamental to his notion of textuality in and of itself. Indeed, the issue is one of contact, of Whitman's capacity to carry the word to the reader as a token of the corporeality of the author within the text. When Whitman achieves such a readerly intimacy, he violates the unstated assumptions of a more traditional bibliophilic relationship. By employing the trope of textuality/sexuality, Whitman discovers a way to reconcile anxiety with desire.[31]

Yet for Whitman, the "truth" remains that the male poet is as dependent upon the expectant, incomplete Feminine as she is upon him. The creation of the new American artist must, finally, be the result of union, not vanquishment.

> Through you I drain the pent-up rivers of myself,
> In you I wrap a thousand onward years,
> On you I graft the grafts of the best-loved of me and America,
> The drops I distil upon you shall grow fierce and athletic girls,
>   new artists, musicians, and singers. . . .
>   ("A Woman Waits For Me," 31–34, p. 103)

Though he "drains," "wraps," "grafts," "distils," the continuation of his power depends upon the "fierce and athletic girls" of the future. Interestingly, the anxiety Whitman seeks to suppress both in himself and in the Female Other is not restricted to this highly explicit sexual trope, for in Whitman's essentially eroticizing poetics, sexual dynamics inform his understanding of the idea of textuality itself, as the text serves in a dual capacity, carrying the word to the reader as it reembodies the author in his text. In this process of verbal embodiment, Whitman achieves an intimacy that strives to evade as it transgresses the very limits of language.[32]

By describing the relationship between reader and text in terms of physical contact, Whitman posits a quasisexual intimacy that may effectively sublimate desire. Such sublimation, however, extends only so far, for when Whitman describes the act of reading, the tactile pressure of the reader's hands releases a hitherto controlled desire in the reified text, as phallic play between reader and writer verifies the text's corporeal presence:

> Or if you will, thrusting me beneath your clothing,
> Where I may feel the throbs of your heart or rest upon your hip,
> Carry me when you go forth over land or sea;
> For thus merely touching you is enough, is best,
> And thus touching you would I silently sleep and be carried
>   eternally.
>   ("Whoever You Are Holding Me Now in Hand,"
>   "Calamus," 22–26, p. 116)

Here the book as object and as trope significantly controls the amative aggression that might otherwise disturb the balance between reader and text, checking Whitman's self-censored desires. As book, he becomes the passive member, reified into inaction, carried by the reader toward a greater physical intimacy. The passive regression elsewhere evident in Whitman, the urge to be lulled back to one's origins and lured effortlessly into a benign eternity, here reemerges. The medium for such convergence is the book as sexual agent that functions to preserve the poet's illusion of "innocence." Self becomes text in an inverted transubstantiation whereby word is not made flesh, but flesh word. Only through such a sublimating displacement of desire can Whitman accomplish his deeply regressive psychic task.

If, as Harold Bloom has remarked, the "woman poet reduces the male to muse," Whitman may be understood as reducing the male poet to text, thereby formulating the inherently masculinist poetics that we identify with the mode of the American literary sublime. If my assertion appears too sweeping or austere, I need only invoke Whitman's descendents, among them Williams, Pound, Eliot, Stevens, and Lowell, who, despite vast differences in tone, style, and philosophic outlook, embrace the Whitmanian fusion of Self with text, the identification of male sexual identity with American self-consciousness, and the power of naming with the inherited authority of the Adamic or Emersonian self.

And yet, if Whitman envisions the act of writing as an inherently sexual trope in which his appropriative aggression is tempered by a diffident generosity, he simultaneously incorporates a version of the feminine into that constitutive identity. Fundamental both to his sense of selfhood and his conception of an ideal audience, the woman becomes his interior paramour and most attentive reader. Late in life, Whitman confided,

> What lies behind Leaves of Grass is something that few, very few, only one here and there, perhaps oftenest women, are at all in a position to seize. It lies behind every line; but concealed, studiedly concealed; some passages left purposely obscure. There is something in my nature furtive like an old hen! You see a hen wandering up and down a hedgerow, looking apparently quite unconcerned, but presently she finds a concealed spot, and furtively lays an egg, and comes away as though nothing had happened. That is how I felt in writing Leaves of Grass.[33]

The homely image of the domestic fowl must have seemed particularly appropriate to a man who, despite his apparent openness, kept his life such a private affair. The furtiveness of the hen is both creative and instinctual, designed to protect her egg and to ensure its biological survival. Thus, the hen's feigned lack of concern, her Whitmanian casualness, screens the purposive nature of her activity. The humorously deflationary character of the farmyard allusion serves Whitman in a similar way—pointing toward his recognition of the importance of women as audience while suggesting that the desire for concealment on the part of the author participates in the culturally inscribed female requirement that she disguise her actions in order to protect her achievement. That the woman should be associated with the hen only underscores the preeminence that Whitman assigns women's reproductive capacities. Though humorous to the observer, the hen's behavior nevertheless functions to protect the life of her offspring (as the poet may seek a related defense to protect his art).

If Whitman overtly praises strong women, the image that emerges from the poems and that fully engages his imagination is one that emphasizes maternity. Justin Kaplan has asserted that Whitman "venerated Frances Wright, Margaret Fuller, George Sand, all of them feminists and agents of spiritual liberation." And Kaplan goes on to state that "the 'I' of Leaves of Grass is almost as often a woman as a man, and the book is a supremely passionate argument for the androgynous union of strength and tenderness, sagacity and impulse." "Androgyny," however, develops as the incorporation of female into male with the further reduction of woman to her representational functions as myth, muse, and mother.[34]

This sexual merging can, of course, be found in the workings of all powerful imaginations, male or female, but what is important is not whether and to what degree the female resides in the male or vice versa, but the poems' representations of gender identity and definition, for Whitman's poems assign women specific attributes that contribute/merge into an eidolon that primarily emphasizes the familial and the physical. Consequently, Whitman's seemingly empowering poetics remains tainted for the woman reader who would be a poet, for Whitman at once extols her preeminence as he restricts her opportunities for an autonomous life of the imagination. If, in politics, Whitman advocates women's perfect equality with men, and if, unlike Emerson, Whitman insists upon the necessity of an open recognition of sexuality as essential to the development of a just and healthy society, he almost never allows the woman within the poem to speak or to use words in the ways he so freely deploys. Morever, the Whitmanian conception of woman as strong, athletic, and self-reliant reinscribes his need for a race of perfect mothers, *not* for individuals with artistic or literary ambitions, even if those literary qualities would be a distinct advantage in achieving the nation's aesthetic as well as political independence. Whereas Whitman understands that man's progress depends upon that of woman, hardly ever does he entertain the possibility that history will be directly molded by the power of a courageous woman acting in and for herself.

Reacting to Emerson's apparent denial of the full impact of the growing women's-rights movements in the nineteenth century, Whitman, writing in 1856, breaks with him on this subject: "Of women just as much as men, it is the interest that there should not be infidelism about sex, but perfect faith. Women in These States approach the day of that organic equality with men, without which, I see, men cannot have organic equality among themselves. . . ."[35] And, more than three decades later, Whitman incorporates this vision of social equality into his aspirations for America's spiritual future:

> Centre of equal daughters, equal sons,
> All, all alike endear'd, grown, ungrown, young or old,
> Strong, ample, fair, enduring, capable, rich,
> Perennial with the Earth, with Freedom, Law and Love,
> A grand, sane, towering seated Mother,
> Chair'd in the adamant of Time.
> ("Sands at Seventy," "America," 1888, p. 511)

Whitman had broached this subject from the beginning of his career, when, in 1855, he announced the conjunction of the female with the maternal, the coupling of the health of the American nation with the exuberant procreativity of her daughters:

Her daughters, or their daughters' daughters—who
knows who shall mate with them?
Who knows through the centuries what heroes may come from them?

In them, and of them, natal love—in them that
divine mystery, the same old beautiful mystery.
Have you ever loved the body of a woman?
Have you ever loved the body of a man?

Your father—where is your father?
Your mother—is she living? have you been much with her? and has she
been much with you?*

The violative echoes of this passage (perhaps one reason for its excision?) are never far from Whitman's thoughts, although defended against by an idealizing power of fantasy that extends to prostitutes as well as to those "perfect" mothers. Whoever the woman and whatever her position in life, Whitman's strategies remain constant: to view her image with a nostalgia that creates distance while at the same time preserving by redirecting the emotions associated with woman into forms that neither threaten the poet nor completely abandon him. Whitman thus maintains access to the feminine while defending against his own impulses of violation that, in these lines, locate their origins in incestuous fantasy.

In Whitman's America, heroes emerge from, they are not themselves mothers—and natal love becomes the familiar, unanswerable mystery. Moreover, the land Whitman imagines depends upon these mothers for its very survival. Yet the "same old beautiful mystery" awakens a series of direct questions that leads ever closer to the incestuous fantasy that informs Whitman's conflicts regarding women. While asserting that America is "not the Man's Nation only, but the Woman's Nation—a land of splendid mothers, daughters, sisters, wives"—the woman remains, despite the rhetoric of equality, identified exclusively through family and biology (Preface to "As a Strong Bird on Pinions Free," 1872).

In his still iconoclastic, now classic study of American literature, D. H. Lawrence audaciously characterized the Whitmanian conception of women. Referring specifically to "A woman waits for me—," Lawrence grumbles, "He might as well have said: 'The femaleness waits of my maleness,' O, beautiful generalization and abstraction / O biological function." 'Athletic mothers of these states—' Muscles and wombs. They need't have had faces at all." In a no-nonsense voice, Lawrence continues with his briskly reductive parody of Whitman's Female: "If I'd been one of his women, I'd have given him Female." As so often in Lawrence's criticism, however, parodic observations give way to a more meditative analysis. "He found," Lawrence notes, with self-reflexive insight,

*This passage followed line 3, canto 8 of "I Sing the Body Electric" in Leaves of Grass, 1855 to 1860, and was later excised. See Blodgett, p. 625.

"like all men find, that you can't really merge in a woman, though you may go a long way. You can't manage the last bit. So you have to give it up, and try elsewhere. If you insist on merging." Lawrence shares this melancholy awareness with Whitman as with Emerson, for whom the question seems somehow less crucial since his sense of himself in the world so deeply sublimates his own sexuality. If, however, eros is implicated in metaphysics (as I am certain it must be), then the inscrutability of the Female assumes for Whitman an increasingly ominous significance. Lawrence concludes that "for the great mergers, woman at last becomes inadequate. For those who love to extremes, Woman is inadequate for the merging. So the next step is the merging of the man-for-man love. And this is on the brink of death. It slides over into death."[36] Here Whitman and Lawrence must part company, for the image Whitman recognizes at the threshold of death is not a male but a female spectral presence, as a vision of the mother fuses with those of death in a union that absorbs both principles into a circularity of endless, triumphant becoming. Yet the price of such a reconciliation must be the willful evasion of the woman's resistance to such merging. In his attempt to redeem and thereby diminish the anxiety of approaching death, Whitman resolves that otherness, the inaccessibility of death, by rejecting difference through the incorporation of the feminine into the nurturant, creative Self.

> Underneath all, Nativity,
> I swear I will stand by my own nativity, pious or impious so be it;
> I swear I am charm'd with nothing except nativity,
> Men, women, cities, nations, are only beautiful from nativity.
>   ("By Blue Ontario's Shore," 16, 262–65, p. 352–53)

He could have said that the nativity he sought to sanctify both persons and places was as much a result of his poetic imagination as it was related to an act of conception that had occurred without him, for Whitman remains his own child, born of the ideal mother he seeks in himself.

Informing Whitman's persona of the venturesome, questing child, one of his frequent "changes of garment," is, of course, the desire to return to origins, a wish to reimagine an earlier existence that would confirm the poet in his work. In this desire, Whitman continues to place his own emphasis upon the Romantic infatuation with the child by concentrating on birth itself; he sublates childhood to a quest for and the reenactment of origins by merging mother with son, death with life. In his search for poetic anteriority, Whitman conceives of himself simultaneously as child and as mature, empowering bard. By so situating himself in relation to his own power, Whitman covers the whole territory; at once eager novitiate and reflective sage, he limits women to the margins of discourse. When woman appears, it is as a necessity for procreation and the all-but-final comfort on the verge of death. Thus, woman becomes a garment, whose unfolding (and whose purpose it is to unfold) reveals the hidden life within:

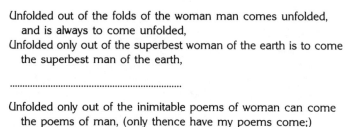

Unfolded out of the folds of the woman man comes unfolded,
    and is always to come unfolded,
Unfolded only out of the superbest woman of the earth is to come
    the superbest man of the earth,

....

Unfolded only out of the inimitable poems of woman can come
    the poems of man, (only thence have my poems come;)

....

A man is a great thing upon the earth and through eternity, but
    every jot of the greatness of man is unfolded out of
    woman;
First the man is shaped in the woman, he can then be shaped in
    himself.
                    ("Unfolded Out of the Folds," "Autumn Rivulets," p. 391)

It may seem that only the most determined of feminist readings could fold this passage back in upon itself, and yet despite all the avowed powers Whitman here attributes to woman as originator of life, as the one on whom the male must in some ultimate sense depend, she is once again relegated (although magnificently) to the edges of things. Whitman gives, and Whitman takes away. Women, beware Whitman, for the Whitmanian double bind that at once promises women equality simultaneously challenges the premise that, as individuals, they can participate in an ongoing intellectual life distinct from their maternal capacities. The danger for those who follow so powerful a poet is that no one, either man or woman, may experience her or himself as sufficient in the face of the Whitmanian ideal. Moreover, what aspiring woman poet would wish to empower herself through such a singularly mystical and biological identity, a conceptualization that has nothing to do with the rigors of articulation or any willed artistic activity? Whitman himself acknowledges that what may be preventing the nation from fulfilling his expectations is the very absence of the woman he envisions.

With all thy gifts America,
Standing secure, rapidly tending, overlooking the world,
Power, wealth, extent, vouchsafed to thee—with these and like
    of these vouchsafed to thee,
What if one gift thou lackest? (the ultimate human problem never
    solving,)
The gift of perfect women fit for thee—what if that gift of gifts
    thou lackest?
The towering feminine of thee? the beauty, health, completion,
    fit for thee?
The mothers fit for thee?
                    ("Autumn Rivulets," "With All Thy Gifts," p. 401)

Assuredly, such apprehension conveys an appreciation of the difficulties for Whitman's women readers, who, given his portrayal, must either submit to their gender-identified role as maternal beings or repudiate his vision in order to evade the burden of striving to embody someone else's myth. At the same time, to disavow the Whitmanian promise is to turn away from a poetic vision akin to rebirth. Tantalized by Whitmanian poetics and aware of its prohibitive price, American women poets have each, in their own ways, come to terms with this vision.

Charting the differences between poetic fathers and sons, one recognizes the means by which Emersonian self-reliance reconstitutes itself as a Whitmanian bodily metaphysics. Like his predecessor, Whitman seeks to transform his sense of displacement, to redefine what it means to be a poet in America into an earliness that awakens its own compensatory power, a self-created myth of the origins of the imagination. "As Adam early in the morning," Whitman speaks with a voice that unites flesh and text in a corporeal trope that compels those poets who follow him either to reaffirm or to deny the identification of body as text. What Whitman accomplishes may be playfully understood as the inversion of Queequeg's activity in Melville's *Moby Dick,* when, by tattooing his skin with words from his native language, he signifies his body as the one true, always-present text. Whitman, however, reverses this process by rendering the text synonymous with the body in a determined, self-willed transubstantiation that stakes all on heightened sensory awareness. The saving power of presence thus privileges as it protects the status of the text from the otherwise dangerous limitations imposed by mortality. If, for Queequeg, his signs fade along with his mortal flesh (transfigured anew on his hand-wrought coffin), Whitman's flesh adheres to his text, striving to escape the death that would otherwise take all along with it. The massive tomb Whitman had built for himself in the final months of his life, and into which he poured monies that were supposed to meet the expenses of living, was not simply the whim of a dying man but the expression of a more profound dread of effacement, the fear of the plunder of time that overtakes us all.

In "Thou Mother With Thy Equal Brood," Whitman anticipates if not arrogates his own determinative role in literary history. Invoking another kind of house (albeit related to the tomb), he writes,

> The paths to the house I seek to make,
> But leave to those to come the house itself.
> (l, 8–9, p. 456)

Himself a builder of houses, son of a carpenter/builder, Whitman, despite his pioneering, "pathfinding" assertion, nonetheless constructs many literary "houses" along the way to his final resting place. In his attempt to structure reality, to ascertain stability in a seemingly tumultuous, teeming life, Whitman constructs a self as well as a home. As R. W. B. Lewis remarks, "What is implicit in every line of Whitman is the belief that the poet projects a world of order and meaning and identity into either a chaos or a sheer vacuum; he does not discover it. The poet may salute the chaos; but he creates the world."[37]

Although I would demur from the full implications of Lewis's assertion, it does contain a core of truth, for Whitman makes his world as surely as Dickinson constructs hers. Despite their obvious differences (Whitman's almost obsessive acquisition of experiences, Dickinson's withdrawal from outward circumstance; his emphasis upon explicit sexuality, her largely disembodying human vision), they share two essential, although frequently overlooked, similarities: the aforementioned construction of a self-reflexive domain and a relationship to language marked by an idiosyncratic, obsessive quality that we would now recognize as disinctly "modern." Commenting upon Whitman's language, F. O. Mattheissen identifies the quality other critics have perhaps less accurately observed: "In its curious amalgamation of homely and simple usage with half-remembered items he read once somewhere, and with casual inventions of the moment, he often gives the impression of using a language *not quite his own*" (italics mine).[38]

Mattheissen's recognition of Whitman's sense of linguistic displacement, rather than the more conventional criticism of Whitman's "malapropisms" or his awkward use of "foreignisms," seems especially pertinent. For in a way, it is all foreign to Whitman, who, as an autodidact intent upon burying his influences, makes a good case not only for being self-reliant but for being a self-made poet as well. Out of his sense of alienation, the risks of employing a language not wholly native or his own, Whitman resembles those women poets who themselves feel so profoundly if proleptically displaced by him, and suffer thereby the anxieties of secondariness based upon exclusion rather than fear of a redundant similarity. Though in vastly different modes, Dickinson and Whitman both wrote what look like no other established poetic form. Dickinson's enigmatic, encapsulated four-stressed lines and Whitman's expansive, deeply alliterative, sprawling texts may be understood as highly dissimilar reactions to a related sense of estrangement, a discontinuity from literary tradition.

Whitman's response to his belatedness, his fear of failing to fulfill the Emersonian prophecy, nevertheless is more likely to threaten than to redeem the woman poet's sense of her work. What for Whitman became a potentially saving vision becomes for a woman poet a debilitating and ultimately self-defeating vision. She, too, would wish to partake of new intellectual freedoms, those opportunities for the imagination that Whitman holds out to her with such assurance. She, too, would readily appropriate the power of presence, the instrumentality of the firsthand witness, the possibility of the individual imagination that, reaching beyond convention, sheds all restrictions and is free. While himself summoning women toward this apparent equality, toward a more realistic awareness of their sexual identity, Whitman simultaneously resists defining women in terms equivalent to those he employs when describing himself. She is ineluctably associated with otherness, with an unreliable, potentially chaotic nature, with death, and therein resides her fate, according to the gospel of Whitman, who (as Harold Bloom has rightly noted) is our American Sublime.

What possibilities are there for the woman poet after Whitman's language ← experiments become synonymous with tradition, and what avenues can she discover for herself in order to win her own access to the Sublime? However tentative the assertions or risky the task, a reading of major women poets in light of the engendered American Sublime may yet yield fresh insights into the problematic intersections of sexuality and the imagination. I take solace in the fact that Whitman himself invites such speculation when he implores us to acknowledge the centrality of woman and her preeminence in the world:

> Think of womanhood, and you to be a woman;
> The creation is womanhood;
> Have I not said that womanhood involves all?
> Have I not told how the universe has nothing better
>   than the best womanhood?
>   ("Think of the Soul," poems excluded from
>   *Leaves of Grass*, 20–23, p. 590)

Who might the "women" behind this "womanhood" be, and how might they not only embody themselves, but also articulate their various versions of the American Sublime? The paths of women poets as they search for their origins will themselves determine the course of my attempt to address these questions and thereby identify an alternative poetics, an American Counter-Sublime.

2

ANOTHER WAY TO SEE

Dickinson and the Counter-Sublime

. . . I work to drive the awe away,
yet awe impels the work.

(letter 891, to Louise and
Francis Norcross, late March 1884)

In order to establish an alternative authority in the face of Emerson's poet, Dickinson creates a conception of poetic power that seeks to place her consciousness at the center of a self-made world. Informed by syntactic equivocations and hermetic linguistic strategies, Dickinson's poems shape a response to Emerson's poetics that glows with its own austerity.[1] What marks Dickinson's enabling transformations is her internalization of the conflict between the Emersonian Me and the Not Me. The split self seeks, from internal conflict, to generate a poetics that denies both the definitions of commonal discourse and the realities of a cultural landscape that would prohibit women from naming their world. Characteristically, Dickinson's poems speak from a position of aftermath or prolepsis, thus winning the requisite freedom to define the character of experience. Within the corpus of Dickinson's poems, the Sublime assumes an unaccustomed yet hauntingly familiar resemblance to Emerson's conception of the powerful self's relationship to ecstatic experience as Dickinson invokes tropes of the Sublime to describe her intermittent relation to power. Thus, for Dickinson, the Sublime must incorporate a defense against its own radical discontinuities. This defense takes the form of responding to the necessity of the influx of external power by denying need, privileging the process of doing without such an implosion of power, and converting renunciation of that power into a force of equal grandeur—into a counter-Sublime.

Because the empowering influx of the Sublime finds its source in nature or in other human or Godlike entities, Dickinson does not differentiate, as had Emerson, between persons and things. All externality represents threat—to be indebted is to be vanquished. Consequently, Dickinson's poems move back and forth, erratically, not symmetrically, between the experience of awe before the world and a rejection of its capacity to affect the self. "Transaction is assisted

by no Countenance," Dickinson asserts, as imaginative process takes prec-
edence over the recognition of external forces or forms (750).[2] And yet, Dickin-
son's acknowledgment of the transformative effects of power beyond the self
abides:

> I heard, as if I had no Ear
> Until a Vital Word
> Came all the way from Life to me
> And then I knew I heard.
>
> I saw, as if my Eye were on
> Another, till a Thing
> And now I know 'twas Light, because
> It fitted them, came in.
>
> I dwelt, as if Myself were out,
> My Body but within
> Until a Might detected me
> And set my kernel in.
>
> And Spirit turned unto the Dust
> "Old Friend, thou knowest me."
> And Time went out to tell the News
> And met Eternity.
>
>   (1039)

If a transformation that recalls an awareness of Grace (the addition of a new
sense) opens the poem, the closing lines refuse to leave this experience free
from self-questioning irony, for the "Might" that looms so large, restoring self to
soul, may be related to that other mite, as minute as the kernel it implants. Thus
the spirit communes with dust, restoring it to life, as time becomes eternity.
Paralleling this bestowal of immortal life is the passage into literal death, for the
self owes its gratitude to the transformative experience that bestows immortality
by taking life away. This gift is double-edged, demanding a sacrifice that equals
mortality. The interfusion of a corporeal vocabulary with the concerns of the
soul establishes an aura of physical presence startling in its acuity. Sensation—
including the inhalation and exhalation of breath—becomes a mode of dis-
course through which the poet dramatizes the workings of the imagination. For
Dickinson, "A Word made Flesh" (1651) "breathes," as it assumes the life of the
spirit living within her. The consequence of this process is, most significantly, an
elision between bodily processes and intellectual work that articulates the
Sublime in physical as well as psychological terms. Confrontation with an
authoritative natural or intellectual spirit appears in Dickinson's poems as a
conflict between a defensive subject and what I have referred to elsewhere as an
"essential adversary." Indebtedness (recall "I heard, as if I had no Ear") creates
its own defensiveness (1039).

Dickinson shares this conflictual perception of the Sublime with other women
poets, who experience an interfusion of the corporeal and the imaginative and

envision the workings of the Sublime as an essential process that carries with it the shattering capacity for severing the self.[3] In Dickinson's work, moreover, the Sublime operates as a compressed and consolidated mode wherein power, whether from the landscape or external consciousness, threatens the poet as it infuses her with its presence. When, however, the external, transformative power is perceived as feminine, the relationship between Dickinson and the Other is momentarily freed from the corporeal anxieties that otherwise mark such confrontations:

> I think I was enchanted
> When first a sombre Girl—
> I read that Foreign Lady—
> The Dark—felt beautiful—
>
> And whether it was noon at night—
> Or only Heaven—at Noon—
> For very Lunacy of Light
> I had not power to tell
>
> ....
>
> I could not have defined the change—
> Conversion of the Mind
> Like Sanctifying in the Soul—
> Is witnessed—not explained—
>
> 'Twas a Divine Insanity—
> The Danger to be Sane
> Should I again experience—
> 'Tis Antidote to turn—
>
> To Tomes of solid Witchcraft—
> Magicians be asleep—
> But Magic—hath an Element
> Like Deity—to keep—
>
>   (593)

The disruption of perceived experience, the heightening of perception, the conversion of the mind and sanctification of the soul, even the "Divine Insanity," echo traditional descriptions of the Sublime. Yet here (unusually for Dickinson) the experiential Sublime transpires without the burden of indebtedness, the necessity for physical defensiveness, or the chill of competition. Instead, as the closing lines of the poem suggest, changes can be permanent; should the "I" slip back into conventional sanity, the love found in "Tomes of Witchcraft"—the covert mysteries of female magic—will keep it from losing its newly acquired powers. In Dickinson's fusion of bodily sensation and the workings of the mind, her elision of poetic influence with the process of the experiential Sublime, and her reshaping of the transformative experience through the redemptive possibilities of a woman-to-woman encounter, we discover the seeds of a tradition that will be elaborated by future American women poets, who in various ways attempt to apprehend an alternative poetic tradition.

Rueful acknowledgment of the price she must pay for being a woman with formidable literary ambitions dictates Dickinson's austere revisionist poetics, as the erotics of aggression vie with the claims of a severe solipsism.[4] If Whitman defines the highly sensual, eroticized American Sublime emerging from his engendered masculine identity, Dickinson initiates an alternative tradition that, through her difficult, evasive poetics, revises Emerson's Poet by placing the woman at the center of the workings of the American Sublime. Dickinson's poems repeatedly attest to her right to be her own master and the dissymetry of her perceived relationship with the father to whom she consistently subjected herself in the abdication of that right. Dickinson testifies to her ambition to be a poet, what she means when she decrees, "Mine—here—in Vision and in Veto!" (528). Possession cannot be shared, but depends, instead, upon the aggressive, indeed murderous, impulses emerging from her poems.[5]

Although explicitly murderous impulses do not surface in the text (a too-overt recognition—never mind validation—of murder would threaten her sense of self and her consequent need for repression), Dickinson encodes her murderous desire. Yet, whether covert or not, murder repeatedly presents itself as a means to attain an individuating authority. To admit to a strategy so potentially lethal is to betray a dependency at once crippling and dangerous to the autonomous imagination's sense of its freedom. Consequently, Dickinson adopts, among her various discourses, the mode of the child and the language of play, even the convention of feminine sacrifice in order to approach her aggression and so defuse while simultaneously investing her language with its own purgative powers.[6] Elsewhere bold aggression breaks through, as the reader contemplates a necrophiliac's vision of ownership through death:

> If I may have it, when it's dead,
> I'll be contented—so—
> If just as soon as Breath is out
> It shall belong to me—
>
> ....
>
> Forgive me, if to stroke thy frost
> Outvisions Paradise!
>
> (577)

The brief, apologetic "forgive me" is not directed toward excusing her wish for the other's death, but toward the heresy of secular desire.[7]

As in this poem, religious terms may vie with the secular as Dickinson apologizes for not embracing an orthodox "paradise" instead of a corpse. Elsewhere, however, the poems reveal the verbal elision of God the Father and her biographical father as well as the subsuming of individual masculine personae under the ubiquitous and problematic "He."[8] Dickinson's "He" goes so far as to extend his presence into herself, as the "I's" corporeal processes, such as the aforementioned breath and pain, assume a masculine gender. At these moments, part of "herself" becomes alienated from the female "me," although "He" remains intimate and intrinsic. In poem 574, the speaker decides to take her

> . . . Chance with pain—
> Uncertain if myself, or He,
> Should prove the strongest One.

This context is internal and sexualized; the force identified with the male, potentially destructive.[9] That she must strive with pain and that she is alone are the crucial facts that determine Dickinson's need to marshal inner forces and go against the world. Severed from God the Father and thus bereft of his power, Dickinson adopts a strategic weakness from which to contemplate possible revenge:

> And often since, in Danger,
> I count the force 'twould be
> To have a God so strong as that
> To hold my life for me
>
> (576)

Without that "force," she must win an independence that, although necessary for her growth as a poet, may acquire an austerity as unconditional as it is self-destructive. In Dickinson's war with the Father (which is her war with the world), "All," as she knows, "is the price of All" (772). Gazing upward into the night, she observes the moon embodying the freedom and sovereignty she desires:

> But never Stranger justified
> The Curiosity
> Like Mine—for not a Foot—nor Hand—
> Nor Formula—had she—
>
> But like a Head—a Guillotine
> Slid carelessly away—
> Did independent, Amber—
> Sustain her in the sky—
>
> (629)

The moon, "engrossed to Absolute— / With shining—and the Sky" "solves" life's concerns; but hers is a "superior Road" the speaker cannot follow. The price the moon pays for such stunning autonomy is, figuratively speaking, the price of a beheading. The guillotine did its work "carelessly," a carelessness or regardlessness characteristic of Dickinson's other descriptions of the processes of maiming. Within the serenity of the floating, free moon, Dickinson insinuates a description that presents a macabre scene of revolutionary dismemberment, a vision of independence achieved not simply through death but through a separation from the corporeal self. The moon, in all its loveliness, is a *bloodless* orb floating alone. Yet once the guillotine image appears, the moon acquires a sudden partialness; it becomes incomplete through the very fact of its beheading; what sets it free reminds the reader of the body sacrificed to this serenity.

If such muted mutilations shadow this lunar clarity, other poems reveal a sense of indebtedness, of continued love for the other who deprives her of life: "Most—I love the Cause that slew Me. . . . Its beloved Recognition / Holds a Sun on Me—" (925). She is willing to love being the sacrificial victim: "Bind me—I still can sing— / Banish—my mandolin / Strikes true within— / Slay—and my Soul shall rise / Chanting to Paradise— / Still Thine" (1005). Such stunning self-sacrifice does not represent an alternative point of view so much as another level of complexity in Dickinson's sense of injury and emotional destitution. The "He," whether envisioned as sun or "eclipse" (masculine, astral counterparts to the beheaded moon), remains dangerous both in its oppressive presence and its obscuring absence. Imagining herself beholden to the masculine power these images represent, Dickinson pleads, for she believes that she cannot unilaterally achieve, the freedom of the self. She pleads for freedom to a God who is not only distant but also dangerous, who controls both entrapment and the possibility of freedom from that entrapment.

> God of the Manacle
> As of the Free—
> Take not my Liberty
> Away from Me—
> (728)

Her words acknowledge her bondage as they yearn for its destruction.

If I have been suggesting that we see the "father" as a composite figure associated with an essential yet potentially lethal presence, it is equally important to observe his proliferations into other forms that distinguish among various aspects of patriarchy. Dickinson's vision is not simply of destructive male power but also of a force enticing, provocative, and deeply desired. These qualities reappear in her descriptions of the "Master," her preceptors, the masculine "Other," and the elusive figure of the stranger that move throughout her work. These versions of the patriarchy offer the poet possible sources of salvation. The renewed expectation of such salvation followed by continual rejection or loss in death amounts to the poetic equivalent of a repetition compulsion that does not erase so much as underscore Dickinson's fundamental need for the father (although always on her own terms).

Haunted by a pervasive sense of loss since childhood, "a Mourner . . . among the children," the poet seeks to replace what she has missed, to give herself to new fathers only to be rejected, cast out, or self-propelled away from their sphere. Enlisting the conventional paradigm of the abandoned lover, Dickinson expresses her overwhelming resentment at her dependence upon the other. The "savior," in whatever form, comes to rescue her from his absence, but his gifts are double; his bounty leaves her only more destitute. To witness *his* plenitude is to discover her own omnivorous emptiness. Because she cannot claim his power as her own, the "I" remains destitute, with a vision of what she cannot possess clear before her wounded sight. What gratitude can she feel toward him whose "riches—taught me—Poverty"? One learns of bounty from its distance, as the poems assume the shape of an austere consolation, ways of bandaging psychic injury by making destitution bold.

Ironically, the vastly self-contradictory poems that attest to Dickinson's abasement before the male Other and her wish to sacrifice all for him originate in *his* dual legacy to her;

what if were philosophical read as spiritual rather or relentlessly than psychoanalytical?

You left me—Sire—two Legacies—
A Legacy of Love
A Heavenly Father would suffice
Had He the offer of—

You left me Boundaries of Pain—
Capacious as the Sea—
Between Eternity and Time—
Your Consciousness—and Me—
                                                    (644)

Leaving conveys the doubleness of the gift, for the Sire dowers only to depart. "Boundaries" convey "limits" as well as distances—but here the limits themselves are as capacious as the sea (evidently endless and unfathomably deep). These limits do not separate two phenomena of the same kind but elements that are inherently exclusionary: the boundary between Eternity (measureless, unknowable) and the measured, limited sphere of temporality. If Dickinson's grammatical parallelism indicates analogy, then Eternity equals the Sire's consciousness and Time equals "me." Thus, the sire is so far beyond her, so vast, that boundaries signify not simply limits but also oceanic spaces unbridgeable by the imagination. Indeed, she feels insufficient for the supposedly joyous gift of love he bears, a gift that would have "sufficed" even the "Heavenly Father." Of course, legacies are gifts received after death, so that *she* remains alive (hence in time) while he has already entered Eternity. Could his death, then, have been willed by the text? Just how far is Dickinson willing to go to ensure that dual legacy which, no matter how problematic, she finds essential to call her own?

Elsewhere Dickinson combines her plaint of deprivation with the strategy of comparison. In "It would have starved a Gnat—" (612), Dickinson demonstrates the existential superiority of the insect as measured by a freedom defined as the capacity for self-destruction. If, in "My Life had stood—a Loaded Gun—," the Master is perceived as superior because he controls death, so the unlikely gnat is free to seek his food and free to die by his own movements. He possesses a control over his own body that proves him life's superior artist. The speaker of the poems differs from the gnat not because of the gnat's insignificance or its customary identity as a pest, but rather through the latter's desperate, microscopic strength.

> Nor like Himself—the Art
> Upon the Window Pane
> To gad my little Being out—
> And not begin—again—
>   (612)

One's response to this is far from simple. It may, after all, be a relief to see the gnat gone, but in its repetitious, apparently futile thrusting against the window-pane for freedom and escape, the gnat achieves what the speaker is denied—control over fate, even if that control results in the mashed gnat's demise. As the gnat intrudes unpleasantly upon our consciousness, frustration builds. Such effort to a useless end—could that be the art Dickinson covets?

Yet it is this question of control, whether cast in its minutest form or in more magisterial images, that continues to emerge in Dickinson's poems—a vision of literary activity related to competition, specifically a contest against a masculine power judged negatively greater than herself (negatively, because power arises from the capacity to destroy). Cast in ultimate terms, what the heart asks is "the will of its Inquisitor / The privilege to die—" (536). Dickinson conceives of herself as "a Being—impotent to end— / When once it has begun—" (565). Even physical, ordinarily unconscious processes, such as breathing, are not under her control, but yield to a masculine identification that cannot be relied upon to do her bidding. In one of the many poems that proleptically relive life's last moments, Dickinson characterizes her parting breath as other, possessing a will of its own that determines her fate. "Three times—we parted—Breath—and I— / Three times—He would not go—" (598). His obstinacy saves her life as the drowning self is torn between two apparently external forces: the male-identified breath and the waves whose subsiding strength determines her ability to with-stand being pulled under. That the wind and waves subside, leaving breath triumphant, not only saves the "I," but also suggests that the outcome may not be life as we recognize it but a moment of resurrection: "The Sunrise kissed my Chrysalis— / And I stood up—and lived—" (598). The altered form, the erect posture, the "Christ" echoing in "chrysalis" make this no simple rescue.

The poem's description of the self's dependency and the apparent lack of control over one's life or destiny do not mean that Dickinson is ready to relinquish the possibility of control to others. Instead, the contest is close and depends upon her capacity to convert defeat into victory. If Emerson would write in his journals, "I am defeated all the time. Yet to Victory am I born," Dickinson's poems attest to a similarly pervasive sense of defeat that might lead her to conclude: "Yet to repetition am I born." Emersonian consolation falls before the austere poignancy of a prophetic Freudian realism.

Difficult as it may be for us to accept such a conclusion about so powerful a poet, we need only observe a few other poems where Dickinson wrestles with her enemy, caresses a corpse, or, in a cunningly revisionary lullaby, sings him to his final rest. Here is the revisionist lullaby:

> Now I lay thee down to Sleep—
> I pray the Lord thy Dust to keep—
> And if thou live before thou wake—
> I pray the Lord thy Soul to make—
>   (1539)

Although in his note to the poem, Thomas Johnson remarks that the occasion of this "mock elegy" is not known, its spirit is consistent with those poems that assume and even flaunt the power the speaker wields over her deadly, beloved adversary. She names him as she acknowledges her need. Against the experience of powerlessness, she demands a victory: "Mine Enemy is growing old— / I have at last Revenge—" (1509). What strategy can a victimized self best employ to assure a compensatory power so that the struggle between self and other may continue, so that the poems may live? How is Dickinson able to keep the battle so close that she can characterize her relationship with the Other as simultaneously one of complete dependency on her part and of an equal or almost equal dependency on his?

> But since We hold a Mutual Disc—
> And front a Mutual Day—
> Which is the Despot, neither knows—
> Nor Whose—the Tyranny—
>   (909)

The war with the Father is not simply a war with the world, but also an internal struggle between an introjected patriarchal force and that aspect of consciousness Dickinson experiences as "self." Hence the terms of her battle are especially stark when the violent solution of murder meshes with the desire for suicide. Resentment against the Father becomes a self-inflicted hatred that derives its source in exile and a knowledge of rejection.

"A mourner . . . among the children," Dickinson from the first feels cheated, starved to the point of extinction—and this hunger feeds upon the self. Cast out by God the Father and Mother Nature, she perceives herself as outnumbered and outclassed. When nature appears as an independent entity, it may side not with the experiential consciousness but with a God whose piercing, aggressive knowledge of the poet permits no reply. Nature pairs with Him only to intensify Dickinson's sense of haunted isolation. Mother Nature and God the Father overpower her, and the "child" is rendered defenseless, left with only a partially repressed, barely stifled wish for her parents' death.

> Nature and God—I neither knew
> Yet Both so well knew me
> They startled, like Executors
> Of My identity.

Yet Neither told—that I could learn—
My Secret as secure
As Herschel's private interest
Or Mercury's affair—

(835)

The alliance between nature and God turns into a collusion against the child, as her parents withhold knowledge that they alone possess. They both execute (or kill) her identity and preserve it by executing her will after her death.[10] This threatening yet essential alliance is based upon inscrutable parental knowledge. The speaker's secret is "secure," but from whom—herself or the world? The ellipitical closing stanza encourages an interpretative indeterminacy that leaves the reader as much in the dark as the speaker herself. The poem thus recreates in its reader the sense of intrusion and withheld knowledge that is its ostensible subject; we share her exclusion.

What can break down the barriers and give Dickinson sufficient strength to "go against" the world? In my estimation, she derives the impetus for poetry from her ability to sustain intense conflict, the practice of a Keatsian negative capability in extremis. Dickinson draws energy from the intimate war with the Father, at moments even imagining her victory. Though any Dickinsonian victory must vanquish as well, victory nonetheless abides. Her triumphs, like her murders, are dramatic, both intimately staged and never final. Dickinson recognized all too well the importance of literary form ("But we—are dying in Drama—," she wrote, "And Drama—is never dead—" (531). At times this drama assumes the language of the church as her struggles acquire the aura and diction we associate with Christ's Passion. She would be the "Christa" of language if she were not "fated" to be Eve. Sacrificing her own life for God's word remains these poems' constant offering. Denied the possibility of a role as sacrificial daughter, Dickinson is left no place in the Trinity and possibly no way to save herself or her world, to redeem it for belief, to save it for hope. Recalling her earliest feelings of exclusion, Dickinson adopts the tones of the innocent child who questions her awful isolation, thus implicitly warning both the reader and herself of the risks she runs if she strives to become a new savior, a female, literary Christ.

Who were "The Father and the Son"
We pondered when a child,
And what had they to do with us
And when portentous told

With inference appalling
By Childhood fortified
We thought, at least they are no worse
Than they have been described.

(1258)

For one who experiences herself as permanently exiled, the only retaliation is a tortured self-reliance. This is not, however, the Emersonian brand of self-reliance, wherein each of us shares the confidence that the self will triumph, or the Whitmanian faith that what he assumes we too shall assume. Dickinson's at times antagonistic but always ambivalent attitude toward her audience derives from the extenuating philosophical isolation of her position as well as her pervasive skepticism toward all experience not witnessed by the self. Where her triumph, then, and at what price?

I turn to two poems that speak of victory, the Father, and power. And, although neither names murder outright, the tension within each can be traced to the terms of a distinctly murderous poetics: first, the familiar "I'm ceded—I've stopped being Theirs—" (508), which announces a break with family, religion, and the past. Couched in religious language, the poem describes a second baptism, a self-willed choosing of a name fully and exclusively the speaker's own. Of particular interest is the actual position of the speaker, both when first baptized and at the time of her second, self-appointed identification. In its final stanza, the poem draws the contrast:

> My second Rank—too small the first,
> Crowned—Crowing—on my Father's breast—
> A half unconscious Queen—
> But this time—Adequate—Erect,
> With Will to choose, or to reject,
> And I choose, just a Crown—

The infant is held against the Father's breast; for in this vision of the family romance, the Father is the nurturer, the one who floods her with an overwhelming power or leaves her to starve. Note that as an infant, she is not the princess but a queen, potentially the king's equal, in an oedipal identification wherein the child replaces the mother as well as becoming Christ's bride. That the infant cries at her own baptism is hardly extraordinary; what is interesting is her crowing (with its associations of the cock crow of morning, the bird of prey eating its carrion, the allusion to the betrayal of Christ). This sense of insufficiency, hunger for authority, and recognition of the failure of orthodoxy to bestow identity may indeed awaken submerged thoughts of murder and a desire for revenge. To rename oneself may be possible only if one murders the Father and feeds on his power. In the speaker's second transformation, the Father is totally absent. In full possession of her will, the speaker accepts the crown with a gesture full of conscious power.

> Baptized before, without the choice,
> But this time, consciously, of Grace—
> Unto supremest name—

But even though she wins her name, the speaker's power is still associated not with initiatory action but with response. She is "called" to her full, achieving royal/divine status or imperial selfhood in response to a summons. Though the choice is all hers, the speaker understands the demand or call as emanating from outside, as external. She wears the crown, and the religious emblem acquires, through its identification with royalty, not only the choice of independent authority but also a distinctly orthodox cast that modifies the radicalism of her self-bestowal. This release through second baptism is a regal but not a truly radical triumph. The speaker can select among alternatives but does not construct her own.

Despite this more generalized rejection of the possibility of true usurpation, on other occasions Dickinson envisions her transformation not into God's bride but into the aforementioned Christa, the female Christ. If this transformation is frequently encoded in abstract language, Dickinson elsewhere makes it plain. In poem 553, for example, the speaker universalizes Christ's suffering only to defuse the full impact of the poem's closing lines:

> Our Lord—indeed—made Compound Witness—
> And yet—
> There's newer—nearer Crucifixion
> Than That—

Our commonality depends upon our passion, and yet even in this knowledge, she remains the outsider. Denied the legacy of the Father, Dickinson can save neither us nor herself. She is excluded from his generosity as well as denied what she most requires: the self-sufficiency of the Spirit that would validate her own suffering.

> I asked no other thing—
> No other—was denied—
> I offered Being—for it—
> The Mighty Merchant sneered—
>
> Brazil? He twirled a Button—
> Without a glance my way—
> "But—Madam—is there nothing else—
> That We can show—Today?"
>   (621)

God as "mighty merchant" cannot fulfill her presumably eccentric yet attractively exotic demand. Offering substitutions as he refuses to face or acknowledge her need, he utterly fails her. No wonder she meets him with such trepidation. Eager to please, desperate to attract his attention and attain his good will, Dickinson asks that he not rebuke her for her efforts. "Whatever it is—she has tried it— / Awful Father of Love— / Is not Ours the chastising— / Do not chastise the Dove—" (1204). As the Dove of the Holy Spirit or the dove that flew from Noah's Ark in search of the first sign of dry land, of hope, she is cast aside.

Excluded from God's house yet remaining throughout her life in the house of her father, Dickinson strives to assume the Father's power and to win his love. Having experienced the failure of both requirements, Dickinson makes of her exile a provisional home by converting her defeat into a victory that embodies the vanquished. The symbolic language of nature palls beside her quest, and the tie between nature and language, the possibility of the natural world's serving as a symbolic counter for Dickinson's inner life, proves insufficient. Even the powerful promise of the sublime American West cannot match the audacity of Dickinson's interior pioneering.

> The Stars are old, that stood for me—
> The West a little worn—
> Yet newer glows the only Gold
> I ever cared to earn—
>
> Presuming on that lone result
> Her infinite disdain
> But vanquished her with my defeat
> 'Twas Victory was slain.
>
> (1249)

This rejection of the force of analogy is coupled with a grammatical shift that complicates the already tenuous relation between the self and others by experimenting with different gender identities. Note the pronominal shift in the variant originally sent to her sister-in-law, Susan Gilbert Dickinson, (which also accompanied a letter Dickinson wrote to Thomas Wentworth Higginson in 1874), and how this shift alters the dynamics of the final stanza:

> Presuming on that lone result
> His infinite disdain
> But vanquished him with my defeat—
> 'Twas Victory was slain.

The struggle with the Father continues, as does the expression of the inadequacy of nature to convey its intensity. Confronting the infinite disdain of her beloved Susan, her preceptor Higginson, or a bird she had seen that morning (the immediate, precipitating occasion for the poem, according to Johnson), the experiences are interchangeable. Disdained by all around her, the speaker vanquishes the adversary by her defeat, thus slaying victory. Her power resides in her defeat as Christ's power lies in his sacrifice. Imperfect as the analogy seems and almost too grim, perhaps, to contemplate, there can be for Dickinson no other power except (and here the exception is all) the power of the word. The world that excludes her is enemy, and she demands revenge.

> I took my Power in my Hand—
> And went against the World—
> (540)

When the weapon is a pebble, as in this poem, the injury is to herself; when the weapon is the word, with its attribute of power, the result is different.

One asks, what other options were there? The choice of passive aggression based upon waiting, upon watching, upon writing an encoded death sentence that provides her with renewed life becomes a mode of victory.

Mine Enemy—is growing old—
I have at last Revenge—
The Palate of the Hate departs—
If any would avenge

Let him be quick—the Viand flits—
(1509)

Even revenge, however, loses its savor when attained because it arrives belatedly. Dickinson survives to write austere poems of the isolated imagination; she writes to survive. The symbiosis is clear when Dickinson herself speaks: "I work to drive the Awe away / Yet Awe impels the work."

The crux of the matter is power, how to wrest independence from a patriarchal universe. The issue comes down to the power of life and death and who wields it. Though a "loaded gun," Dickinson's life misses the "power to die." Unlike the gnat, she cannot gad her little being out; she is a "being impotent to end." Without the privilege to die, her life depends upon another's death. Yet Dickinson repeatedly relies upon him just as she remains firmly convinced that he will injure or, worse, reject her. Here is the absolute God in all His kindness:

Far from Love the Heavenly Father
Leads the Chosen Child,
Oftener through Realm of Briar
Than the Meadow mild.

Oftener by the Claw of Dragon
Than the Hand of Friend
Guides the Little One predestined
To the Native Land.
(1021)

If salvation rests in the dragon's claw, Dickinson's pen must be equally ready to wound. When she deals her pretty words like blades, she ruefully discovers that she is their closest victim.

II

In a letter to Higginson written in March of 1876, Dickinson recalls her father: "When I think of my Father's lonely life and his lonelier Death, there is this redress—

Take all away—
The only thing worth larceny
Is left—the Immortality.
(*Letters*, III, 457, p. 551)

That flood subject "immortality," of which she remains so uncertain all her life, is alone worth striving for and alone offers a tentative consolation. What potentially rescues the individual in a world of such disenfranchisement is the word, the possibility of writing a poem that will withstand assaults on the self and wage its war against time. The transformation from a self defeated because it cannot will its own death into a triumph for the word depends upon the victory over father/God/lover/precursor, the composite adversary that alone could satisfy. Whereas the self is impotent to end and so must rely even for death upon the Other, conversion of such antagonism into the controlled, self-willed form of a poem confers victory upon defeat. Dickinson's word becomes the Word, an alternative language to the hegemonic orthodoxy of Calvinist Amherst and Christian America. At their most powerful, Dickinson's poems embody the Christa of language she would become.

> A Word made Flesh is seldom
> And tremblingly partook
> Nor then perhaps reported
> But have I not mistook
> Each one of us has tasted
> With ecstasies of stealth
> The very food debated
> To our specific strength—
>
> A Word that breathes distinctly
> Has not the power to die
> Cohesive as the Spirit
> It may expire if He—
> "Made Flesh and dwelt among us"
> Could condescension be
> Like this consent of Language
> This loved Philology.
>
> (1651)[11]

"Ringed with power," the poet discovers a poetics that derives its strength from murderous though encoded messages that alone can control the Father she both desperately needs and mortally fears. The murder takes different forms: the expressed desire for the Other's death, the sardonic lullaby that sings him to oblivion, the mock elegy that would carry the father/lover to his grave.

In closing, I examine one of Dickinson's best-known poems to identify the underlying conflict that issues in such tactics, the impetus behind her murderous poetics, her creation of an uncanny, death-haunted American Sublime. In a most attenuated, urbane vision, Dickinson crosses the threshold between life and death, yet she retains the power of speech to assert an audacious authority over all experience.[12] The poem is "Because I could not stop for Death" (712), which I read through Freud's "The Theme of the Three Caskets," a text that, in its antithetical argument, clarifies Dickinson's relationship to desire and to the awareness of her own death.[13] In his essay, Freud suggests that the male character in Shakespeare's tragedies, when faced with a choice that would fulfill his desire, elects silence, and that his choice signifies the conversion of his own inevitable death, over which he has no control, into an active choosing on his part. Thus, a man may strive to convert the necessity of dying into a willed gesture; in Freud's words, he is therefore able to "make friends with the necessity of dying." Freud draws upon Bassanio's choice in *The Merchant of Venice* of the casket containing lead, the apparently least valuable and dullest of the three caskets before him, which wins him the supremely articulate Portia. Here Freud makes the connection between the caskets or boxes and women as representatives of enclosure or womblike space. He reminds us that the silent Cordelia is King Lear's choice among his daughters and that as the silent woman, Cordelia is both origin and end: mother/mate/fate. Freud cites the end of *Lear:*

> Enter Lear with Cordelia dead in his arms. Cordelia is Death. Reverse the situation and it becomes intelligible and familiar to us—the Death-goddess bearing away the dead hero from the place of battle, like the Valkyr in German mythology. Eternal wisdom, in the garb of the primitive myth, bids the old man renounce love, choose death and make friends with the necessity of dying.

Freud concludes, "But it is in vain that the old man yearns after the love of woman as once he had it from his mother; the third of the Fates alone, the silent goddess of Death, will take him into her arms" (p. 75).

Silent too, is that accommodating gentleman who stops for the woman in Dickinson's poem. Here the speaker is carried by death, and the poem attempts the kind of consolation Freud understands as a requirement for the male imagination before it can accept its fate. Although the speaker wishes to discover a means of converting inevitability into active choice, the poem's strategy is complex, going beyond a simple shift in sexual identification. What marks the break between Freud's Shakespearean women and Dickinson's persona is that Dickinson's woman refuses to be silent; she speaks throughout the experience.[14] If there is no conversation between death and the woman, we nevertheless hear a voice that leads us through the journey to death and beyond, and that voice is the lyric "I" of the supposed victim who becomes the poem's controlling consciousness. The initial refusal of the woman to stop for death is identical to the male character's resistance manifested at the approach of death. Dickinson not only has him "stop" to pick her up, but also, as Harold Bloom has noted, *she stops him.*[15] *Death stops at her bidding,* winning for the poet the privilege to lie against time. Death, though he may be kind, is no conversationalist, and what she knows, she learns through her own observation and surmise. The third party to this ride, "the chaperone, immortality," Bloom identifies with Dickinson's poems, thus leading to the triumph of art over death. And though this triumph is assuredly true for us who have her poems, I would suggest a different identity than the one Bloom assigns the chaperone, for if the poems offer a way of ensuring immortality (the texts themselves placed in a drawer, a box reminiscent of a casket?), this version of immortality does not ease the shock the self undergoes at the poem's close. The speaker is stunned not because she has achieved immortality, but because the acute awareness of the passage of time is just what has *not* fallen away. Immortality, with its promised freedom from the anxieties of *chronos,* is endlessly deferred at the poem's close.

> Since then—'tis Centuries—and yet
> Feels shorter than the Day
> I first surmised the Horses' Heads
> Were toward Eternity—

The feeling of being "shorter than the Day" is not equivalent to that of atemporality. The speaker knows it has been centuries; time is measurable, but that first day, despite the cover, the protection, the civility, could not be made easier. Nothing protects her from the realization of her own death, nor is she freed by it.

Immortality provides no consolation, only prolonged consciousness of the end. It therefore functions as a blocking agent rather than the casket of art and more likely represents the presence of the absent Mother who vigilantly and for all time restrains the daughter from fulfilling her desire for the Father, from making friends with death. Although she is carried in a carriage (a sort of moving casket), the speaker nonetheless keeps her voice and maintains her awareness. Although death stops *for* her, her journey itself becomes an endless quest for Eternity. That one cannot triumph over time or over death may be this poem's most sorrowful wisdom. What remains within the speaker's control despite this defeat is the power of speech, a consciousness even death cannot efface. The triumph for art may be not that it will last beyond the poet, but that it continues to witness her refusal to make friends with death. Thus, Dickinson metaphorically murders death in order to control him; rather than make him her friend, she envisions him as the composite power that would seduce, wed, and silence her. Poem after poem strives to release death's hold by imagining his death as her freedom.

The lead casket will not be dumb, nor will Dickinson accept her appointed role as death mother through silence or concealment. Dickinson's revisionist rejection evolves out of the imperative to speak against the silent Father and the Mother who restrains her from fulfilling her desire. Thus, the "I" is doubly dependent. Yearning for the unattainable Father, she discovers him within her psyche; his strength turns against the self, making her victim of what she most desires. Thus, Dickinson must encounter and continually reenact the struggle with the exclusionary male who prefers to withhold rather than confer. Refused the assurance of becoming the Christa of American poetry or the new Christ, as Whitman might triumphantly proclaim himself, Dickinson does not inherit Emerson's powers unchallenged. She first must resolve through aggression her need for supremacy in imaginatively murderous acts that recur because murder of the tradition is a most illusory triumph. Hers is a poetics as aggressive as any

male oedipal struggle, yet complicated by an intensified vulnerability, a con-
sciousness of perpetual exile, the awareness of the impossibility of winning
adequate patriarchal recognition. With her characteristic astuteness, Dickinson
once remarked, "When the subject is finished, words are handed away." But her
words, though they may have slowed in her final years, were never discarded
because her subject achieves no resolution. Conflict over death becomes,
indeed, a form of poetic life. Unable to write without the "Father," yet forced to
vanquish him in order to survive, Dickinson, with subtlety, wit, and death-defying
irony, practices her murderous poetics. Sharp as surgeon's steel, this very praxis
redeems the dependence her poems counter and magnificently, if sacrificially,
destroy.

3

DICKINSON, MOORE, AND THE POETICS OF DEFLECTION

Silence is broken because I have spoken.
Some *lamma sabachtani* always ends his-
tory and cries out our total inability to keep
still: I must give a meaning to that which
does not have one: in the end, being is
given to us as impossible.

—Georges Bataille

Q. Do you intend your poetry to be useful to
yourself or others?
A. Myself.

—Marianne Moore

Strange things always go alone.

—Susan Gilbert Dickinson

Because she cannot take for granted a relation to what lies beyond the self,
Dickinson paradoxically employs nature to illuminate the anomalous status of
her individual imagination, an imagination that rests its authority upon its
exclusionary singularity rather than upon any reciprocal relationship with the
external world. As Geoffrey Hartman notes, "The peculiar and fascinating thing
is that in Dickinson's lyrics nature and style are the same, a divine etiquette.
Nature teaches art to hide art for the sake of un-self-consciousness. What is
being described here is not Nature, but a mode of being present that at once
values and cancels the self."[1] The term "etiquette," if somewhat antiquarian, is
nevertheless apt, for what nature confers on Dickinson is nothing less than a
style equivalent to a way of being, of apprehending the world so that the poet
can describe it. This conjunction of style with conduct reveals a simultaneous

valorization and cancellation of the self that can be transferred to Marianne Moore's manifestations of rhetorical effacement, for in Moore's poems, one encounters exactly what Hartman finds in Dickinson: the practice of articulating and encoding a "mode of being present that at once values and cancels the self."[2]

In her use of others' words, her discovery of public advertisement, her insistence upon a flaunting, self-effacing modesty that would substitute attentiveness for an aggrandizing aesthetics, Moore's poetics resembles Dickinson's, for both are fueled by the need to reinvent a style of life that is equivalent to a literary ethics. Whereas Emerson would assert: "That is always best which gives me to myself. . . . The sublime is excited in me by the great stoical doctrine, 'Obey thyself,' " (a confidence that lies at the very heart of the American Sublime), Dickinson and Moore are less certain that such a correspondence exists, let alone that it merits the highest praise.[3] What Emerson struggles against in his magisterial assertion is an awareness of the passage of time and his own mortality, for, as he himself laments, "already the long shadows of untimely oblivion creep over me, and I shall decease forever." Oblivion, whatever it would later become for the Emersonian imagination, must always be "untimely," and to counter its arrival, Emerson deploys the full force of his daunting imaginative resources. If he admonishes the students of the Harvard Divinity School "to Yourself (become) a newborn bard of the Holy Ghost," he speaks as if he were that bard, inviting others to win a similar supremacy over the conditions and limitations of human life. The sublime individualism of Emerson's commitment to power, although invoked with equal intensity by Dickinson, becomes a vexed subject in her work—split off from itself, unable to draw upon an awareness of continuity between her imagination and those who strove before her to express the illusion of control over temporality. Dickinson's poetic authority depends upon other sources, founded as it is upon a more austere and specifically marginalized, gender-inflected poetics. What I would emphasize is the possibility that in the very formulation of the question of self-identity in relation to nature, Dickinson refuses the Emersonian imagination's assurance. By imagining her relationship to nature as primarily allegorical rather than analogical, Dickinson redefines the terms that characterize the conception of selfhood for women poets.

Although Moore differs sharply from Dickinson in a number of ways, there is nevertheless an underlying similarity in motives as well as in particularities of style—the use of an obsessively restrictive metrical form, the idiosyncratic yet demotic diction, the choice of the minute or grotesque creature as a signature for the self—such discrete tactics gesture toward the need to create a style that protects as it privileges the status of the marginalized authorial self. Not surprisingly, this marginalized poetics at times exaggerates the style of the dominant culture it would evade. Consider, for example, Dickinson's antinomian self-reliance or Moore's appropriation of esoteric allusions (although, I later will argue, always an esoteric with a difference). Surely, for Moore as for Dickinson, observation becomes de facto *a mode of being* that balances the effacement of self with an exploration of the self's rhetorical powers. In attempting to rewrite the cultural script Romanticism would assign them, Dickinson and Moore establish their relationship to nature and to "others" by choosing what might arguably be envisioned as a private, intensely marginalized aesthetics that depends upon achieving and maintaining an awareness of the disruption between their identity and the world. Consequently, this awareness creates the need to reassess (and to test) their relation to the world beyond the self.

In a poem whose initial word may serve as one source for Elizabeth Bishop's "Man-Moth," Hart Crane meditates upon the desire to name nature, to refashion natural forms to serve the purposes of the self:

> Moonmoth and grasshopper that flee our page
> And still wing on, untarnished of the name
> We pinion to your bodies to assuage
> Our envy of your freedom—we must maim
> Because we are usurpers and chagrined—
> And take the wing and scar it in the hand.
> Names we have, even, to clap on the wind,
> But we must die, as you, to understand.

Crane's revisionary dream combines a sacramental and anonymous condition that, although apparently swerving from the intense individuality of the acquisitive naming he would question, nevertheless achieves a performative transcendence that establishes itself firmly within the Emersonian mode:

> I dreamed that all men dropped their names, and sang
> As only they can praise, who build their days
> With fin and hoof, with wing and sweetened fang
> Struck free and holy in one Name always.

"A Name for All" accurately conveys its ambition—not the diminishment of the self but its transformation, the freedom that comes from metamorphosis of self into nature—the dream of the still-hoped-for yet always defeated vision toward which Emerson strives: the Whitmanian merging of self and world.[4] This ideal differs from that of Dickinson and Moore, each of whom prefers to explore the distance between consciousness and world, Dickinson by rhetorically engaging the tensions between them and Moore by focusing upon the etiquette of observation itself.

The mediating presence here, of course, is Whitman, who, as I have earlier asserted, founds his poetics on the trope of the body. If Whitman insists upon poetry as body, Moore proceeds by resisting, with the vast rhetorical means at her disposal, any such identification. Instead, her poetics reinforces a disengagement of affect from voice. Moore's poetry displays the absence of eros and its attendant desires, as it relentlessly defends against the incorporation of the bodily that distinguishes Whitmanian poetics. Moore's insistence that what she writes is "nonpoetry" is an inversion of Whitman's similar assertion, for whereas his "nonpoetry" vests its authority in his *personal* power, the "flesh-and-blood" self that seeks to evade the distance created by language, Moore depends upon as she elaborates the rhetoric that creates and extends that distance. Although temperament surely plays a crucial role in defining this aesthetic difference, culture plays its part as well, for the authority upon which Whitman founds his alternative corporeal poetics, however apparently heterodox, nevertheless draws on the Romantic imagination's identification of the power of poetry with masculine authority.

Interestingly, Moore's categories themselves, moral and tutelary as they are, establish a hierarchy of values that, while identified with the feminine, nevertheless divorce the conventionally condoned aspects of the female—maternity, modesty, gentleness—from those that threaten men: female desire, sexuality, explicit assertions of power. Thus, Moore's poetics, while overtly offering an "alternative" code of moral style in art, covertly reinscribes the male imagination's conceptualization of the feminine. This reinscription costs Moore an artistic disengenderment that may be one source of the overt absence of eros in her art. If, for Moore, "literature is a phase of life," ("Picking and Choosing"), then how to live becomes for her an aesthetic question. With "inflection disguised" ("Those Various Scalpels"), Moore reinvents an aesthetics of renunciation, not renunciation (that is a more Dickinsonian severity) but of deferral, creating a proliferating figuration that at times replaces the illusion of a controlling "I" directing the poem. Yet the erudition, the stream of unidentified allusions, the deployment of advertising copy and prose nevertheless betray a will to power that, although associated with traditionally female attributes—modesty, privacy, the determination of worth based upon personal affection—bespeaks a bid for complete authorial control. The reader is at Moore's mercy, guided by no reliable signs of discursive or poetic continuity.

Repeatedly, Moore associates the inherent dangers of explicit power with questions relating to style. In "Critics and Connoisseurs," she berates "ambition without understanding" and chastises a disabling fastidiousness. Whether it be fastidiousness or ambition (style serving to abet so as to mask a will to power), anything that suggests either too great a self-absorption or an overt display of talent may be transformed into an object of critical scorn.

> What is
> there in being able
> to say that one has dominated the stream in an attitude
> of self-defense;
>
> in proving that one has had the experience
> of carrying a stick?

> ("Critics and Connoisseurs")

The terms in which Moore envisions writing as craft and her experience of living in the world remain profoundly adversarial; to counter that aversiveness, she defines a poetics that itself denies the efficacy of the deliberately performative tactics of the male-identified poetic tradition. "Novices" reveals this cultural critique *cum* defense: "Novices / anatomize their work / in the sense in which Will Honeycomb was jilted by a duchess; / the little assumptions of the scared ego confusing the issue / so that they do not know 'whether it is the buyer or the seller who gives the money'— / an abstruse idea plain to none but the artist, / the only seller who buys, and holds on to the money." If one is not diverted by the allusive "Will Honeycomb," one is instead intrigued by this definition of the economics of the artist. Value resides within her/his imagination and cannot be either bought or sold. If the artist is excluded from an economics or exchange wherein acquisition is associated with shoring up the "scared ego," the "novices" who aspire to art are not themselves immune to the forces of corruption. These novices are not only young, they are also male, identified by their overweening egocentricity: "Because one expresses oneself and entitles it wisdom, one is not a fool. What an idea!" Moore's joke at the novices' expense exposes their foolishness as self-adulation. But this is just the beginning, for the novices' mistakes proliferate; they are "blind to the right word, deaf to satire, . . . averse from the antique." They choose, moreover, to write for an explicitly female audience, art serving as courtship: "they write the sort of thing that would in their judgment / interest a lady; . . ." Significantly, Moore includes herself among those ladies to whom the novices address their work: male artists who remain "curious to know if we do not adore each letter of the alphabet / that goes to make a word of it."

Winning women's admiration becomes a major aim of this seduction through language, for these would-be poets appropriate the alphabet to gain power over the women who read their words. By placing herself over against this company, Moore marks her sense of otherness and her marginalization from both economic and linguistic culture. Yet for Moore to identify with that feminine audience is potentially to deprive herself of one source of the novice's power, illusory as this might be. The imperative to create an outsiderhood that is itself not identified with passivity manifests itself stylistically in a poetics constructed to negotiate and to celebrate life, to provide Moore with a means whereby she can dissociate herself from the inherently engendered poetics that she finds morally as well as aesthetically reprehensible. Furthermore, Moore implicates economic and governmental structures in such an oppositional, masculinist-based poetics: "according to the Act of Congress, the sworn statement of the / treasurer and all the rest of it— / the counterpart to what we are." If institutions reify and thereby reflect our identity, then to succumb to such a culturally engendered script makes both men and women "stupid." "Stupid man; men are strong and no one pays any attention: / stupid woman; women have charm, and how annoying they / can be."

To break free of the confines of this engendered trap of language requires the sacrifice of ascriptive clarity, for Moore at times makes it difficult to discern not only the speaker's attitude toward the words on the page, but also the source of those words itself. Such an obfuscation of point of view bestows the freedom that enables Moore to interrogate as well as to describe the debilitating effects of cultural and aesthetic traditions. Such deliberate lack of perspectival clarity (masking, as it does, one's relationship toward language) provides Moore a means for containing as well as controlling the external, threatening, or simply offensive viewpoint that the narrative simultaneously interrogates and enacts. The poems might therefore be read as conversations between quotations or attributable statements with interpolations of an authorial narrative voice that emerges out of the dialogue; indeed, Moore's poems may constitutively function as a heteroglossia of textual voices that itself functions to displace authorial point of view. In "Novices," Moore uses the technique of narratorial displacement in the service of defining her criticism against the productivity, mastery, and capacity for an endlessly proliferating figuration she associates with an appropriative, masculine poetics. "Yes, 'the authors are wonderful people, particularly those that / write the most,' / the masters of all languages, the super-tadpoles of expression. " The novices are "bored by 'the detailless perspective of the sea,' reiterative and / naïve, / and its chaos of rocks—the stuffy remarks of the Hebrews— / the good and alive young men demonstrate the assertion / that it is not necessary to be associated with that which has annoyed one." The verbal echoes in "annoy" draw the reader back to the poem's earlier association of "annoyance" with women: "How annoying they can be." Not only does Moore define and condemn, she also records her own estrangement from such cultural deployment of language.

Through her idiosyncratic poetics and her use of a prosodic discourse that evades traditional poetic categories (gesturing instead toward a more demotic, unclassifiable sense of what language can be), Moore derogates the conventual assumptions that underlie traditional linguistic structures. In her poem "Bowls," Moore writes of her need for an etymological dictionary (one recalls Dickinson's insistence upon the fundamental and exclusive importance of her lexicon) as if the language as it exists were not her own. To be a "precisionist," accurate or faithful to what one sees, may be the sole redemptive capacity of a private poetics based upon an awareness of marginalization: "I shall purchase an etymological dictionary of modern English / that I may understand what is written." Ironically, the master of vocabulary voices the incomprehensibility of a language from which she feels dispossessed. Of course, her ironic glance at what is written conveys her intense criticism of the pretensions of those who would make communication more difficult than it need be—a charge readers often level at Moore's own work. Her aversion to those who write, to those "others," borders on a "sickness" that manifests itself in her formulated disavowal of that very aversion: " . . . it does not make me sick / to look playwrights and poets and novelists straight in the face/ . . . I feel just the same" ("Bowls"). Such aversiveness, no matter how playfully expressed (or, indeed, intensified through the need for such playfulness), is Moore's response to a writing that conforms to the cultural and economic terms intricated in a will to power and desire for mastery.

Beyond this antagonistic poetics, Moore advocates, whether in what she admires or in what she herself chooses to write, a willed relinquishment of the exercise of power. "When I Buy Pictures" defines such an aesthetics of selection. Her selection "must not wish to disarm anything," and Moore adds at the poem's close,

> It comes to this: of whatever sort it is,
> it must be "lit with piercing glances into the life of things";
> it must acknowledge the spiritual forces which have made it.

Overly intense self-scrutiny, however, may result in confusion. Suicidal dreams or self-inflicted injury can thus be avoided by turning outward, by humor and by appreciation. Too-vigilant introspection, in Moore's views, leads to paranoia:

> . . . you'll see the wrenched distortion
> of suicidal dreams
> go
> staggering toward itself and with its bill
> attack its own identity, until
> foe seems friend and friend seems
> foe.
> ("To Statecraft Embalmed")

If Moore disguises her inflection, it is not only because of her radical questioning of institutional structures, but also because of a more pervasive sense of alienation from the dominant and distinctly male-identified formulations of poetic modernism itself. Robert Lowell's recognition of the rebelliousness of Moore's work, what he describes as her "terrible, private, and strange revolutionary poetry," is absolutely accurate, for despite her many obscurities (or because of them), Moore takes her stand against the Romantic mythos of self-divination.[5] Her interrogatory poetics, if at times apparently in collusion with a male modernist tendency toward obscurantism, more often incorporate an open-endedness, a pluralism that eradicates hierarchy. Moore's foreclosing aphoristic assurance lends her an enabling verbal authority. It is Moore's prescriptiveness, aphoristic neatness, and willfully idiosyncratic rhyme that delimit the rigorous interrogations embodying the rebellious aspect of the poems. And yet the rhetorical digressions, overspecificity of descriptions, and proliferating negative constructions themselves function to divert the reader from the poems' true radicalism, a radicalism that is contained not in rhetorical over-formulation but in the interstices of self-doubt and observation of the external world that define Moore's poetic vision.

II

As an outgrowth of this wildly exuberant conception of style, Moore continuously strives to disengage composition from a cultural model in which publication is viewed as a form of appropriation, in which the dominant system of capitalist economics becomes the model for poetic acquisition or, to adopt another frame of reference, in which the individual's will to power is subdued or altogether denied in deference to an alternative aesthetics of modesty, gusto, and humor. Peter the cat embodies a standard of conduct by which such an artist might live, for "it is clear that he can see the virtue of naturalness, / that he does not regard the published fact as a surrender" ("Peter"). "Naturalness" thus becomes a defense against the combativeness of a world in which publication can be interpreted as a usurpation of the will. (One recalls Dickinson's description of publication as the "auction of the mind.") Yet Moore does not deprive nature or Peter of his aggression, for the predatory instinct is preserved in terms of a cautionary tale that is a consequence of predetermined identity.

> As for the disposition invariably to affront,
> an animal with claws should have an opportunity to use them.
> The eel-like extension of trunk into tail is not an accident.
> To leap, to lengthen out, divide the air, to purloin, to pursue.
> To tell the hen: fly over the fence, go in the wrong way
> in your perturbation—this is life;
> to do less would be nothing but dishonesty.

The poem's closing lines convey the honesty of acknowledging Peter's aggressive instincts as they suggest the formulation of a poetics of "truth-telling" that takes for its validation the "honesty" of the way things are, the truth about life. "Virtue of naturalness" thus becomes a stylistic virtue when the cat "tells" the hen to fly over the fence, but such virtue becomes problematic when the speaker wonders whether the cat does not, in its instinctive desire to catch the hen, *misdirect* her movements, for it is not made clear whether what is being described is the cat's or the hen's confusion. Or does the descriptive phrase itself refer to a confusion shared by animals and people alike—a plausible interpretation, given the rhetorical elision of Peter and that ubiquitous "one" who makes an appearance at various moments in the poem?

   With "inflection disguised" ("Those Various Scalpels"), Moore reinvents an aesthetics of renunciation, a series of punctuated deferrals, of endlessly proliferating figuration, that replaces or displaces the otherwise apparently controlling authorial presence directing the poem. Yet the erudition, the stream of unidentified allusions, the deployment of advertising copy and business-textbook prose, conjoined with Moore's compensatory self-imposed formalism, suggest a will to power that although associated with traditionally female attributes—modesty, privacy, the determination of worth based upon personal affection—nevertheles constitutes a bid for complete authorial control through stylistic manipulation. The reader thus remains at Moore's mercy, guided by no predictable signs of discursive, logical, or associational continuity. In this sense, Moore's poems enact Emerson's worship of whim, for if Moore's contextualizations can be distinguished from Pound's or Eliot's erudite interpolations by her inclusiveness, by Moore's choosing from what is available to all, this difference carries us only so far. The effect of such willful contextualization, whatever its sources, is to create a verbal field that borders upon the impenetrable, proving as deflective as any of those created by her contemporaries.

The telling difference lies, instead, in Moore's expressed purpose—a deflective poetics voiced in the service of a modest attentiveness that subverts the presence of a delineated selfhood, an armor of intimidating allusions designed to defend an apparently self-effacing ideal. One result of Moore's allusiveness is to create an ahistorical, imaginative field in which the poet ranges widely and enjoys her freedom, yet such "playfulness" makes its own demands upon the reader, who is dependent upon an associational context that reveals neither its sources nor its continuities. Yet intimidation need occur only if the reader insists upon reading by the old rules, making traditional demands upon the text. Moore's bid for control thus depends upon a complementary gesture on the reader's part. If one reads by these "rules," Moore's willful allusiveness seems (although not overtly) as much an authorial gesture of appropriation as Dickinson's poems of interrogatory definition, the expression of power over experience that excludes the reader from the specific, originatory experience itself (recall those poems of definition or abstraction that do not name but rather, through the imagination's transformative power, *reclaim* the external for the exclusive subjectivity that constitutes the Dickinsonian "self").

Despite their differences, what Dickinson's and Moore's poetics share is a bid for authorial control that would redefine the ontological status of the woman who herself feels marginalized from that authorization associated with the Emersonian central man. Such an opaque or obscuring poetics may be understood as a means of reasserting authority over experience without succumbing either to the debilitations of marginalization or to the strictures of traditional rhetorical expectations. By denying the validity of that most modern of hermeneutic codes, the psychological, Moore relinquishes what might have been (as it was for other modernists) a means of reclaiming experience for the self. "Psychology which explains everything / explains nothing, / and we are still in doubt," she asserts ("Marriage"). Just how to resolve that doubt informs Moore's deflective poetics.

Yet despite Moore's assertion (re: words) that "certainly the means must not defeat the end," one wonders whether at times her digressions into an ever greater specificity do not themselves render the object under observation more than a little hard to see ("Values In Use"). Moving as they do from absolute to absolute—from unequivocal assertion to unequivocal assertion—Moore's poems, like Dickinson's, record a discontinuity of extremes that undermines a consistent, informing vision while asserting its own constancy. This imperative to encode or to mask one's voice through ventriloquistic techniques of verbal displacement suggests the condition that must exist for all artists, but, I would suggest, most intensely for those whose relationship to the dominant tradition as well as to their audience is especially problematic, based as it is upon an incapacity to take for granted the notion that one belongs to any "visionary company" at all. Moore's *maskenfreiheit* (Heine's word) is, despite all her overt advocacy of plain speech, as deeply involved in the convolutions of style as

Dickinson's encoded poetics; moreover, Moore's sense of marginalization is implicated in her awareness of herself as a woman poet and of the role that the woman traditionally plays in the Romantic literary imagination.

The apparent "inappropriateness" or "eccentricity" of Moore's technique may, therefore, be understood as a radicalizing aesthetic that engages the reader in discomforting, because inherently violative, poetics. One does not want to submit imaginative interiority to such wry, sharp invective. It may not be true that Moore's poetry is "guarded," as it has so often been labeled, as that it exposes the wariness of readers who face a project that attempts to redefine human categories of thought and the consequent perceptions of the world we so tentatively inhabit. The interpretative difficulties posed by Moore's style, her intrinsically heretical politics and anti-self-promotional rhetoric, have been understood as at once intensely patriotic and akin to that most promotional yet self-effacing genre, the advertisement. The paradoxical aspects of such a definition reveal readers' wary recognition of a style that works against itself.

The stylistic difference between Moore's and Dickinson's modes of verbal deflection are, of course, necessarily linked to their distinct historicocultural circumstances. Thus, Dickinson's poetics develops, in part, out of a response to the tradition from which she necessarily felt excluded, barred from the dark consolations of Romanticism. Moore's poetics, it need hardly be said, emerges from her engagement with an ongoing modernist experimentation with composition and its various revisionary formulations in Eliot, Pound, Williams, and Crane. Yet in Moore's conceptualization of an adversarial world—to which she responds by creating a poetics at once nonaggressive and demotic, a discourse of collage that dazzles in its self-defense—she forges a style that bears a striking, if inverse, resemblance to Dickinson's own.

In her evocative stylistic analysis of Frost, Stevens, and Moore, Marie Borroff considers the relationship between Moore's use of "promotional" rhetoric and an aesthetics of self-effacement. Referring to Moore's technical deployment of aspects of feature writing, Borroff notes:

> The unpretentiousness of the feature article extends to its author as the expounding "I" through the medium of whose words its content reaches us. This author may tell us about someone who is famous, but we do not expect him to be famous himself; indeed, we pay little if any heed to him as a personality in his own right. To the extent that he draws our attention to his thoughts, emotions, and experiences as an individual, he has gone beyond the conventionally defined limits of the genre.[6]

What is "featured" is a language that deflects attention from the self toward the field of the object world, what Borroff later describes as Moore's "surreal word photographs" (p. 100), which create a world where creatures excel and plants can be heroes. The power of the self exists in its capacity to bear witness to these achievements. Reading Moore, therefore, one discovers a style that theatricalizes itself in the name of self-effacement. In Moore's poetics, the advertisement thus becomes a generic mask that provokes readerly response, directing that responsive feeling away from the author and back toward the textual field.

What would be the motive for such an ironically performative yet self-effacing poetics? In an essay on Edith Sitwell, Moore contemplates another virtuoso woman artist's conception of the relationship between poetry and the world:

> In his introduction to Paul Valéry's *The Art of Poetry*, Mr. Eliot includes a postscript-like speculation: "How poetry is related to life, Valéry does not say"—connected in my own mind with Edith Sitwell's self-decriptive comment: "The behavior of the world affects our beliefs and incites the mind to tumult to speak as a Cassandra or as an elegist."[7]

Given the choice between Cassandra and the elegist, Moore chooses instead the rhetoric of accurate disguise. This masking does not mean that interiority is lacking in Moore's poems, but rather that it has become a dissociated interiority in which feelings are displaced or projected onto a world animate but rarely human. Such dissociation is one origin of the uncanny effect Moore's work has on readers, who, while moved by the splendors of language, are left bemused at the discrepancy between wildly exuberant verbal play and an obscured, if not altogether submerged, subjectivity.

Traditionally, verbal display and subjectivity most powerfully converge in descriptions of the erotic, and it is here, in the self's relation to its own desire, that Moore's poetics grows most opaque as her poems deflect emotion away from the subject onto other forms of life. Such a negative correspondence between verbal energy and the effacement of a private self has signified for some of Moore's readers (Randall Jarrell among them) a kind of failure, for it creates a vision of the world that is dangerously oversimplifying. Moore's denial of the sexual, Jarrell remarks, is perhaps too comforting, too easy, and too complicitous. "We are uncomfortable—or else too comfortable—in a world in which feeling, affection, charity, are so entirely divorced from sexuality and power, the bonds of the flesh."[8] Moore's stylistic idiosyncracies or, more accurately, Moore's idiosyncracy as style might be interpreted as comprising an evasive rhetorical performance meant to distract readers both from the potential vulnerability of authorial subjectivity and from speculating upon the energies that produce this display. Like the "false eyes" of the Moro butterfly, the reader is directed to "attack" what can apparently be hurt but still leave authorial subjectivity secure. Given Moore's extraordinary verbal efforts and explicit descriptions of defense as a mode of living, one might consider her poetics in terms of injury, verbal camouflage, and readerly aggression. Rhetorical display becomes a mode of privacy central to Moore's sensibility, creating a protectiveness that she herself regarded as essential. Jarrell goes on to note that Moore dangerously distorts the moral, a subject on which she speaks with magisterial authority. He asserts that in Moore's work, "morality usually *is* simplified into self-abnegation."[9] While self-abnegation may be a simplification in terms of the complexity of moral issues, it is neither "easy" nor necessarily "comfortable" for the subject, the one living through and in that abnegation. Renunciation, that "piercing virtue," is a virtue that Moore and Dickinson share, for both deploy not a quiet or artfully natural poetic voice but a highly performative, dazzlingly figural language designed to protect the self against the adversarial possibilities of the world.[10]

Yet there is, of course, a crucial distinction between Dickinson's and Moore's performative selves. If for Dickinson, "self" remains the locus of the drama, the center of conflict, the site and dominant agent of experience, for Moore the self is impressed upon the external world. Such submergence of subjectivity, however, provides Moore the camouflage of intense particularity while preserving her espoused morality of self-effacement. As you will recall, Moore warns us of the dangers of too-prolonged introspection, the introspective investigation that lies at the heart of Dickinson's poetics and that is also a major source of her transformative, energizing pain.

> Me from Myself—to banish—
> Had I Art—
> Impregnable my Fortress
> Unto All Heart—
> But since Myself—assault Me—
> How have I peace
> Except by subjugating
> Consciousness?

Despite the severity of this self-inflicted assault, Dickinson withstands the tempting narcotic of self-effacement, achieving, as she herself characterizes it, a postmortem vision—"another way to see."[11] At the close of a passage that includes his characterization of Dickinson and the extraordinary "burden" of purification she places on language, Hartman invokes Marianne Moore as the poet who exemplifies an apparently salutary return to the figural density of language, the ludistic aspects of a poetics that is always on the brink of self-destruction. Hartman writes,

> We see that the poetic diction once rejected had extraordinary virtues, including its nonnatural character, its lucid artifice, the "mirror-of-steel uninsistence" (Marianne Moore) by which it made us notice smallest things and ciphered greatest things, and gathered into a few terms, magical, memorable, barely meaningful, the powers of language. (p. 132)

Admitting the difficulty he experiences trying to bring his essay on the "Purification of Language" to a close, Hartman maintains that

> like Mallarmé, she (Dickinson) is a crucial poet, a dangerous purifier, . . . In the German tradition Hölderlin, Rilke, and Celan have a similar relation to a purity more radical than what went under the name of Classicism. These poets are so intense— Shelley is another—they place so great a burden on the shoulders of poetry, that language breaks with itself.
>
> (p. 131)

But whereas the recuperative counter to such a vision of language and its function at the present time includes invoking Marianne Moore's attentiveness to the minute presencings of the external world and a delight in the display of figural language, I would locate Moore's ludic conception of language in a perception closer to Dickinson's than either Hartman or Moore herself might endorse. What Hartman wants to "understand is why the poetry Dickinson brings forth is so lean" (p. 130). And the question that follows is also a crucial question: "It would not be wrong to ask how she can be a great poet with so small a voice, so unvaried a pattern, so contained a form of experience." Hartman's questions, provocative as they are, evade the full force of Dickinson's strength, which seems (*pace* Hartman) less an instance of oversensitivity than a capacity for sustained scrutiny where other, less sturdy psyches would turn aside. Hartman, nevertheless, accurately describes the difficulties for Dickinson's readers: "Whereas, with many poets, criticism has to confront their overt, figurative excess, with such purifiers of language as Emily Dickinson criticism has to confront an elliptical and chaste mode of expression. The danger is not fatty degeneration but lean degeneration: a powerful, appealing anorexia" (p. 130). Hartman ascribes this leanness of language to literary historical causes, to the learned "Puritan scruples about language-art—." But his first evaluation gives way to a second, more complicated analysis, which more closely approaches the origins of Dickinson's aesthetic strategies. Hartman suggests, "We cannot dismiss the possibility that she so identifies with an ascesis forced upon her, that instead of the milk of hope she substitutes the 'White Sustenance— / Despair' (640)." This identification of an ascesis forced upon Dickinson is, to my mind, a more accurate description of her dynamics of aesthetic production as she seeks to discover how to make invention the mother of necessity.

Despite their overt stylistic differences, Dickinson's and Moore's poetics converge upon this ascesis. If for Dickinson the emptying out of the self creates a conception of figural language in which the self explores its quest for purification in stunning isolation (thus becoming the landscape that surrounds it), hers is a subjectivity so intense that normative oppositions dissolve at its approach, a subjectivity that interrogates the very question of representation. But is this not the proleptic inversion of Moore's own highly dense figural dramas, where once again the life of the self must be emptied out, where the proliferation rather than the elision of language functions protectively as the deflection of display? Questions of style in both Dickinson and Moore inevitably draw us back to questions of the self's experience of its own subjectivity. If in Dickinson, that subjectivity manifests itself as a language that questions representation and so quests toward a purification that continually threatens to destroy the representational community of a shared language, for Moore subjectivity must be deflected by embedding it in figural camouflage, the obligatory closure of aphoristic phrases, the falling back upon the distanced, purposive discourse of advertising—a verbal proliferation that effectively strives to *silence* the self. This, too, bespeaks Moore's identification with an ascesis forced upon her, but the strategies for defense against that identification manifest themselves in a deliberately armored language. For Moore, the purification of language is not synonymous with the self's quest for its own purification. Wallace Stevens, in "The Owl in the Sarcophagus," may, as Harold Bloom suggests, be antithetically completing Whitman's "Sleepers," but Stevens is also giving us a vision of both Dickinson's and Moore's aesthetics of language:

> she was a self that knew, an inner thing,
> Subtler than look's declaiming, although she moved
>
> With a sad splendor, beyond artifice,
> Impassioned by the knowledge that she had,
> There on the edges of oblivion.
>
> ....
>
> . . . in the silence that follows her last word—[12]

4

MARIANNE MOORE

Toward an Engendered Sublime

Nowhere is Marianne Moore's art of verbal deflection more apparent than in her two early, ambitious poems, "Marriage" and "An Octopus," works that originate in notebook meditations upon issues associated with human relationships and images affiliated with the natural Sublime. In the following discussion, I engage these poems at some length in order to elaborate upon the distinctive means whereby Moore approaches the interworkings of desire and cultural institutions and the links between gender and the American Sublime. Before turning to a reading of the poems themselves, however, a more general description of Moore's poetics, as I understand them, may prove useful.

If Moore, despite her professed aversion to Whitman, follows in his footsteps, she does so in two ways: first, through the insistence upon herself as "witness," the immediacy of individual observation; and, second, in her determination to free herself from outmoded forms and non-native styles.[1] If Moore's search for a distinctively American originality can be understood in relation to Dickinson's poetics in its exploration of alternative form and adherence to contemporary American experience, it is deeply Whitmanian as well.

Both Whitman and Moore possess the courage of great poets who set their sights on the future. Commenting upon the hidden origins of her creativity, Moore writes, "Creative secrets, are they secrets? Impassioned interest in life, that burns its bridges behind it and will not contemplate defeat, is one, I would say."[2] In terms of technique, as Grace Schulman has recently noted, overt similarities also exist. Schulman comments that "both are poets of place, creating wonder in the landscape and things of America, . . ."[3] Comparing Moore's "Dock Rats" and Whitman's "Crossing Brooklyn Ferry," Schulman continues,

> Both passages are written in an acervative style, the accumulation of detail forcing the reader's attention on the poet's process of thought. True, Whitman's clusters of detail show a growing relationship between poet and scene, while Moore's acervate style emphasizes the scene itself, leading to a joyful concluding statement: "shipping is the / most interesting thing in the world." Nevertheless, the excitement of either passage is in the sense of a mind set in motion by the amassment and reiteration of detail. (p. 13–14)

Similarly, Moore's interest in incorporating common speech into verse is a Whitmanian and, by extension, an American enterprise. Along with her Whitmanian origins, Moore's relation to the modernist project and a commensurate appreciation of the thoroughgoing radicalism that informs that relation are only now receiving their just recognition.[4] In her study of Moore (*Marianne Moore: Subversive Modernist*), Taffy Martin stresses the poet's differences, her distinguishing capacity to maintain her optimism while emphasizing "the discontinuity and contradiction that so many of her contemporaries wished to diminish" (p. 56). Martin, moreover, associates Moore's radicalism with her identity as a woman, asserting that what gives Moore the courage of her convictions is the site of her difference as a "renegade within the context of high modernism" (p. 125). According to Martin, Moore achieves "not a modernist but a postmodern interrogation of language that supercedes the radicalism of her contemporaries."

Addressing the difficulties readers of Moore have traditionally encountered, Martin observes:

> Moore's discourse does not submit to traditional interpretation, whatever the predilection of her critics, because she plays with the stereotype of feminine passivity and indecision by continually but idiosyncratically asserting her power and control. Moore begins, like her contemporaries, by rejecting and presenting a corrective to the excesses of nineteenth-century romantic verse. She goes on, however, in ways that her contemporaries did not, to question as well the literary tradition preceding it. She rejects the romantic pursuit of capturing and reproducing speech rhythms, even though she admired William Carlos Williams's attempts to do so. She then goes on to question the very efficacy of speech and language. (p. 124)

In summary, Martin says, Moore's poetics reveal a power that emanates from, rather than denies, her sexual identity (p. 139).[5] "Most of all, Moore's muscle enjoys showing the power that a solitary feminine speaker can harness." Although I share with Martin an appreciation of Moore's difference and an awareness of the extent to which Moore interrogates codes of language, her revisionary modernism, in my estimation, seems not only to tolerate confusion and privilege discontinuity, but also to be less completely triumphant than Martin asserts, for if Moore's radicalism is implicated in sexual difference, her poetry records the perils as well as the triumphs of that difference. Faced with a male poetic Sublime that would envision the woman as Other, as object or muse, Moore reestablishes the authority of the center (the acquisition of poetic authority) by displacing feeling in order to assume control over it. The defensiveness and suppression of expressive feeling that readers have so long noted in Moore cannot, as Martin suggests, be dismissed as misperception. Rather, the poems attest to a view of the world that is essentially adversarial, a view that requires a code of conduct suited for survival. Moore's rhetorical strategies offer ways to tamp rather than release feelings as they displace authorial affect through the proliferation of quotations and tropes. One asks of her poetry, where are others—not the otherness of type, exemplum, or anomaly, but the relational otherness that presents consciousness beyond and to the self? This question leads to an awareness not only of the restrictions imposed upon the Other but also of those imposed upon the presentation of the self. While the "I" of strong preference, of moral or critical authority, appears throughout the poems, only rarely does one discover an "I" that expresses the aura of spontaneity or direct emotion.

Cultural historians might locate the origins of Moore's appropriations of her self-image in the historical spectrum of possibilities available to a woman of such fierce poetic ambition. Her task was indeed formidable: to create her own version of poetic modernism without violating the contours of her familial and social identity. Cultural history is, however, not my primary concern here, for whatever combination of unconscious and conscious motivations, Moore evolves a poetics that suppresses the erotic in the name of the profoundly sublimating activity of art. In "Marriage," "An Octopus," and many other poems, Moore suppresses her relation to the poem, as subsequent drafts erase the earlier individualized voice in favor of a universalizing "one." Surely there is an inherent paradox in Moore's position; if, in order to claim the stance of radical spokesman, Moore adopts an antiquated persona, her assertion of a feminist aesthetics depends upon poetic disengenderment. It is hardly surprising that Moore's self-presentation encourages mixed or skewed evaluations, yet such misperceptions reveal as much as they foreclose. As I will argue, Moore's rhetorical techniques cumulatively achieve a turning-away from the erotic self as they betray a will to power over words through their apparent critique of that power. Moore's investment in propriety, her shock at Whitman's overt, erotic art, conveys, I would suggest, a will to power as great as his own. By converting cultural characteristics into tropes, by invoking self-parody as a costume for her own bravura, Moore retains her access to authority. On the level of poetic style, Moore's dense, figural field, with its extravagant similes and its plethora of voices, deflects the reader's attention from the relationship between language and speaker; hers is an exuberant verbal elaboration that invests rhetoric with a deflective value as it draws us into the play between tropes and away from the relationship between feeling and language. If Moore appeals to the authority of the witness and the proprietary claims of direct observation, the poems nevertheless resubmerge the witness's voice, relegating it to the silent margins of the text. In this engendered redefinition of the American Sublime, Moore is, in her time, stunningly alone.[6]

If Moore's poetics is achieved at the cost of erotic presence, it offers an alternative both to Whitman's insistence upon the primacy of sensation and to Dickinson's renunciatory poetics, conceived in terms of the "self" that Moore would efface. Through this rhetorical effacement, Moore wins the freedom to appropriate language, a strategy of colonization won at the price of feigned anonymity. Moore inflects values in terms of gender, yet simultaneously obscures personal presence, and in this sense, her work is, from the beginning, always "occasional." Moore's assertion that what she writes is "not poetry" itself engages modesty as a trope, for it awakens the reader to Moore's thoroughly radical conception of the poetic.

If "Marriage" addresses crucial issues of gender, sexuality, and desire, it bears witness to Moore's magisterial deployment of obscuring rhetorical techniques as well. The reading of "Marriage" that follows suggests the poem's deeply subversive cast, a subversiveness that Moore might have risked only by and through an intricate series of rhetorical baffles. When Moore turns her attention to the natural world of the American wilderness, she confronts it by combining the traditional high Romantic rhetoric of the Sublime with the discourses of American pragmatism, regulation, and domesticity. "An Octopus" reveals in minute detail what Moore as witness sees as it simultaneously occludes the mountain from our view. For unlike Dickinson and Stevens, poets who, according to Harold Bloom, make the visible "a little hard to see," Moore creates a world where the very fact of visual overspecificity may mean we see almost nothing at all.[7] "An Octopus" is as much a poem about the Family Romance as it is about "nature," and for Moore the naturalizing Sublime reveals as one of its meanings the primal scene of female poetic origins. The volatility and power of the materials Moore engages in "Marriage" and "An Octopus" may, therefore, provide a clue to these poems' extraordinary rhetorical expenditures. That "Marriage" and "An Octopus" should have their origins in a single text, that questions of sexual identity, culturally encoded gender roles, and the female self's relation to all beyond it should converge only to diverge into two distinct works makes sense. For surely, as a woman poet of formidable insight, Moore recognizes that the imagination is gender-identified and that the imagination's confrontation with the natural Sublime inevitably reenacts the self's experience of the origins of her personal, hence sexual, identity.

II

You are not male or female but a plan
deep-set within the heart of man.
                    —Moore ("Sun")

"My work has come to have just one quality of
value in it. I will not touch or have to do with
those things which I detest." In this austerity of
mood she finds sufficient freedom for the play
she chooses.

                    —William Carlos Williams

They make a nice appearance, don't they,
happy seeing nothing?
                    "An Octopus," 93–94

In the interest of clarity, I begin with a reading of "Marriage," which not only presents a highly dense, often apparently disjointed commentary on this cultural institution, but also engages more general issues relating to the nature of desire and the possibilities for male/female relationships. In this lengthy and particularly resistant poem, Moore discloses her own imaginative indictment of the institution that codifies the assumptions about gender that inform our cultural as well as our emotional lives. From the first, marriage is described in terms that raise questions as to its credibility in both the public and private spheres. As an institution, marriage is weak because it requires "public promises / of one's intention / to fulfill a private obligation" (ll.6–8). After this rather sociological pseudodefinition that challenges more than it actually defines, Moore asks, "I wonder what Adam and Eve / think of it by this time, / this fire-gilt steel / alive with goldenness" (ll.9–12). By speculating upon the original couple's response to the history they have themselves initiated, Moore deftly invents an ontogenetic trope that unites marriage as an institution with the genesis of human differentiation and self-consciousness. To invoke the first "couple's" judgment of the history they initiate is to elide myths of origin with sustaining cultural institutions. By describing what Adam and Eve are to evaluate as "this fire-gilt steel alive with goldenness," moreover, Moore substitutes for "Marriage" a discursive synecdoche. The phrase "fire-gilt steel alive with goldenness," with its representation of the wedding band as steel but appearing golden (and the possible pun of "gilt" and "guilt"), adds to the poem's proliferating, contradictory observations on marriage.[8] Indeed, the idiosyncratic "alive" suggests as well that it is feeling that informs the life of institutions, that marriage depends upon the power of such feelings divorced from any attempt to codify or reify their force. Thus the practice of marriage is rendered precious through the bestowal of mutual affection, and the image, uninflected by rhetorical directives, moves in at least two directions, creating a dynamic between approval and disapproval, an alterity of point of view that operates throughout the poem and makes linear interpretation problematic. Moore extends her golden associations, remarking, "how bright it shows." Again the brightness, although present, is called into doubt by the emphasis upon appearance, upon a deceptiveness that is confirmed by what follows: " 'of circular traditions and impostures, / committing many spoils' "(ll.14–15).[9] Not only is the institution itself a creature of cultural deception, but marriage also "commits" its own "spoils" in the very reification of an intimacy that perhaps cannot and should not be culturally or societally circumscribed. If marriage is as dangerous as it is alluring, it certainly requires "all one's criminal ingenuity / to avoid" (ll.16–17). Through its aversiveness and the requirement of a "criminal" because culturally illicit effort to evade a societally sanctified act, marriage becomes an institution hostile to the speaker for reasons as yet only partially identified. If human psychology cannot account for marriage (the need to codify intimacy), a return to the original politics of experience might offer in its culturally primal scene an insight into the rite of couples.

The return to the Garden is marked both by praise and the reassignment of blame in a revisionary genesis that offers a very different version from the scriptural description. The poem's redefinitions begin with Eve, who is not only beautiful but intellectually accomplished, "able to write simultaneously / in three languages," a woman of verbal fluency who knows her own mind and wants her solitude, expressing no need for the other who intrudes upon her prim(v)acy (ll.25–26). If Eve responds to Adam, "*I* should like to be alone," it is he who seduces the independent, competent, beautiful woman for *his* own needs (l.31). "Why not be alone together?" he asks—certainly the most ingenuous of questions (l.34). This, according to Moore, is the original Adamic temptation, a first fall and no *felix culpa*.

Yet this revisionary scene of masculine seduction is interrupted by a descriptive passage that evokes the pathos of the isolated male imagination, the subjectivity of the Adamic poet who would console his loneliness through woman.

> Below the incandescent stars
> below the incandescent fruit,
> the strange experience of beauty;
> its existence is too much;
> it tears one to pieces
> and each fresh wave of consciousness
> is poison.
>
> (ll.35–41)

Although one cannot with absolute assurance identify the voice that speaks these words, they nevertheless describe the forbidding experience of encountering the beautiful, a haunting beauty that the preceding lines associate with Eve. But these lines are also an indictment of her power, for in viewing her, "one" experiences the torture thus awakened by the introduction of desire itself as what would console Adam in his loneliness turns to poison before his eyes. "See her, see her in this common world, / the central flaw / in that first crystal-fine experiment" (ll.42–44). Unable to accommodate the burden of his desire, Adam refashions the woman's beauty into a fault that destroys his equanimity. Eve is thus converted into the immediate cause of, rather than the putative solution to, the pain of desire.

Yet the poem itself makes such an unambiguous interpretation difficult to sustain, for grammatically "the central flaw" also works appositively in relation to the phrase that immediately follows: "This amalgamation which can never be more / than an interesting impossibility" (l.45). Marriage could itself, on a syntactic level, be associated with poison. "This amalgamation" explicitly refers to the marriage of the poem's title, thus bearing a more general appositional relation to the poem's subject: the iteration of revisionary definitions.[10] The snake's temptation of Eve, her eating upon his invitation, thus becomes "that invaluable accident / exonerating Adam," freeing him because it assumes narrative responsibility for his own originatory desire that culminates in the marriage institution (ll.59–60). Yet the speaker(s) also recognize(s) the power of Adam's beauty as well as the mastery he himself embodies:

And he has beauty also;
it's distressing—the O thou
to whom from whom,
without whom nothing—Adam;
"something feline,
something colubrine"—how true!
(ll.61–66)

"Feline" may recall Peter the cat, who, one remembers, combines the predatory instincts of feigning and grace. This Adam is both predatory and "colubrine," or snakelike—an image of the scriptural tempter himself. In the pleasure he derives from his access to language, Adam describes the laws of the natural world as well as the customs of social law, "forgetting that there is in woman / a quality of mind / which as an instinctive manifestation / is unsafe" (ll.85–88). Deprived of this illusory recognition, eager to make an order out of the world and so discern as well as codify its structures, Adam continues to "generate discourse," as it were, for "he goes on speaking / in a formal customary strain, / of 'past states, the present state, / seals, promises, / the evil one suffered, / the good one enjoys, / hell, heaven, / everything convenient / to promote one's joy' " (ll.89–97). Although such linguistic prowess and putative command do not diminish his loneliness, they nonetheless convert him into an "idol," for the capacity to deploy language, to name the landscape as well as formulate the codifications of social intercourse, affords him an enabling yet burdensome power. Adam thereby creates through his power a crisis of consciousness that resembles that of the idealized male Romantic poet's quest for meaning in a world alive with the capacity for suffering.

Plagued by the nightingale
in the new leaves,
with its silence—
not its silence but its silences,
he says of it:
"It clothes me with a shirt of fire,"[11]
(ll.103–8)

Caught between the dangers of expression and the horrors of inexpressibility, the originatory male imagination cannot make its peace either with the nightingale's silence or with its song. The clarifying "with its silence— / not its silence but its silences" suggests, moreover, that what disturbs Adam is, in part, the intermittent character of the natural world, the periodicity that breaks up fluent discursiveness, a disruption that creates in the perceiving consciousness an unbearable sense of reciprocal discontinuity, hence the destructive double bind of the nightingale's silences: "It clothes me with a shirt of fire."

Unable to make peace with his own desire, and in the face of both his tenuous relationship with an uncontrollable natural world and its temptations, Adam as central man turns to Eve for his saving fiction—not so much deliberately turns as "stumbles," as if by accident. "He stumbles over marriage" in order "to have destroyed the attitude / in which he stood," the attitude of suffering in nature (ll.124, 126–127). Bound by the necessity of inaction, he seeks a solution beyond the self to break the pain of hearing/not hearing the nightingale's song.

> "He dares not clap his hands
> to make it go on
> lest it should fly off;
> if he does nothing, it will sleep;
> if he cries out, it will not understand."
> (ll.109–13)

To counter the double bind of such paralysis, the loneliness of living in a natural world immune to penetration by or through language, man invents marriage, thereby implicating it in the crisis of his imagination. By "stumbling" over it, he deflates the very solution he hoped would save him. The syntactic ambiguity of what follows creates an interpretative difficulty that nevertheless emphasizes (whatever readerly choices one imposes on the lines) the terms of the crisis:

> "a very trivial object indeed"
> to have destroyed the attitude
> in which he stood—
> the ease of the philosopher
> unfathered by a woman.
> (ll.125–29)

Marriage, presented as the putative resolution to the solitary man's suffering, is thus derogated by him in order to preserve his illusory independence from the necessity for such a solution. Consequently, "the ease of the philosopher" becomes a pose, an ironic ease that recalls his earlier condition when he was indeed "unfathered by a woman," without her and painfully alone. Yet the "ease of the philosopher" also conveys a portentousness that hardly characterizes the man trying to free himself from that excruciating "shirt of fire." In its own self-importance, the "philosopher" image gestures toward an aggrandizing self-pity that reflexively mocks an assumed, only apparent ease. But this interpretation does not address the inherent ambiguities of the phrase, "unfathered by a woman." Is man "unfathered" before or after his marriage? If marriage allows the possibility of man's legally becoming the father, then "unfathered" refers to this previous state of bachelorhood, yet "unfathered" echoes the more familiar "unmanned." The line suggests contradictory if related readings: to be unmanned is to be castrated; to be unfathered is at once not to have a father and to lose him in terms of the subject's own origins. Is the husband thus deprived of the father by the wife? To be "unfathered" may also describe the condition that necessarily precedes the presence of the woman who enables the man to assume his role as originary biological being—to father himself as well as father his own children. Thus woman simultaneously serves as legitimator, biological necessity, and castrating signifier. The prior state, "the ease of the philosopher / unfathered by a woman," however assured by the prelapsarian absence of woman, contains within it the pejorative associations of the "unmanning" of that very freedom. Man once again discovers himself trapped; to marry may resolve his philosophical and even his biological isolation but at the same time "unman" him by implicating him in the chain of desire. "Unhelpful Hymen" indeed, for marriage, instead of resolving, has reintroduced in sexual terms the anxieties of relation that Adam has already known and sought, through marriage, to resolve (l.130).

Like something old, something new, something borrowed, and something blue, this initial scenario proliferates into identifications, decorations, and rationalizations on marriage. Yet despite its ceremony of accrued meanings and the simultaneous undermining of those associations, images of Hercules and "black obsidian Diana," the poem continues to examine the complexities of affection living out its course over time. One is made to witness, for example, the masochism of "wifely" devotion:

> the spiked hand
> that has an affection for one
> and proves it to the bone,
> impatient to assure you
> that impatience is the mark of independence,
> not of bondage.[12]
>
> (ll.169–74)

The complex truth of this spiked hand worn "to the bone" for and against marriage represents the interrelatedness of *soma* and speech, between life lived and desire unspoken. Married life appears as a series of actions against one's own conflicting interests: "Married people often look that way" (l.175). From an elaboration of marriage as insult and mutual (self-) depreciation, the poem moves toward evaluating its own enumerations.

> turn to the letter M
> and you will find
> that "a wife is a coffin,"
> that severe object
> with the pleasing geometry
> stipulating space not people,
> refusing to be buried
> and uniquely disappointing,
> revengefully wrought in the attitude
> of an adoring child
> to a distinguished parent. . . ."
>
> (ll.209–19)

In these lines, difficulties proliferate along with associations. As the final resting place that at once contains as it proleptically recalls the husband to his death, the wife becomes a place that signifies a sense of an ending. If the "M" refers to the marriage that is the poem's title as well as its subject, then what precisely is "uniquely disappointing"—the person, the coffin, and/or the institution of marriage itself? Is marriage the coffin "revengefully wrought, in the attitude / of an adoring child / to a distinguished parent"? Why, once again, has the marital relationship been converted (recall "unfathered") into the dynamics of parental relations?

With their bickering, coterminal narcissism, the couple that emerges from Moore's cumulative description doom all hope for lasting relationship. "He loves himself so much, / he can permit himself / no rival in that love," and "she loves herself so much, / she cannot see herself enough" (ll.234–38). This marital collusion results in a mutually exclusive poverty, for "one is not rich but poor / when one can always seem so right" (ll.243–44). Is there a remedy for such destructive self-adulation, and what might it be? If marriage is grounded in power and the tension of suspended opposition, is there any hope? Given the poem's opacities, the reader's difficulty in assigning identities and pronominal referents, its problematic tone and mixed authorial allegiances, the answer may be negative. The poem faces the possibility of its own helplessness as it again focuses upon the self-created couple: "What can one do for them?" The question stands as the poem describes "this model of petrine fidelity" (the unfaithful wife) and her public husband/orator declaiming, "I am yours to command" (ll.251, 255). In a gesture of interpretative relinquishment, the poem asserts, " 'Everything to do with love is mystery' " (l.256). And yet such relinquishment is not synonymous with resolution, for once again, relentlessly, the poem pursues its course. Creating its own obstacles in what it chooses to perceive, it is not deflected by them, for there is something of value, something to be named, confronted, and acknowledged no matter how problematic or fraught with actual difficulties. At this moment in the poem, the issue turns to the origin of the speaking voice, conjecturally a sign of the poem's apparent undecidability, only to be resolved by the appearance of a monumental synecdoche, the statue of Daniel Webster in Central Park.

The final shift to politics, to a statue rather than a voice, to a monument that reinforces the reification of marriage as an institution, provides the closure to what might otherwise become a potentially endless conflict that in its accretions denies the impulse to conclude. The political posture and the assurance of stone silence as they articulate the poem's dangerous tendencies toward overaccumulation. Webster's words, "Liberty and union / now and forever," with their explicit political referentiality, similarly define as they deconstruct the condition of marriage itself (ll.286–87).[13] The poem draws our eye toward the statue as subject, "the Book on the writing-table; / the hand in the breast pocket" (ll.288–89). These are gestures of patriarchal assurance that need nothing to complete them. Thus, the formal posture of political and cultural validation reductively codifies the very attitudes toward marriage against which Moore's poem speaks. Although versions of marriage have heretofore proliferated throughout the poem, fragmentary rather than stone-solid, what unifies these fragments is a myth of creation in which marriage institutionalizes a relationship based upon the genesis of male need, desire, and despair, a relationship fraught with pain and based upon a power reinforced by the political, social, and cultural forces that ensure its preservation. Although "liberty and union / now and forever" may be read as an ironic invocation of patriotic institutionalization misapplied to the life of the affections, it may also be understood as an ideal of extraordinary rarity, which, however much a myth, given the potentially self-destructive love of both sexes and the narcissism that potentially always waits to devour relationships, nevertheless remains a possibility in the realm of the ideal "Marriage."[14] As its difficult deflections chip away at the stone edifice of marriage as institution, Moore's poem simultaneously refuses any ideological alternative, instead choosing the complexity of the psyche while undermining the fundamental assumptions upon which the bedrock of the marriage institution itself is based.

In terms of technique, the effect of Moore's enumerative poetics is to deflect the reader from the thread of continuity or the possibility of a continuity existing beyond the proliferation of description. Moore counters this proliferating allusiveness with the insertion of lines that seem to "sum up" or to render applicable the "meaning" of the disparate associations that the reader, provided with this guide, can then reinterpret. Provisionally, one can discern in this compositional structure Moore's attraction to the project that would consume so much of her energy toward the end of her life—her translations of La Fontaine's *Fables*, wherein a narrative is clearly separated from its moral, and the translator can proceed to direct her and the reader's attention to the fable with the assurance that what is simultaneously delineated will be unequivocally and univocally rendered as the already formed origins of the story itself. The relationship between stylistic manners and morals, always a vexing one for Moore, is thus potentially resolved by the form of the fable as a bid for security. Thus, the form's attraction may have its origins for Moore in its defense against the always potential problematic imbalance between exemplum and moral. Conjecturally, this always-to-be-resisted imbalance signifies anxieties associated with resolution itself. From this point of view, Moore's vexed poetics can be understood as reenacting a recurrent swing between proliferation and compression, the competing demands of accuracy on the one hand and the urge to discover in discrete phenomena an ethical imperative on the other. Such a poetics reveals a deeply Emersonian tendency that in Moore's work reaches the dimensions of a crisis, for the very success and specificity of Moore's descriptions lead the reader in one direction only to have her/his attention as craftily and abruptly drawn away. Moore's poetics and its inherent difficulties may have as much to do with accommodating oneself to the mission of the American Sublime—its assertion that there is the possibility of a knowable or identifiable reality—as it does with her sense of marginalization from such confident assumptions. Against such an historical and engendered decentering,

Moore's poetics strives to resolve the problematic aesthetic as well as moral choices her poems continuously engage. "Marriage" as institution and as text reflects the conflicts and verbal difficulties inherent in all chiastic conceptualizations—whether in the economics of affection or the rhetoric of style.

In terms of sexual identification, "Marriage" retains an unresolvable difference, a divorce between the masculine-identified poet trying to accommodate his solitary desire and the woman, who, despite her multiple talents, cannot finally protect herself. This perceived divorce between poetic sensibility and female sexuality provides one occasion for the fragmentation of the poem, which, rather than flaunting its literary willfulness (as Pamela White Hadas suggests), might be understood as investigating the separation between an awareness of oneself as woman and/or as alienated "sensibility" (whose gender remains masculine). The crisis of engagement between aspects of the self elaborated by "Marriage" is, among other things, an internal drama, which, nevertheless, encompasses the capacity of the self's fulfilling its desire through others. The diverse, often fragmented allusions in "Marriage" gesture toward the impossibility of such a union in the face of a cultural set of distinctions that the self not only perceives as surrounding her, but that also has penetrated the very core of her being. Thus "Marriage" implicitly argues for the inherent difficulty of mutuality by accreting evidence from various cultural sources that add up to a death sentence spoken against all such attempts at heterosexual relations because of the culturally inscribed dialectics of gender identity.[15] Not until gender has been redefined, not until we are rid of the old myth of Adam and Eve, with its initial bifurcation and guilt-naming, can the possibility of reconciliation be achieved over against the now-existent institutionalization of the individual's narcissistic and self-protective proclivities. In its fragmentary indictment of cultural definitions of sexual differentiation and profoundly skeptical conception of human personality, "Marriage" is as radical as those poems that are its equals both chronologically and in terms of ambition, Pound's "Cantos," Eliot's "The Waste Land," and Williams' "Paterson." That the reception of "Marriage" should have been near silence bespeaks, in part, the tremendous cultural resistance to an indictment that requires not only a revisionary mythmaking but also a reexamination of the relationship between one's sexual identity and its institutional manifestations, both in terms of the literary tradition and in terms of the political institutions in which or against which the literary chooses to define itself. A marriage between the personal and the political informs Moore's poetics. The intelligent pressure Moore brings to bear upon the private, a kind of analytic scrutiny we more readily associate with philosophical discourse, may be one origin of our difficulty in coming to terms with the poem, a difficulty that contributes to its "impenetrability."

The apparent "inappropriateness" or "eccentricity" of Moore's techniques may, therefore, be understood as a radical aesthetic strategy that engages the reader in a disquieting, because inherently violative, poetics. One does not easily submit subjective experience, let alone intimate desires, to such wry, sharp invective. It may not be that Moore's poetry is quite so "guarded" as readers would wish, but rather that her work challenges the vary wariness of those readers who confront a poetics that interrogates culturally inscribed gender relations.

5

THE "PIERCING, MELTING WORD"

Moore's "Octopus"

This division into masculine and feminine
  compartments of
achievement will not do . . . one feels oneself to
  be an integer
but one is not one is a particle
in an existence to which Adam and Eve
are incidental to the plot.
            —Marianne Moore (Stapleton, 39;
                Rosenbach, 1251; 7, 18–19)

Sweet Mountains Ye tell Me no lie—
Never deny Me—Never fly—
                        —Emily Dickinson
                              (722)

If "Marriage," that deeply conflictual, extended meditation upon the nature and origins of engendered relations and their institutional forms, remains Moore's major statement on the inherent difficulties of a world of human desire and otherness, "An Octopus" is its companion poem, equal in its metaphysical imperative and equivalent in its exploration not of human interrelations but of the individual imagination's confrontation with nature, the subject of the naturalizing Romantic Sublime. Surely it is significant that "Marriage" and "An Octopus" should have initially merged in Moore's mind, that, indeed, Moore's extensive preliminary notes for each poem should interweave in what Moore seems to have envisioned as a single long poem that, as Patricia Willis documents, only subsequently became two poems. To recontextualize "An Octopus," to read it in light of the concerns that emerge from the preceding discussion of "Marriage," may enable us to define more accurately Moore's version of the Romantic Sublime and its powerful, if submerged and partially expurgated, subtext of sexuality. Moore's thoughts in preparation for the writing of "An Octopus" find their source (if we take the notebooks as evidence) in "twenty-two pages of notes about Adam, emotions, and other images that consider human relationships. . . ."[1] In her essay on "An Octopus," Willis cites this "remarkable conjunction of lines":

An octopus of ice
so cool in this the age of violence
so static & so enterprising
heightening the mystery of the medium
the haunt of many-tailfeathers
these rustics calling each other by their first names
a simplification which complicates
one says I want to be alone
the other also I would like to be alone.
Why not be alone together
I have read you over all this while in silence
silence?
I have seen nothing in you
I have simply seen you when you were so handsome you gave me a
start[2]

Surely, "An Octopus," with its explicit echoes of Dante, Milton, Wordsworth, and Shelley, is Moore's most magisterial poem on the subject of the Romantic Sublime. The poem engages fundamental issues of the Western poetic tradition: the competing claims of Greek versus Judeo-Christian culture, the relation between the imagination and the natural world, and the ethics of human behavior within that world. Moreover, "An Octopus" includes a reenactment of Adam and Eve's banishment from the Garden of Eden, transcribed into Moore's demotic diction:

'disobedient persons being summarily removed
and not allowed to return without permission in writing'

A poem of vast ambition, "An Octopus" not only endows Moore's personal experience of Mt. Tacoma with mythological structure and cultural resonance, but even more crucially, it redefines the Romantic crisis poem in terms of a woman's encounter with the Sublime, an encounter that reenacts, from the point of view of the woman, the dynamics of the Family Romance. Preparation for such a bold, revisionary project was formidable, and Moore's voluminous notes demonstrate not only her characteristic thoroughness but also a telling elaboration of themes later submerged or rendered partially obscure by the poem's dense, allusive structure.

Of Moore's traditional literary, readily traceable sources, perhaps the one that most fully anticipates the poem's vision of glacial violence comingled with a descriptive fidelity to the prolific devastation of life is Shelley's "Mont Blanc."[3] But whereas Shelley, with his customary dazzling assurance, closes his magnificently rendered vision of the original, eruptive violence that rises, transmuted before him, by reasserting the sovereignty of the human imagination, Moore's "An Octopus" ends with a vision of violence in stasis that neither asks nor answers the challenge of the competing powers of the human imagination and the external world.[4] Instead, Moore's poem closes with the threat of violence as "something ever more about to be" (Wordsworth, *The Prelude,* VI.608)

> the white volcano with no weather side;
> the lightning flashing at its base,
> rain falling in the valleys, and snow falling on the peak—
>
> the glassy octopus symmetrically pointed,
> its claw cut by the avalanche
> "with a sound like the crack of a rifle,
> in a curtain of powdered snow launched like a waterfall."

The rhetorical poise that constitutes closure depends upon the participial repetition of "falling," a repetition that simultaneously describes as it freezes action; similarly, the reification of that action into the noun that ends the poem, "waterfall," converts motion into stasis. Note how closely Moore echoes Wordsworth's earlier use of grammatically related techniques to create an effect of vertiginous stasis:

> . . . The immeasurable height
> Of woods decaying, never to be decayed,
> The stationary blasts of waterfalls, . . .
>   (*The Prelude,* VI, 624–26)

Although Moore employs related rhetorical means to achieve a salutary stasis, she eschews the final act of Wordsworthian distancing wherein the scene is read allegorically as

> Characters of the great Apocalypse,
> The types and symbols of Eternity,
> Of first, and last, and midst, and without end.
>   (lines 638–40)[5]

Instead, Moore creates closure by obscuring abrupt violence with a double veil of similes. Thus, the action described within the poem is not temporally located; rather than present the onslaught of the avalanche as past, present, or future, the poem simultaneously presents us with its consequences: "its claw cut" and the sharp noise that apparently precedes this effect. This conflation of act and aftermath, rather than being resolved, is enhanced by the similes that reiterate violence converted into loveliness: " 'with a sound like the crack of a rifle, / in a curtain of powdered snow launched like a waterfall.' " As readers, our desire for order, sequence, and meaning are deflected in favor of the aestheticization of the image, as the figural continues its task of displacing violence with beauty.

If Moore deploys the rhetorical gestures of the Romantic Sublime for her own purposes, she also incorporates the explicitly "modern," or "new," for "An Octopus" contains a critique of an aggressive, exploitative culture and an admiration for equally American attributes—the ravaging loveliness of the rugged wilderness and a pragmatism that enables survival in the face of adversity. Furthermore, in the poem's wide-ranging allusiveness and admixture of quotations from such diverse sources as *Rules and Regulations: Mount Rainier* (Washington, D.C.: Department of the Interior, 1922) (Willis, 248) and Richard Baxter, the seventeenth-century nonconformist English divine, Moore creates her customary "American menagerie of styles." In its depiction of a landscape to be read, the violence discovered there, and the testing of competing forces of the imagination over against the world, "An Octopus" draws upon the tradition of the Romantic Sublime as it records a difference. Finally, it is in the reengendering of that sublime confrontation, in Moore's revision of the Sublime as a female-centered Family Romance, that the poem performs its most radical gesture.

It we return not to the version of "An Octopus" that appears in Moore's *Complete Poems*, but to the manuscript revised slightly for publication in the December 1924 *Dial* and reprinted in the 1984 *Twentieth Century Literature*, we find in the original a passage Moore later excised that provides a key to the difference between the tradition of the Romantic Sublime and Moore's revisionary conception. For despite the easily amassed differences between "Marriage" and "An Octopus," on another level both poems engage similar questions relating not simply to the authority of the imagination over experience, but also, more specifically, to a woman poet's understanding of her possible authority in the world. What my reading of "An Octopus" attempts to show is that the drama of glaciers, mountains, and a later-deleted orchid reenacts both in its violence and in its dread the drama of sexuality that Moore envisions as essential to the life of the imagination. Not surprisingly, the lines Moore suppresses are those that most directly and explicitly implicate her in the life of the poem. Sexual, mythic, and personal identifications, later attenuated or excised, contribute to a cumulative view of opposition that reenacts (with the obvious displacement of setting) the conflicts elaborated in "Marriage."

What emerges from a recontextualization of the excised passages is a clearer understanding of the themes that inform the poem's major preoccupations: readerly aggression, the power of a female-identified nature, and the kind of strength required to overcome both the adversarial aspects of the world and the destructive misunderstanding of those readers who cannot comprehend the magnitude of the task at hand—the need to master the imminent threats of masculine appropriation (the intrusive climbers) and the glacier's paradoxically maternal, rapine claw. The 1924 text and the version of "An Octopus" that appears in the *Complete Poems* show several differences: shifts in line breaks and other relatively minor deletions. Most important, Moore's major excision removes from our extended scrutiny a myth that makes a fundamental contribution to the subject of gender and authority as it is elaborated throughout the poem. Here is the excised passage:

> Larkspur, blue pincushions, blue peas, and lupin;
> white flowers with white, and red with red;
> the blue ones "growing close together
> so that patches of them look like blue water in the distance;"
> this arrangement of colors
> as in Persian designs of hard stones with enamel,
> forms a pleasing equation—
> a diamond outside and inside, a white dot;
> on the outside a ruby; inside, a red dot;
> black spots balanced with black
> in the woodlands where fires have run over the ground—
> separated by aspens, cats' paws, and woolly sunflowers,
> fireweed, asters, and Goliath thistles
> "flowering at all altitudes as multiplicitious as barley,"
> like pink sapphires in the pavement of the glistening plateau.
> Inimical to "bristling, puny, swearing men
> equipped with saws and axes,"
> this treacherous glass mountain
> admires gentians, ladyslippers, harebells, mountain dryads,
> and "Calypso, the goat flower—
> that greenish orchid fond of snow"—
> anomalously nourished upon shelving glacial ledges
> where climbers have not gone or have gone timidly,
> "The one resting his nerves while the other advanced"
> on this volcano with the bluejay, her principal companion.
> "Hopping stiffly on sharp feet" like miniature icehacks—
> "secretive, with a look of wisdom and distinction, but a villain,
> fond of human society or the crumbs that go with it,"
> he knows no Greek, the pastime of Calypso and Ulysses—
> "that pride producing language,"
> in which "rashness is rendered innocuous, and error
>   exposed
> by the collision of knowledge with knowledge."
>
> (ll.130–61)

With its perspectival patternings and Miltonic "enameled" order, the surface vegetation that gratuitously grows upon the mountain is the art that escapes the intrepid mountaineers, here seen as at a great distance, as "puny, swearing men / equipped with saws and axes." If these flowers are inimical to the men who would scale the mountain, the glacial mass itself—"this treacherous glass mountain / admires" beauty that can survive it: "gentians, ladyslippers, harebells, mountain dryads." The femininity and fragility of the list culminate in "Calypso, the goat flower," a rare, extremely delicate pink orchid. The "goat flower" recalls, as Willis suggests, the goat-god Pan, mythic persona of natural, priapic power. "Anomalously nourished upon shelving glacial ledges/where climbers have not gone or have gone timidly," the rare Calypso thrives, but not alone, for there is the "bluejay, her principal companion," a bird that quickly acquires hostile attributes. " 'Hopping stiffly on sharp feet' like miniature ice-hacks," the bird is masculine, "secretive, with a look of wisdom and distinction, but a villain." Like Adam who prides himself on his wisdom but knows fewer languages than the erudite Eve, of "Marriage," this bluejay cannot engage in the pastime of Calypso and Ulysses, the seductive pleasure of conversation, " 'that pride producing language,' in which 'rashness is rendered innocuous, and error / exposed / by the collision of knowledge with knowledge.' " If the bluejay cannot converse, the Greeks similarly lack the requisite qualities for genuine experi-ence: " 'emotionally sensitive, their hearts were hard' " (l.189). It is the Calypso orchid, delicate flower and mythic female voice of seduction, the one who woos through language, not those who like smoothness nor the contemporary "ora-cles of cool official sarcasm," who endures. For Calypso acquires more than a symbiotic relation to the mountainside she inhabits as, through synecdoche, the orchid comes to represent the glacier's forbidding presence:

> this fossil flower concise without a shiver,
> intact when it is cut,
> damned for its sacrosanct remoteness—
> > (lines 202–4)

Aware of the dangers that would assault it, the fossil flower remains remote. If Calypso speaks, she must do so in a language that fends off her readers, exercising a verbal restraint that serves to protect her against the violation of those who would vanquish her, those climbers with saws and axes. To envision Calypso as an image of the woman poet confronting an adversarial readership and the abandonment of her beloved is to follow the clues, offered in Moore's notebook entries, that directly compare her situation to Calypso's and the poem's own discussion of the octopus to the relationship between literary style and the reading public:

> not decorum, but restraint;
> it was the love of doing hard things
> that rebuffed and wore them out—a public out of sympathy with
> > neatness.
> Neatness of finish! Neatness of finish!
> "Occasioning no little consternation,"
> relentless accuracy is the nature of this octopus
> with its capacity for fact.
> > (ll.206–12)

If the abrading surfaces of glacier and mountain create such neatness of finish, the tension between the restrained difficulties of Moore's language and the readerly impositions it demands serve a mutual function, a protective process that allows the mountain and language to survive. The inviolability of such restraint protects, yet that protection works only to ward off human adventurers, for the glacier itself is on the move:

> "Creeping slowly as with meditated stealth,
> its arms seeming to approach from all directions, . . ."
> (ll.213–14)

Its violence causes a destruction so complete it renders natural phenomena beyond normative naming:

> Is tree the word for these strange things
> "flat on the ground like vines;"
> some "bent in a half circle with branches on one side
> suggesting dustbrushes, not trees . . . [6]
> (ll.218–21)

The deflationary "dustbrushes," while introducing the domestic, only momentarily stave off the vision of overwhelming devastation. In an echo of the Websterian advice that closes "Marriage," " 'Liberty and union now and forever,' " the trees struggle toward a similar solution: "some finding *strength in union,* forming little stunted groves, / their flattened mats of branches shrunk in trying to escape" (italics mine). As in "Marriage," with its finally unsatisfactory application of the political to the personal, this attempt to find strength in collective endeavor amounts to a pathetic failure that gives way before the final scene of violence that freezes threat in vertiginous stasis. In this confrontation, the mountain faces both its natural and human adversaries, those that would penetrate so as to ravage its native beauty. Against such mercantile and natural forms of exploitation, Moore presents the fossil flower that, although concise, does not shiver, that remains intact when it is cut, whose art is the art of self-protection, the only art strong enough to survive in a landscape as adversarial as that evoked by the conditions of our history. Thus, while establishing itself firmly within the tradition of the Sublime confrontation between the human imagination and nature, "An Octopus" situates that encounter within the dynamics of gender by aligning female powers of language with that of natural endurance, with a nurturance and restraint that inform the core of Moore's poetics.

Yet if one examines the image of the octopus, the cumulative, creaturely image that at once telescopes the encroaching glacial mass and endows it with identity, one discovers another scene that complicates the elision between the Calypso orchid and the "fossil flower."[7] This scene can be read as being presented from the point of view of a child who would fend off a stifling, overwhelming maternal pressure along with the threat of sexual violation. Both male and female positions threaten to destroy the daughter's fragile presence. Conquest recalls the threatening primal scene. Thus, the close of "An Octopus" might be viewed as a witness's description of an incipient scene of destruction, a witness who identifies with the failed attempt at union, the child who recognizes the inevitability of the destruction of what is most valuable and most vulnerable.

The identifying signs of the glacier as mother, threatening and nurturing at once, assume an almost uncanny presence, for Moore's descriptions of the octopus emphasize its restraint, control, nurturance, and compliance, echoes of Moore's conflictual relationship with her own mother. From the poem's opening description: "An Octopus / of ice. Deceptively reserved and flat, / it lies 'in grandeur and in mass' / beneath a sea of shifting snow dunes; / dots of cyclamen-red and maroon on its clearly defined pseudo-podia, / made of glass that will bend—a much needed invention—" the images of reserve and contained, massive force develop. "A much needed invention" recalls the cliché, "necessity is the mother of invention," with the unspoken term, "mother," excluded. By the poem's close, the maternal glacier has become an object both to be emulated and defended against through the very female powers and the linguistic resources that the good mother as mountain has bestowed upon her daughter. In this split image of mother as devourer, as submerging glacier and inimitable, endangered mountain (echoed in Moore's use of the Indian name Mt. Tacoma) one discovers the conflictual relationship between maternal nurture and strangulation that informs the troubled origins of the poetic consciousness from which the poem speaks. Ambivalence toward the maternal emerges throughout the text as the image of the glacier acquires the attributes of delicacy and protectiveness that camouflage its ultimately destructive intent— the destruction of the mountain it abrades, as the bad mother threatens not only the mountain, but also, more immediately, the fragile, rare orchid, the beautiful flower that is the mountain's true progeny. Interestingly, the orchid is nurtured both by good and bad mothers, by glacier and mountain, fed by the mountain's thin soil, watered by the bitter, icy waters that seep from the "rocky, hard breasts" (Elizabeth Bishop's phrase), from the melting glaciers.

That "An Octopus" reinscribes Moore's Family Romance is, of course, no surprise, given the primal materials and originary questions it so ambitiously addresses. That Moore should have published no poems for seven-and-a-half years following the 1924 publication of "An Octopus" may, moreover, bespeak a psychological impasse signalled by the position of the tenuous, threatened daughter that "An Octopus," despite its attempts to work through and to gather strength against primal oedipal materials, fails to resolve. What Moore discovers, as she had in "Marriage," is that such "union" does not suffice to conquer the perceived double threat of male aggression and maternal destructiveness. Both poems end with the admission of a failure of the imagination that manifests itself as stasis: "Marriage" with the image of a statue, "An Octopus" with the framing of the avalanche that holds off victimization but admits to no resolution of the difficulties inherent in all human relationships and the failure of the woman's linguistic expertise to achieve union. Both Eve and Calypso fail to contain the men with whom they wish to converse. If there is any protection from the "mother," that glacial, icy nurturance threatens to destroy the emergent flower, for Calypso remains trapped in her isolation despite her endowment of the maternal powers of refined speech. While remaining in the protection of the good mother, the mountain, Calypso faces the glacial violence that would abrade her to extinction. She is a self-endangered species. Trapped by daughterly affection as well as by the strangling arms of maternal devotion, the imagination is faced with a double bind it cannot evade—hence, one speculates, the lapse into silence as the psyche strives to break this impasse of victimization. What both eludes Moore's revising of the Sublime and remains elusive is the attainment of happiness, the paradisiacal vision. Although literally situated in a park named "paradise," "An Octopus" envisions a world in which paradise remains forever unattainable, warded off by the conflictual threats of family and, more explicitly, of sexuality. The arresting scene of violation and the very process of arresting convert the promise of a Miltonic paradise into a crisis that emanates from the distinctively female, daughter-identified imagination. Here is the promise of sexual reciprocity, of reflection and mutuality:

> Another side, umbrageous Groves and Caves
> Of cool recess, . . .
> . . . meanwhile murmuring waters fall
> Down the slope hills, disperst, or in a Lake,
> That to the fringed Bank with Myrtle crown'd
> Her crystal mirror holds, unite thir streams.
> The Birds thir choir apply; airs, vernal airs,
> Breathing the smell of field and grove, attune
> The trembling leaves, while *Universal Pan,*
> Knit with the *Graces* and the *Hours* in dance
> Led on th' Eternal Spring. . . .
> (*Paradise Lost,* IV, 257–68)

"An Octopus" presents the waterfalls, grottoes, lake, mirror reflections, birds, Pan, and caves of cool recess, but shows them in stark isolation, so that no such vital happiness can occur. The poem describes a dangerously adversarial landscape where the beavers' den is "concealed in confusion," where one must become acclimated to survive conditions so austere.

> A special antelope
> acclimated to "grottoes from which issue penetrating draughts
> which make you wonder why you came,"
> it stands its ground
> on cliffs the color of the clouds, of petrified white vapor—
> black feet, eyes, nose, and horns engraved on dazzling icefields, . . .
> (ll.60–65)

The anomalous adjustments necessitated by those who would live on "Big Snow Mountain," who make it their "home," testify to the privations of such geographical severity, where the essential streams that nurture life may carry death, where moisture transmuting verdure into onyx works its lethal alchemy.

Standing at the mountain's top, the goat is itself "a scintillating fragment of those terrible stalagmites," a phallic manifestation of the glacier and its creaturely counterpart. Strewn with the feminized map of flowers, the "cavalcade of calico," the mountain merges with language in Moore's notebook entry (p. 41) that combines passages from Richard Baxter's "The Saints' Everlasting Rest" with John Henry Newman's *Historical Sketches:*

> the Greeks liked smoothness,
> telling us of those
> upon whose lifelessness
> [the] piercing melting word becomes
> a pearl on lepers hands
> since some of them
> weary of a hard heart, some of a proud,
> some of a passionate & some, of all
> these & much more.[8]

"The piercing melting word" eloquently represents the combined phallic and glacial origins, the male and female sources from which language flows. That the pearl, itself an object produced by inward abrasion, falls on lepers' hands recalls the poem's subsequent description of the public's dislike, or rather, misunderstanding of Henry James's work, the literary precursor of the restraint produced by too great an affection rather than by too little. If the piercing melting work, phallic milk converted into language, cannot find an auditor who understands, if Calypso, the pink and yellow hidden orchid, fails to be understood by the bluejay (the pink and blue tag of gender assigning an infantilizing identification of color), then the lessons of verbal restraint taught by the literary father and the biographical mother cannot protect the daughter-poet who would wish a responsive, surely not an illiterate, male.

Both the cultural and the natural descriptions of the male, however, offer no alternative but to turn away from the expectations of unrequited love as a source for potential happiness. And yet the mountain, with the imminent pressures of the abrading glaciers, offers neither safety nor neutrality. Instead, the poem retreats not to the claims of the powers of the imagination, as in "Mont Blanc," but to a reassertion of the objective conditions, the glacial movements, that create psychic threat, arresting anxiety by representing the violence at the origins of crisis.

> Neatness of finish! Neatness of finish!
> relentless accuracy is the nature of this octopus
> with its capacity for fact.
>
> (ll.209–11)

If recollections of Moore's own mother, her penchant for accuracy, her insistence upon fact, invest the approaching glacier with maternal resonance, this precipitating violence dashes all hopes of recovery as the pathos of the desolate trees, the "little stunted groves," shrink "in trying to escape / from the hard mountain 'planed by ice and polished by the wind'—." Despite Moore's excisions, the covering up of the traces of the familial, psychic origins that determine the poem's view of the imagination and the world, the threat of the Family Romance emerges in stark defiance. That such violence should itself demand that the psyche strive to suppress recognition of its origins is hardly surprising. Rather, when one examines the layers of deflection created by the proliferation of quotations, the dislocations of image and voice, the narrative stance of objectivity, what emerges is the recognition of the potency and danger of the "piercing melting word" along with the even harsher recognition that even to possess a powerful voice may finally offer insufficient protection against

> the glassy octopus symmetrically pointed,
> its claw cut by the avalanche
> "with a sound like the crack of a rifle,
> in a curtain of powdered snow launched like a waterfall."
> (ll.228–31)

The power of language to arrest threat and ward off danger, although it creates a scene of sublimating, sublime loveliness, does not erase this threat. Despite the aesthetic consolation of the poem's close, the threat abides in the arrested struggle toward and impossibility of any union—marital, communal, or linguistic—that could effectively defend against the ravages of so deeply engendered a Sublime. As Moore builds from her notes to her poem, she submerges her explicit relationship to Calypso as she suppresses the origins of "An Octopus" in "Marriage." By the poem's close, these acts of rhetorical displacement covertly represent a scene wherein the symbolic mother threatens her natural children, causing them in panic to find "strength in union." The poem's speaker is no participant in but an observer of that scene, having rescued herself long before, not only through a comixture of quotations and descriptions, but also through the discontinuities that rob the poem of discursiveness.

In place of sexual dynamics and personal identifications, Moore reconstructs a "natural" scene that serves a dual purpose as the text removes Moore as daughter from danger (the threat of the avalanche) and enables her to escape the fate of Calypso who, despite all her verbal powers, nevertheless must relinquish Ulysses at the gods' bidding. Before Calypso is silenced or removed from the poem, however, she is converted into something else, not a "special antelope," but part goat nonetheless:

> and "Calypso, the goat flower—
> that greenish orchid fond of snow— . . .

Thus begins the aforementioned passage that describes a clearly engendered drama between the goat flower and the masculinized bluejay. That the final version should omit Calypso and preserve the goat in isolation is the first of a series of rhetorical gestures that distance issues of gender from the text to which, initially, they are so closely tied. In a similar act of self-inclusion that simultaneously occludes specific identity, Moore (as Willis notes) incorporates family nicknames into her list of creatures who inhabit the mountainside.[9] If early in the poem, Moore allows her family a place on the mountain, she has by the poem's close, in the sequence of final devastation, replaced this allusive fauna with flora, a displacement that intensifies the initial displacement in the very act of *including* family nicknames in a list of otherwise purely "naturalistic" descriptiveness. This elision of categories suppresses as it retains family presence by at once erasing the distinction between person and creature while preserving the secret identification of individuals.

Moore achieves a similar suppression of gender identity by the restraint identified with the mountain's feminine speech associating the feared main peak of Mt. Tacoma, "damned for its sacrosanct remoteness," with Henry James "damned by the public for decorum"; "not decorum but restraint." Interestingly, as Willis notes, Moore quotes her mother's comment on James from Carl Van Doren's *The American Novel* (New York: Macmillan, 1921): "He says what damns James w[ith] the public is his decorum—It isn't his decorum it's his self control, his restraint [,] his ability to do hard things w[ith] suavity. It wears them out" (Willis, 259) Willis continues, "In the same notebook, Moore again quotes Mrs. Moore: 'The deepest feeling ought to show itself in restraint,' " a statement she would elsewhere (in "Manners") ascribe to the voice of the father. That in "An Octopus" Moore should quote her mother's words may be just as significant as the attribution to James of the very restraint that Moore identifies with her mother's values and voice, for this suggests a transposition of female-associated values to the public, masculine voice of modernist authority. If, for Moore, Henry James is "a characteristic American" (Willis, 259) and "his restraint masks an abundance of affection" (Willis, 259), that "restraint" is "like that of the mountain and suits it as the Greeks' hardness of heart does not" (Willis, 259). While it may be too simple to suggest that James stands in for the maternal origins of restraint, the verbal source that is, in actuality, Moore's mother, the poem nevertheless works from a female to a male identification. This move participates in a more widespread tendency in Moore's work not merely to obscure the biographical (a fact frequently noted by others) but also to supplant the original mother-daughter dynamics of poetic origin with a more "neutralized" veneer of impersonality in order to speak with the universalized authority of the masculine poetic tradition. Another retreat into "transgendered" privilege occurs when the pronoun "one" creates a neutrality that, rather than clarifying the speaker's identity or enhance her/his/its authority, confuses the reader who seeks its referrrent.

> It is self-evident
> that it is frightful to have everything afraid of one;
> that one must do as one is told
> and eat "rice, prunes, dates, raisins, hardtack, and
>   tomatoes"
> if one would "conquer the main peak" of Mt. Tacoma—
>   (ll.197–201)

While the initial "one" apparently refers to Mount Tacoma, subsequent pro-nominal appearances suggest the climber. Thus, "one" is split between the object to be feared and the "one" who would conquer it. A similar splitting occurs (if not on the level of grammar) between the mountain as intimidating female and the Jamesian ascription of style. The split might be understood, moreover, as extending to the properties of the "good" and "bad" mother as conceived in the abrasive relations between the glacier and the mountain, for the octopus's "capacity for fact" is the stylistic corollary to its encroaching capacity for destroying all it covers. By the time the octopus launches its attack, language has so displaced all other origins of identity the words themselves are called into question: "Is 'tree' the word for these things 'flat on the ground like vines'?" By a verbal burial that anticipates the avalanche's own, Moore obscures the dynamics of her Family Romance, the conflictual relationship between poetic and sexual identity that forms the threatening yet generative origins of "An Octopus."

II

In conclusion, if we return to the initial "conjunction of lines" that later will separate into "Marriage" and "An Octopus," Moore's interpolations strengthen the case for an engendered reading, especially as they develop a line of interpretation relating to the Greeks as perceived by Calypso. If Calypso, who cajoles Ulysses to remain with her for seven years only to have to relinquish him upon Hermes' command, represents the female capacity to capture the male's attention, then the Greeks, as cumulatively portraying refinement in a world created by abrasion, are themselves, self-deceived. What begins as a possible source of praise— "An octopus of ice / so cool in this the age of violence / so static & so enterprising" —becomes precisely the quality disparaged when discovered in the Greeks. And Calypso makes an error in failing to remember the Greeks' penchant for "smoothness" over a productive adversity. From Moore's notebook:

> and genuine & if it were it might sometimes be gross
> and Greeks liked smoothness but then—genuine but gross
> *Calypso a northern orchid named for*
> *the goddess who fell in love w Ulysses*
> has forgotten—there is no Ulysses merely Mr. D.
> (Willis, p. 253; Moore, p. 56)

This suggests the possibility of Moore's identifying the unrequited Calypso with herself, who finds no hero, only the mysterious "Mr. D.," someone, we assume, whom she met on her trip to the Rockies. Willis notes the repetition of the phrase, "no Greek would have it a gift" (p. 254), which acquires a further resonance if we recall the Iliadic injunction, "Beware a Greek bearing gifts." If here no Greek would accept what is offered, one cannot be placed in a position of having to beware what the enemy himself refuses to possess.

Further notebook entries illuminate the deliberately engendered relationship of Calypso and the Greeks. Willis quotes a later notebook passage (p. 65) wherein Moore combines "phrases from several sources":

> Pisistratus   causing [the] earth to move up & down under
> you w hatchet crest & saucy habits
> migrating vertically
> cruel bold & shy   claws like miniature ice-hacks
> wise & something of a villain.
>
> (Willis, 254)

Willis identifies Pisistratus "to whom Newman refers as the bringer of culture to Athens, (as) also the demagogue whose extreme tyranny led to the rise of Greek democracy." Willis continues, "He here becomes associated with the blue jay whose description Moore quoted from the guidebook to Mt. Rainier National Park" (Willis, 254). Although Moore subsequently alters the sequence, the following notebook passage expresses what later revisions tend to obscure: the interrelated identities of the Greeks, masculinity, superficial values, the self-righteousness of privilege, and conformity. All these conjoin in a passage that may have struck Moore herself as too revealing.

> END   no Greek looks into the goats' lookingglass
> Dissatisfied w the ragged marble & the blue gentian & the
>   the level leisure plain
> Calypso the onyx flower forgets
>   has forgotten that Ulysses was a Greek
> The age comes back to mountains
> Every spot with its flowers
>
>   ....
>   ....
>
> Now obscured by the avalanche
> with the crack of a rifle
> a curtain of powdered ice
>   the legal righteousness of leisure
> Before rich motion
> the legal righteousness of Greek
> Calypso has forgotten that Ulysses was a Greek
> Do you think in good sadness
>   he is here
> Calypso the goats flower refuting reproving
> olive trees oracles of Greece.
>
> (Willis, 254–55; Moore, 68)

What Calypso would be "refuting reproving" is the inevitability of Ulysses' return, the inevitability of abandonment. A later notebook entry once again pursues and expands upon Calypso's desire and the reasons for its failure:

> The Greeks liked smoothness
> and find it difficult to serve us
> It is hard to serve when one is trying to be many masters
> Inclined to imitate them in their worship
>   of conformity in heat
> a new species of Calypso's hope
> upon which lifelessness
> the piercing melting word becomes a pearl
>   on lepers hands.
>
> (Willis, 255; Moore, 78)

Presented against a terrain that is itself produced by abrasion and identified with what sustains life, the Greeks' penchant for smoothness would contribute to their inherent unsuitability for understanding or communication. The notion of "serving" becomes a difficulty for one who quests not simply after mastery but also "is trying to be many masters." Thus, inevitably, Calypso's hope proves lifeless, her "piercing melting word" a pearl contaminated by untouchable lepers' hands.[10]

In the association of the Greeks with mastery and an antipathetic admiration for smoothness and the identification of the bluejay with "Pisistratus, the notion of one who brings culture as both demagogue and villain," Moore's notebook entries establish the constellation of sexual, cultural, and psychological traits that make the jay a bad candidate for intimacy. Although the published version of "An Octopus" excludes all references to Calypso and suppresses the overtly sexual character of the indentifications suggested by the notebook drafts, the poem as Moore finally chose to publish it in *The Complete Poems* nevertheless speaks from the position of witness to an endangered self. The prevailing image of the octopus with its severed claw (a claw that in the notebook originally belonged to the masculine bluejay) remains a threatening presentment of destruction.

III

With its unpredictability and sheer force, the octopus is a maternal creature whose embrace can kill. In "The Paper Nautilus," enfolding arms represent a desire for absolute love that engages related issues of maternal steadfastness and the tenacity of maternal affection. Like "An Octopus," "The Paper Nautilus" approaches, through elusive and at times evasive images, an alternative aesthetics that is gender-identified and political. If in "An Octopus" the appropriative, capitalistic mountaineers threaten the mountain's flora and fauna and ultimately the origins of artistic life itself, the paper nautilus rejects a commercial, suburban set of values, choosing in their stead an anti-authoritarian, maternal world of symbiotic nurturance and intimacy. Here the central trope is the creation of new life within and from a creature, the carefully balanced mutuality of the eggs and their maternal source.

For authorities whose hopes
are shaped by mercenaries?
Writers entrapped by
teatime fame and by
commuters' comforts? Not for these
the paper nautilus
constructs her thin glass shell.[11]

Turning away both from the generalized commercial values of society and more specifically from those writers who are trapped by false lust for fame and ease, the paper nautilus, with delicate tenacity, constructs something that will endure long enough to sustain life and become an object of loveliness. This entrapment contrasts with the freedom of the mother who releases rather than smothers her young. Aware that what she has to give is "perishable," the paper nautilus constantly guards her thin glass shell.

Giving her perishable
souvenir of hope, a dull
white outside and smooth-
edged inner surface
glossy as the sea, the watchful
maker of it guards it
day and night; she scarcely

eats until the eggs are hatched.

Such vigilance is a testament to the fragility of her creation and a tribute to her loyalty. And yet the image of the maternal is not without its dangers, dangers strongly reminiscent both in visual and in psychological terms of the glacier as octopus. Like the octopus, the nautilus has eight arms, and again like the octopus, the danger, although here a danger evaded, is that she will crush what she strives to protect, the precise risk that the glacier as octopus presents to what flourishes through and in her potentially devastating presence.

Buried eight-fold in her eight
arms, for she is in
a sense a devil-
fish, her glass ram'shorn-cradled freight
is hid but is not crushed;
as Hercules, bitten

by a crab loyal to the hydra,
was hindered to succeed,
the intensively
watched eggs coming from
the shell free it when they are freed,—

The suddenness with which maternal devotion shifts from a totally benign to a much more ambivalent description is signaled by the image of entrapment. Again, Moore draws upon Greek myth, provocatively comparing the maternal paper nautilus's relation to her eggs to Hercules, who, according to legend, was the strongest man in the world and a figure of supreme self-confidence.[12]

Moore's simile alludes to Hercules' second labor, the killing of the nine-headed Hydra (a difficult task, both because one of the heads was immortal and because as soon as one head was chopped off, two grew in its place). In the original story, Hercules is helped by his nephew Iolaus, who brings him a burning brand to sear the neck as he cuts the head so that it cannot sprout again. "When all have been chopped off he disposed of the one that was immortal by burying it securely under a great rock."[13] In Moore's recasting, the crab's bite contributes to Hercules' success because of the evident disparity between Hercules' physical strength and his activity in the world and the apparent fragility and stasis of the paper nautilus.[14] Yet it is this paradoxical relationship that best expresses Moore's understanding of the alternative powers of maternal effort, of the natural as the primary trope for artistic creation. Hers is no idealized maternity, but a complex understanding that combines the inherently adversarial potential in the relationship between daughter and mother with an abiding awareness of the dangers embodied in the mother. If, in "An Octopus," the arms that reach out create the abrasions of both potential destruction and the possibilities of renewed life, in "The Paper Nautilus" a similarly ambivalent mutuality between the mother and her eggs occurs:

> as Hercules, bitten
>
> by a crab loyal to the hydra,
> was hindered to succeed,
>   the intensively
>   watched eggs coming from
> the shell free it when they are freed,—[15]

In the poem's final lines, the vision of what remains after the eggs are freed, interdependence and the need for security, is reinscribed upon the shell itself:

> leaving its wasp-nest flaws
> of white on white, and close-
>
> laid Ionic chiton-folds
> like the lines in the mane of
> a Parthenon horse,
> round which the arms had
> wound themselves as if they knew love
>   is the only fortress
>   strong enough to trust to.

These wasp-nest flaws preserve the scene of birth as they mark the scars of separation. While the "Ionic" folds and the Parthenon horse not only return us to

Hercules and ancient Greece, the poem's close describes a powerful dependency that clouds the earlier vision of mutual, simultaneous freedom. "Chiton" reiterates the pattern of intimate dependency, referring both to "a gown or tunic, usually worn next to the skin" and to a "*sea* cradle, a mollusk of the class Amphineura, having a mantle covered with calcareous plates, found adhering to rocks." With her allusion to the chiton as garment and as "sea cradle," Moore undercuts the freedom of release through images that depict clinging, holding on for life. As a "cradle," a place for the newborn that is covered by plates, a cradle that itself *clings,* the chiton bears witness to the power of dependence.

Similarly, the arms, unidentified yet clearly human, cling even in statuary form to the Parthenon horse's mane for protection. And yet that idealized mutual liberation is undercut by the poem's close, which, in its allusions to "chiton-folds" and the arms that wind themselves around the Parthenon horse, reassert the need for protection. The knowledge Moore provisionally ascribes to the anonymous arms "as if they knew love / is the only fortress / strong enough to trust to" reintroduces the dangers of separation the poem had earlier cast aside. Like "An Octopus," that other poem of dangerous engulfment, "The Paper Nautilus" is both a refuge and a risk, offering, as it does, security from the outside world and the crushing pressure of dependency. If Bonnie Costello is correct when she asserts that in this poem "as always Moore directly associates these issues of protection and strugggle with problems of language and interpretation," then the myth of poetic origins, as envisioned by Moore, is a maternal myth, wherein the mother proves as potentially dangerous as the world her daughter's words would inhabit.[16] To understand that Moore considered her tasks akin to "the labors of Hercules," one need only glance at her poem of that title wherein the project of revising the world's corruption to advocate the inherently unpopular, to defy worldly expectations without donning "a long white beard" (patriarchal sign of authority), demands a strength comparable to that possessed by the hero himself.

Yet Moore provides other visions of the artist that escape the confines of female identity as they engage issues of gender. Moore's "Frigate Pelican," for example, is completely freed of the domestic constraints and sexual knowledge that would delimit his autonomy.

> unlike the more stalwart swan that can ferry the
> woodcutter's two children home. Make hay; keep
>   the shop; I have one sheep; were a less
> limber animal's mottoes. This one
>   finds sticks for the swan's-down-dress
> of his child to rest upon and would
>   not know Gretel from Hansel.

Unable to recognize the difference between male and female children, let alone lead them home, the frigate pelican resembles the "impassioned Handel" who defies parental expectations and "never was known to have fallen in love." Like Handel,

                         the unconfiding frigate-bird hides
                         in the height and in the majestic
                         display of his art. . . .

His independence is the radically Whitmanian self-contentment of the artist:

                         "If I do well I am blessed
                    whether any bless me or not, and if I do
                         ill I am cursed."

And yet he is the "most romantic bird," exploring the possibilities of his exten-
sive freedom.

If in "An Octopus" Moore assigns the bluejay's claw to the glacier, a formerly
"male" attribute to the image of the mother, elsewhere in poems such as "The
Frigate Pelican" and "He 'Digesteth Harde Yron,' " Moore casts aside or rede-
fines categories of human sexuality. The nonhuman as trope offers Moore the
opportunity for such redefinition to the extent that the relationship between
sexuality and behavior in nonhuman creatures does not submit, so far as we
know, to the human burden of self-consciousness. The restriction of desire to
instinct may be one source of the nonhuman world's passionate attraction for
Moore—a realm where sexual identity, although it may determine behavior,
does not potentially affect constitutive notions of the self. Thus, the ostrich in
"He 'Digesteth Harde Yron' " "watches his chicks with / a maternal con-
centration—and he's / been mothering the eggs / at night six weeks—his legs /
their only weapon of defense." "Natural observation" promotes an interrogation
of humanly defined roles in a neutral territory, thus allowing Moore ex-
perimentation without the dangers of personal identification. Moore may as
readily find an emblem for the heroic in the male ostrich, which displays an
exhausting heroism, the "one remaining rebel," as in the female-identified paper
nautilus.

If "Marriage," among its other projects, articulates the tortuous difficulties of
human relationships (including the difficulties of overcoming narcissism long
enough to sustain mutuality) and "An Octopus" describes the dangerously
adversarial abrasions that create the possibilities of an ever-threatened life and
art, these themes proliferate throughout Moore's work as radical independence,
constancy, and nurturance of a passionate will are severed from the limitations
of human sexuality and the complications imposed by culturally derived gender
codes. If, for Moore, the price of artistic freedom is the submergence of sexuality
and the expression of a gender-inflected desire, "Marriage" and "An Octopus"
partially reveal some of the reasons for this judgment. As a poet of astonishing
achievement and the major woman poet of her age, Moore's strikingly revision-
ist poetics carries enormous consequences. Capable of encoding desire in an
extraordinarily complex network of allusive tropes, Moore simultaneously dis-
engages from that desire as she reinscribes a radically subversive aesthetics
cast in the nonappropriative, nurturing values traditionally associated with the
maternal. That her vision of maternity is itself both destructive and nurturant

comes as no surprise, given the accuracy of her perceptions. That she is capable simultaneously of disengendering the self while engendering her poetry is just the magisterial tour de force one would expect from a poet of such sinuous imagination.

If, for Moore, the origins of art are deeply implicated in the drama of human desire, "Marriage" and "An Octopus" reveal her need to suppress and dissociate poetic praxis from those origins. In her deliberate and proliferating disengagement of a personal, "female" voice from her most ambitious poems, Moore testifies not only to her own anxieties regarding the claims of poetic originality but also to a wary recognition of the risk incurred by breaking the silence of that disengagement.

6

BISHOP'S SEXUAL POETICS

If contemporary poetry borders on the limits of expressive form, there are nevertheless poets who are masters of those limits, who, in creating the poems of our climate, return us to ourselves. Elizabeth Bishop is such a poet. And although she would have resisted being classified with "women poets," her work clearly establishes itself as belonging to that alternative tradition of women poets whose redefinition of the Sublime centers upon the interrelation of the imagination and sexual identity. Bishop's poems reveal the complex tensions between women poets and the American Romantic tradition she identified as her own. In response to this tradition, Bishop writes poems of passionate reserve that fuse a capacity for wonder with a descriptive power that makes the Sublime, however provisionally, possible once more. To name the techniques Bishop uses to achieve such verbal moments is itself to recall the strategies practiced by her precursors, those women poets who, like Bishop, experienced the need to conceal as much as to disclose, for Bishop's elusive rhetoric engages her in the complex interactions between women poets and the American Sublime. The impetus of the exile, which paradoxically turned Dickinson into a recluse (her most impassioned form of travel), Bishop converts into the vocation of the traveler, whose powers of observation acquire acuity through estrangement. Yet Bishop's articulate exclusion does not rule out her own indebtedness to the magisterial poets we associate with the American Sublime.

In a wryly discursive letter to Anne Stevenson, her first biographer, Bishop comments directly upon her relationship with the American literary tradition. "But I also feel," she writes, "that Cal (Lowell) and I in very different ways are both descendants from the Transcendentalists—but you may not agree."[1] Despite the characteristic demurral, Bishop acknowledges that her work derives from that early manifestation of American self-consciousness known as Transcendentalism. The particular approach she takes toward American Romanticism, her swerve from Emerson and his heirs (different as it is from Lowell's), depends substantially upon her gender, upon the fact of Bishop's being a woman. In what follows I sketch the outlines of a reading of Bishop's work that attempts to account both for the influence of gender and the importance of tradition, her awareness of origins and the origins of her difference. That Bishop continues to define herself in terms of the American Romantic imagination is perhaps less a conscious decision than an unavoidable burden affecting all our poets, men and women, who cannot, of course, evade their literary predecessors. Yet a consideration of the relationship between eros and poetics suggests the possibility that the woman poet may win a certain measure of freedom from literary indebtedness and thus acquire in the very weakening of those traditional ties a restitution born of loss.

If, as Wittgenstein writes, "to imagine a language means to imagine a form of life," then contemporary women poets are inventing, through their poems, new forms of constitutive identity; in remaking language, they strive to reinvent themselves. The impetus for this reinvention derives from the woman poet's need to reassert authority over experience, establishing, as I have elsewhere noted, an unmediated relation with both the natural world and the word. Dickinson is the first woman poet to attempt such a transformation, and although Bishop expresses a certain disdain for the self-pity she perceives in Dickinson's poems, she acknowledges not only her forebear's genius but also her historical significance. "I particularly admire her having dared to do it all alone," Bishop remarks, and the relationship between Dickinson and Bishop may be closer than the urbanely disingenuous Bishop might wish to acknowledge.[2] Distanced from Dickinson by both time and temperament, Bishop nevertheless faces an allied, even intensified, version of the Emersonian Sublime, modulated as it is through Whitman's bodily poetics and the various poetic voices of our own century. And even more than Dickinson, Bishop defends against the challenge to her poetic autonomy by usurping the very terms of that challenge; she responds to the coupling of sexual identity and poetic power by interrogating the sexual dialectic upon which that coupling depends. Bishop's poems may be read as a map of language where sexual identity appears to yield to a fluidity of gender that does away with rigid, heterosexist categories. In this sense, Bishop follows Whitman's poetic coupling of homosexuality with erotic power. Yet rather than establish the lesbian as an overt erotic position from which to write (Adrienne Rich's choice), Bishop distinguishes between eroticism and sexual identity, a distinction that allows her to deflect sexual identification while simultaneously sustaining a powerful erotic presence. Recollecting how close Bishop's early aesthetic ideals are to Whitman's may remind us how fully his eroticism is translated into her own.

Bishop apparently began reading Whitman very early, and the passages she marks in her copy of *Leaves of Grass* are one indication of what initially impresses her.[3] Bishop is struck by Whitman's emphasis upon precision, the aim of effortlessness, the ideal of a poetry that does not betray the work that produces it. In one such passage, Whitman writes that poetry should appear "without effort and without exposing in the least how it is done." Along with this apparent effortlessness comes a familiar insistence upon imaginative accuracy and the preeminence of sight. "(What the eyesight does to the rest he does to the rest. Who knows the curious mystery of the eyesight?)"(p. 492, marked by double line). Beyond this allegiance to visual accuracy and the illusion of ease, Bishop learns from Whitman a "prudence suitable for immortality, . . ." (underlined, p. 502). Bishop incorporates Whitmanian prudence with sexual radicalism, as prudence assumes the guise of verbal deflection or effacement, the invocation of the magical, and displacement of point of view—the definition of erotic pleasure through absence and the unspoken.[4] Such verbal masking allows Bishop to preserve the erotic while deconstructing heterosexist categories. In this reconceptualization, Bishop follows both Dickinson and Whitman; for although Bishop's admiration for Dickinson may be muted, Dickinson herself practices a similar poetic encoding, employing techniques of gender crossing, the disguise of authorial displacement, and the substitution of natural tropes for human presence. By eliding the dialectics of heterosexuality, Bishop extends Dickinson's and Whitman's poetic projects to discover an individuating source of renewed poetic authority.

In one of her few public statements on the relation of gender to writing, Bishop comments, "Women's experiences are much more limited, but that does not really matter—there is Emily Dickinson, as one always says. You just have to make do with what you have after all."[5] For Bishop, "making do" meant a life of daring exploration and an intense dedication to craft—the sustained development of a style of straightforward effacement that couples indirection with the plainness of speech. The guise of the traveler, the voice of the child, the testimonies of grotesque, liminal creatures all convey experience profoundly felt and obliquely expressed. Different as these voices are, each carries a quality of existential displacement that restricts as it imagines the possibilities of human relationship.

In "Crusoe in England," Bishop's most extreme poetic instance of gender crossing fused with eroticism, the practical, stranded voyager with his laconic voice becomes the spokesman for feelings of great intimacy, fear of maternity, the pain of separation and loss. Here the voice of the isolated man most clearly articulates Bishop's terrain of difference, for Crusoe's hardship is related as much to the claustrophobia of entrapment within an obsessive imagination as it is to the physical conditions of the island.[6] Loneliness finds its projection in a violent, aggressive landscape where volcanoes' heads are "blown off" and the "parched throats" of craters are "hot to touch," an island hissing with aridity and the replication of barren life. It is a place of singleness: "the same odd sun / rose from the sea, / and there was one of it and one of me. / The island had one kind of everything: . . ."[7] To relieve the tension, Crusoe turns to the imagination's capacity for recollection and for change. But in both efforts, his imagination fails him, for he cannot remember the final word of the Wordsworth he would recite, and the baby goat, which he dyes red, is rejected by its mother. His most powerful imaginative act is to dream, and his dreams reveal an obsession with procreation, the loss of the mother, and the pain of a subjectivity bereft of relationship.

> Dreams were the worst. Of course I dreamed of food
> And love, but they were pleasant rather
> than otherwise. But then I'd dream of things
> like slitting a baby's throat, mistaking it
> for a baby goat. I'd have

nightmares of other islands
stretching away from mine, infinities
of islands, islands spawning islands
like frogs' eggs turning into polliwogs
of islands, knowing that I had to live
on each and every one, eventually,
for ages, registering their flora,
their fauna, their geography.

The hopelessness of a purely biological repetition (or what Alan Williamson in another context has called "desolate accumulation") is broken by the arrival of Friday, whose friendship is mourned both for its future loss and its inherent infertility:

Just when I thought I couldn't stand it
another minute longer, Friday came.
(Accounts of that have everything all wrong.)
Friday was nice.
Friday was nice, and we were friends.
If only he had been a woman!
I wanted to propagate my kind,
and so did he, I think, poor boy.

....

—Pretty to watch; he had a pretty body.[8]

Here, "pretty" gestures both toward Crusoe's desire that Friday be a woman and toward the attraction he feels for the boy himself, an expression of homoerotic longing voiced by the speaker, who simultaneously stands in for the poem's author and speaks, in the narrative, for himself. In a unisexual and univocal text, Bishop tells a story rich in allusiveness and human suffering while addressing issues of single-sex friendship and the terrors faced by an intense subjectivity that seeks expression in stark isolation.[9] The themes of this sexual politics emerge through Crusoe's rhetorical guise, enabling the reticent Bishop the veil of prudence Whitman himself had advocated. Casting her story as Crusoe's enables Bishop to deal with subjects that would otherwise remain unspoken because they were too overtly threatening or simply too overt. Crusoe's "poor old island's still / unrediscovered, unrenamable" because it is both self-created and unique, a terrain of psychic origins known and recognized only by the self. Unlike Defoe's hero, who returns to Brazil and visits his island (bringing with him provisions and women for the men to marry), this Crusoe remains bereft and alone on that other island, England. If, in the end, Defoe's Crusoe learns that providence rewards the believer, Bishop's Crusoe lives in a world robbed of certainty, in a void of meaning.

Now I live here, another island,
that doesn't seem like one, but who decides?
My blood was full of them; my brain
bred islands. But that archipelago
has petered out. I'm old.
I'm bored, too, drinking my real tea,
surrounded by uninteresting lumber.
The knife there on the shelf—
It reeked of meaning, like a crucifix.
It lived. How many years did I
beg it, implore it, not to break?
I knew each nick and scratch by heart,
the bluish blade, the broken tip,
the lines of wood-grain on the handle . . .
Now it won't look at me at all.
The living soul has dribbled away.
My eyes rest on it and pass on.[10]

In such a world, loss proliferates endlessly, like those "polliwogs of islands" bred of sorrow and despair. Value adheres to externality only through use and former affection as Crusoe enumerates the relics of survival:

The local museum's asked me to
leave everything to them:
the flute, the knife, the shrivelled shoes,
my shedding goatskin trousers
(moths have got in the fur),
the parasol that took me such a time
remembering the way the ribs should go.
It still will work but, folded up,
looks like a plucked and skinny fowl.
How can anyone want such things?
—And Friday, my dear Friday, died of measles
seventeen years ago come March

The very barrenness of this catalog, with its massive withdrawal of feeling, prepares the way for the recollection of Friday's death, voiced with the quietness characteristic of Bishop's most intimate revelations. Yet that quietness contains insistence, the verbal repetition its own intensity as Friday's memory is kept alive by the repetition of his name and the adjectival "my dear." The last line's plaintive, arcane "come" assures, moreover, that Friday's memory, rather than fading with time, will, in Crusoe's imagination, expand through it.

Adrienne Rich once noted that "poems examining intimate relationships are almost wholly absent from Bishop's later work. What takes their place," Rich continues, "is a series of poems examining relationships between people who are, for reasons of difference, distanced: rich and poor, landowner and tenant, white woman and Black woman, invader and native."[11] Intimacy, along with a strong eroticism, *is* present throughout Bishop's work; yet that intimacy, to extend Rich's observation, is not simply distanced by differences of class and race, but invoked most powerfully in terms of loss. It is through absence, departure, and death that eroticism in Bishop's poems receives its fullest expression, as if, like Dickinson, Bishop believed that "absence makes the present mean."

Bishop's late poem, "One Art" (whose title conveys the implicit suggestion that mastery sought over loss in love is closely related to poetic control), articulates the tension between discipline in life and the force of circumstance.[12] The poem speaks in the tones of the survivor:

> the art of losing isn't hard to master;
> so many things seem filled with the intent
> to be lost that their loss is no disaster.

The opening line, with its echo of a folk prescription such as "an apple a day," leads into the specifics of daily loss—of keys, of time—the syntactic parallelism suggesting an evaluative equation of what we immediately recognize as hardly equal realities. Such parallelism, by providing a temporary distraction that draws the reader away from the force building in the poem, functions as a disarming form of humor that undercuts the potential self-pity otherwise latent in the poem's subject.

> Lose something every day. Accept the fluster
> of lost door keys, the hour badly spent.
> The art of losing isn't hard to master.

"One Art" presents a series of losses as if to reassure both its author and its reader that control is possible—an ironic gesture that forces upon us the tallying of experience cast in the guise of reassurance. By embracing loss as Emerson had Fate (the Beautiful Necessity), Bishop casts the illusion of authority over the inexorable series of losses she seeks to master.

> Then practice losing farther, losing faster:
> places, and names, and where it was you meant
> to travel. None of these will bring disaster.

The race continues between "disaster" and "master" as the losses include her mother's watch, houses, cities, two rivers, a continent, and, perhaps, in the future, an intimate friend whom, breaking out of the pattern of inanimate objects, the poem directly addresses:

> —Even losing you (the joking voice, a gesture
> I love) I shan't have lied. It's evident
> The art of losing's not too hard to master
> though it may look like (*Write* it!) like disaster.[13]

Here conflict explodes as the verbal deviations from previously established word patterns reflect the price of the speaker's remaining true to her initial claim that experience of loss can yield to mastery. With a directness that comes to predominate in Bishop's later work, "One Art" delineates the relationship between the will and the world. Note the split of "a gesture / I love" across two lines; the profession stands by itself as it turns back toward the beloved gesture. Syntax reveals the pain "One Art" has been fighting, since its beginnings, to suppress as the thought of losing "you" awakens an anxiety the poem must wrestle with down to its close. This last time, the refrain varies its form, assuming an evidentiary structure that challenges as it expresses what has hitherto been taken as a fact recognized from within the poet's consciousness. Coupled with the addition of "it's evident" is the adverbial "too" (It's evident / the art of losing's not too hard to master"), which increases the growing tension within the desire to repeat the poem's refrain while admitting growing doubts as to its accuracy. In the end, the pressure to recapitulate the by-now-threatened refrain betrays itself in the sudden interruption of the closing line by an italicized hand that enforces the completion of the "master" / "disaster" couplet that the poem itself has made, through its formal demands, an inevitable resolution: "the art of losing's not too hard to master / though it may look like (*Write* it!) like disaster." The repetition of "like" postpones, ever so fleetingly, the final word that hurts all the more. The inevitability of "disaster" ironically recalls the fatalism of such childhood rituals as "he loves me; he loves me not"—in which the child's first words, "he loves me," and the number of petals on the flower determine the game's outcome. In its earlier evocation of folk ritual and in the villanelle's rhyme scheme, "One Art" reveals an ironic playfulness that works in collusion with high seriousness, a strategy that proliferates throughout Bishop's work.

Despite the disclaimers, qualifications, and play that mark these poems, there is an ominous quality to Bishop's restraint more suggestive than confession, a tenuous apprehension of a self moving through a world at once alien and mysterious. Her clarity is a subjective clarity more than a literalizing one, an accuracy based upon magic and surrealistic surprise. In such a poetics, the Sublime would be what is even more strange, what speaks to us of experiences that carry us beyond our self-reflexive consciousness to that which lies unidentified within. Bishop thus articulates an alienated or exiled subjectivity, and, as outsider, she must observe with all her powers to draw a map, discern a geography.

That geography includes not only the desolate, surreal vitality of Crusoe's unnamed island but an alternative terrain as well, for if Crusoe's unnamed island signifies a terrain of lost invention, "Santarém," the town where the Amazon and the Tapajos rivers meet, is a destination of memory that invites a meditation upon singleness and duality. Drawn here and really wanting to go no farther, the speaker admires not only the scene she discovers, but also the idea that informs the scene. Like Crusoe's lost island, Santarém's geography has epistemological consequences. "I liked the place; I liked the idea of the place / Two rivers. Hadn't two rivers sprung / from the Garden of Eden? No, that was four / and they'd diverged. Here only two / and coming together. Even if one were tempted / to literary interpretations / such as: life/death, right/wrong, male/female / —such notions would have resolved, dissolved, straight off / in that watery, dazzling dialectic." This final "dialectic" deconstructs the dissolution of the binary oppositions that precede it, as if the natural meeting of the two mighty rivers at once washed away all arbitrary distinctions, yet held them apart in a single, brilliant, phenomenologically irrefutable suspension. The logical outcome of the conflux of these dialectical opposites would be union; Bishop resolves the division, however, not through a conceptual unity but by preserving the dialectic perceived in nature itself. That Bishop preserves this dialectic may reflect her recognition of a troubling because naturally derived dualism that cannot be effaced by linguistic reconceptualization. The presence of difference in the world, whether metaphysical, ethical, or sexual, appears as unyielding fact—the equivocal reality in which her poems strive to create reciprocal meanings. Santarém dazzles because of the singularity of ostensibly exemplary experience, the uniqueness of the place. Yet singularity here depends upon a merging of dissimilar cultures, customs, races. The "mongrel / riverboats skittering back and forth / under a sky of gorgeous, under-lit clouds" synecdochically reveal the vitality of the exceptional that defines the town. So do the occasional blue eyes, the English names, and the oars, all legacies of the nineteenth-century white Southerners who came here because "they could still own slaves." That colonial impulse has been converted through the passage of time and the mixing of race into a reality marked by the exceptional. Finally, the wasps' nest (originally an object of danger) has become an artifact of beauty as well as an occasion to test whether a sense of wonder can survive the medium of exchange. The aesthetics of the singular is always at risk in Bishop's poems, the risk of being misunderstood or simply rejected.

> Then—my ship's whistle blew. I couldn't stay.
> Back on board, a fellow-passenger, Mr. Swan,
> Dutch, the retiring head of Philips Electric,
> Really a very nice old man,
> Who wanted to see the Amazon before he died,
> asked, "What's that ugly thing?"

Unable to recognize the value of the wasps' nest, Mr. Swan, head of an organization that itself controls and so demystifies the lightning bolt that cracked the cathedral tower, remains oblivious to what renders both the gift and Santarém itself sacred. Mr. Swan's utter lack of appreciation speaks to the risk Bishop runs when offering something of value to others. Such moments, however, emerge against a psychic background distinguished by a desire for self-protection in a world perceived as irremediably divided between the subjectivity of the self and the threatening possibilities of other persons. In singling out Santarém and establishing a homeland of the exceptional that incorporates difference, Bishop gestures toward her desire to go beyond the oppositional character of literary and philosophical interpretation (and beyond the conflict between colonizer and colonized as well).

Even more explicitly, "Brazil, January 1, 1502" evokes a sense of place (the particularities of an aestheticized history) and the interworkings of exploration, lust, and greed. The poem's major trope, the interchangeability of nature and tapestry, invites a conflation of epistemological experience and aesthetic representation that, in its very tactility, suggests an elision between the sexual and the aesthetic. The torn tapestry becomes the violated body of nature itself. Bishop approaches her subject as one who simultaneously beholds an aesthetic object and a historic reality.[14] The poem's epigraph, ". . . embroidered nature . . . tapestried landscape" (from Sir Kenneth Clark's *Landscape Into Art*), prepares the way for the transformation of text into textile, cloth into life, the explorers into ourselves:

> Januaries, Nature greets our eyes
> exactly as she must have greeted theirs:

We are implicated at once, for we see what they see. And yet the poem sustains an aesthetic distance; when sin appears, it is as an allegorical figure.

> Still in the foreground there is Sin:
> five sooty dragons near some mossy rocks.
> The rocks are worked with lichens, gray moonbursts
> splattered and overlapping,
> threatened from underneath by moss
> in lovely hell-green flames,
> attacked above
> by scaling-ladder vines, oblique and neat,
> "one leaf yes and one leaf no" (in Portuguese).

The hell-green flames, sign of the weaver's wit, are singled out for their loveliness even as the forces of natural power are described in militaristic terms of threat, attack, and scaling ladders. Increasingly, any distinction between natural text and tapestry fades as the observer enters the world described, her eye drawn ever closer to the fabric of things. When that eye settles on the female lizard, there is no escape and no turning away.

> . . . all eyes
> are on the smaller, female one, back-to,
> her wicked tail straight up and over,
> red as a red-hot wire.

The inflamed, "wicked" female creature is marked as a sexual, potentially threatening presence and a sign of evil—an immoral, albeit natural, presence. While Bishop preserves her rhetorical distance from this tableau by describing it through the invaders' eyes (note the adjectival "wicked" attached to the lizard's tail), she simultaneously incorporates the invaders' presence into the tapestry and renders her independent judgment of their actions. The army of invaders are not only "hard as nails" but also "tiny as nails," for they undergo a miniaturization that effectively symbolizes their meanness of spirit. Like ourselves, they find Brazil "not unfamiliar," for what they recognize is no artificial dissimilarity of culture but the occasion for sexual and material lust: "wealth, plus a brand-new pleasure:" These "hard" men rip through the fabric of nature, each out to snare a native woman for himself:

> those maddening little women who kept calling,
> calling to each other (or had the birds waked up?)
> and retreating, always retreating, behind it.

With their lovely, birdlike calls and their ease of escape, these women embody a naturalizing freedom and vocal community that eludes the men who must tear the very fabric of nature to assuage their desire.[15]

If those "maddening little women" remain alluringly elusive in the Brazilian jungle, so in "Roosters" the speaker aligns herself with the voice of the woman whose peaceful pleasure is interrupted by the harsh cries of explicitly phallic birds.[16] The speaker describes being awakened from an apparently pleasurable sleep by the cocks' cry of "unwanted love, conceit and war." What restores "us" to former harmony is another atmosphere—muted, calm, and transfused with a pink light:

> In the morning
> a low light is floating
> in the backyard, and gilding
>
> from underneath
> the broccoli, leaf by leaf;
> how could the night have come to grief?
>
> gilding the tiny
> floating swallow's belly
> and lines of pink cloud in the sky, . . .

Like the underlit clouds of Santarém, this "low light" gilds nature, and like the gilt that rubs off one's fingers when one opens the "big book" in "Over 2,000 Illustrations and a Complete Concordance," this light makes the world seem at once protective and secure. Here, the low light signals the distancing of the roosters: the cocks are now almost inaudible, and

> The sun climbs in,
> following "to see the end,"
> faithful as enemy, or friend.

This pink light foreshadows the rising of the sun, a moment described with supreme equivocation. Indeed, the sun may not simply be "climbing in" the window but, given the ambiguities of the verb, climbing into bed. Its presence, while signifying the predictability of certain natural phenomena, is itself open to question because it potentially destroys the intimate shades of dawn and, with it, the sleepers' peace. Yet despite equivocation, fidelity abides, for the sun climbs in "to see the end" as Peter (Matthew 26:58) follows Christ into the high priest's palace where he sits "with the servants, to see the end." In their earlier betrayal and final gesture of faithfulness, Peter's actions aptly foreshadow the equivocal question that closes Bishop's poem. The roosters with their pompous, militaristic arrogance, out to prove their "virile presence," usher in a dawn that threatens the alternative intimacy that precedes the day's return.[17] While the poem will not betray secrets, it nevertheless alludes to a crisis of faith between friends and the possibility of a mutual faithfulness that belies the murderous aggression that surrounds them.

If Bishop identifies patently male images with aggression and violence, traditionally female images may be cast in an equally negative light, for both represent false terms in the dialectic her work seeks to evade. In "The Riverman," for example, the quest of the would-be male initiate is for the acquisition of divine magic and mythic power. What hinders his progress is the normative world of dry land from which he desires to escape. The riverman yearns for a place freed from conventional gender identifications. He laments, "I need a virgin mirror" not spoiled by "the girls" who have used it "to look at their mouths in, / to examine their teeth and smiles." This vanity is, in its way, as prurient as the cocks' arrogance. In his pursuit of the redemptive, divine river spirit that would yield magical powers, the riverman must first relinquish a rude domesticity (his snoring wife) and win a singularity that would enable him to aid those he has left behind. Interestingly, the moment of being singled out, of achieving the magical powers that estrange him from his past and the community of others, is celebrated by a maternal union of moon and river; to prove oneself exceptional and alone here signals (as so often in Bishop) a reenactment of maternal bonding that affirms rather than opposes one's isolation.

> You can peer down and down
> or dredge the river bottom
> but never, never catch me.
> When the moon shines and the river
> lies across the earth
> and sucks it like a child,
> then I will go to work
> to get you health and money.
> the Dolphin singled me out;
> Luandinha seconded it.

Singled out at the moment of maternal fusion, the riverman gains his freedom, escaping from earthly realities of wife and home into the waters of mystery, where he seeks a virgin mirror to reenvision and thereby empower the self, for it is only in a world of magic, in the provisional impossibility of things not as they are, that the riverman can discover the power he craves. Indeed, Bishop may welcome isolation as a potential blessing—when, for example, in "Pleasure Seas," she beholds "an acre of cold white spray . . . / Dancing happily by itself." But Bishop knows too well the difference between the exuberance of natural isolation and the human need for others, and in her exploration of a poetics rather than a politics of gender, she focuses upon the division between self and other, male and female, life and death. Such divisions can be healed only by the imagination's recognition of loss and the ambivalent promise of singularity. Bishop's awareness of the problematic aspects of eros and the cultural construction of gender influences her understanding of her own desire as well as her need to imagine an alternative way of being that counters restrictive, normative definitions.

In an early poem, "Exchanging Hats," Bishop alludes to the conventional ascriptions of gender, teasing out the ontological ambiguities that hide behind costume.

> Unfunny uncles who insist
> in trying on a lady's hat,
> —oh, even if the joke falls flat,
> we share your slight transvestite twist
>
> in spite of your embarrassment.

The acknowledgment of a shared interest in sexual shifts, the "slight transvestite twist," is not unrelated to the plural pronoun, the "we" of the poem, which playfully dissociates the speaker from the poet while suggesting her multiple identities. The provisional status of costume becomes an occasion for the fictile imagination: "Costume and custom are complex. / The headgear of the other sex / inspires us to experiment." Mysteries are revealed as much as they are hidden by such awkward experimentation. Tawdry as the "unfunny uncle" seems, he still may be hiding "stars inside" his "black fedora." And the "aunt exemplary and slim," with her "avernal" eyes, becomes both male and female: "springlike," embodying the possibilities of change and rebirth, a figure from the ancient underworld.

> Aunt exemplary and slim,
> with avernal eyes, we wonder
> what slow changes they see under
> their vast, shady, turned-down brim.

Bishop's play on "avernal" suggests the eyes' deep gaze, with their capacity to witness the "slow changes" of a cosmic panorama beyond any apparent fixity (of gender or of time). The diurnal progression from night to day is analogous to a male/female shift that remains a mystery. The aunt's hat brim, like the uncle's fedora, withholds knowledge from view as it ambiguously shades identity or expression from too intense scrutiny.

Such a blurring of distinctions and the implications of crossing over through costume reemerge in Bishop's late poem, "Pink Dog."[18] The subject is a rather sickly, depilated bitch who must disguise herself to avoid becoming an object of scorn; she must don a costume to survive the continuing "celebration" of life known as Carnival. Despite a vast difference in tone, "Pink Dog" recalls Wallace Stevens's "The American Sublime," for both Stevens and Bishop address what one needs to survive in a place of deception, a land of danger that requires the individual armor of the imagination. Seeking what will suffice, Stevens asks, "How does one stand / To behold the sublime? To confront the mockers, / The mickey mockers / and plated pairs?" His provisional response is a stripping away of the external self until all that remains is "the spirit and space, / The empty spirit / In vacant space." What can such a spirit draw upon for sustenance? Stevens poses the question in sacramental terms: "What wine does one drink? / What bread does one eat?" (lines Bishop will parodically echo at the close of her poem). Like "The American Sublime," "Pink Dog" confronts a world of disguise and advocates a necessary defense not of stripping away, but of costume. This response is associated with the dog's color, her sex, and the perceived embarrassments associated with being a nursing mother with scabies (a disease caused by an insect that gets under the skin and produces intense itching). Her discomfort, then, is related to a once external, now internalized agent, a discomfort that can be masked but not cured.

Immediately following the poem's opening, "the sun is blazing and the sky is blue," with its echo of another Stevens poem about transformation, "The house was quiet, and the world was calm," we meet the hairless dog. Afraid of contagion, the crowds "draw back and stare" with us.

> Of course they're mortally afraid of rabies.
> You are not mad; you have a case of scabies
> but look intelligent. Where are your babies?

The dog's raw, pink skin and her hanging teats require a defense that can be achieved only through the use of intelligence operating as disguise. With an apparently effortless, desperado humor, Bishop rhymes "teats" and "wits," an associative verbal gesture so assured that the identification seems to carry all the circumstantiality of truth.

> (A nursing mother, by those hanging teats.)
> In what slum have you hidden them, poor bitch,
> while you go begging, living by your wits?

Unless the "poor bitch" can redirect her wits toward disguise, she will join those "idiots, paralytics, parasites" "bobbing in the ebbing sewage." The practical solution, explains the level-headed, sardonic speaker, is to wear a "fantasia," or carnival costume.

> Carnival is always wonderful!
> A depilated dog would not look well.
> Dress up! Dress up and dance at Carnival!

The voice that proffers this advice is at once sympathetic and admonitory, as it insists upon the necessity of costume. Woman and dog are related by their gender and, potentially, their vulnerability. Wit alone can protect each of them— a wit the poet practices so as to preserve her identity. Rarely does Bishop invoke masking so explicitly, although throughout her poems the need for protection is met by the courage of a voice willing to incur the risk of exposure.

II

Compensation (as Emerson himself came to recognize) is a boon in nature and a significant human activity. In her creation of a poetics that seeks to disrupt the fixities of our inherited understanding, Bishop strives to assign the human map of comprehension a less rigid set of directions, an alternative geography based not upon polarities of difference but upon the poet/geographer's painterly perception freed of disabling divisions. Such an alternative mapping may create, as in "Santarém," a distinct version of the Sublime, one that develops from a renewed awareness of loss and discontinuity that with dazzling restraint reconstitutes the world according to its and the world's priorities. With an Emersonian audacity tempered by a tact requisite to her radical vision, Bishop's poems aim at nothing short of freedom from the inherently dualistic tradition that lies not only at the foundations of the American Sublime, but also at the very heart of the Western literary tradition.

Two poems from Bishop's last volume, *Geography III,* approach the Sublime by means of apparently contrasting yet structurally similar experiences.[19] "In the Waiting Room" and "The Moose" both explore the self's relation to others as they articulate a moment that interrupts the continuous act of sublimation that enables us to preserve an ongoing constitutive identity. In each poem, the crisis of that interruption is resolved through a gesture of reunion with life beyond the self that allows identity to reconstitute itself in a recognizable form. These poems delineate an *ecstasis* that recalls the vertiginous psychic shifts of the experiential Sublime. "In the Waiting Room," strangers isolated by anxiety and anonymity come together, their status provisional, for they are on the outside waiting to go in.[20] In "The Moose" the liminal is again invoked as strangers embark on a communal journey only to await their arrival at various destinations. Against these provisional environments, Bishop introduces images of family. The bus passengers in "The Moose" catch a glimpse of a woman shaking out a tablecloth. Anonymous voices float softly from the back of the bus (the recesses of the mind?) to create a soothing lullaby of conversation that retells the history of people's lives. But the family is not the narrator's own; if the recollections draw her back into her past, it is through the aura of remembrance created by others' voices.

Within "In the Waiting Room," familial forms assume a more terrifying guise. While she waits for her aunt to emerge from the dentist's chair, "Elizabeth" reads an article in *National Geographic* where human images assume macabre, distorted forms:

> A dead man slung on a pole
> —"Long Pig," the caption said.
> Babies with pointed heads
> wound round and round with string;
> black, naked women with necks
> wound round and round with wire
> like the necks of light bulbs.
> Their breasts were horrifying.

What is meant to pass the time becomes a rite of passage as the seven-year-old "Elizabeth" is led into the abyss of a self she had not earlier recognized as her own:

> Suddenly, from inside,
> came an *oh!* of pain
> —Aunt Consuelo's voice—
> not very loud or long.
>
> ....
>
> . . . What took me
> completely by surprise
> was that it was *me:*
> my voice, in my mouth.
> Without thinking at all
> I was my foolish aunt,
> I—we—were falling, falling,
> our eyes glued to the cover
> of the *National Geographic,*
> February, 1918.

The child counters the vertigo that accompanies her faltering sense of self with facts, with information about the external world and contemporary events. What has threatened her perception of identity can be traced, at least for its proximate cause, to the grotesque pictorial representations of man, woman, and child. What so disturbs "Elizabeth" that she loses the sense of self one takes for granted in order to live in the world? Lee Edelman addresses this issue:

> Though only in the course of reading the magazine does "Elizabeth" perceive the inadequacy of her positioning as a reader, Bishop's text implies from the outset the insufficiency of any mode of interpretation that claims to release the meaning it locates "inside" a text by asserting its own ability to speak from a position of mastery "outside" of it. For this reason everything that "Elizabeth" encounters in the pages of the *National Geographic* serves to disturb the stability of a binary opposition.[21]

This disturbance incorporates, moreover, a questioning of the internalized structures and cultural codes that inform the interpretation of experience. If Bishop's sexual poetics more generally deconstructs the binary oppositions of heterosexist discourse, "In the Waiting Room" addresses a related epistemological concern that arises from Bishop's destabilization of the distinctions by which persons organize information about themselves and their world. Edelman continues, "Though Bishop's text, then, has challenged the stability of distinctions between inside and outside, male and female, literal and figurative, human and bestial, young 'Elizabeth' reads on from her own position of liminality in the waiting room until she confronts, at last, an image of women and their infants: . . ."[22] By focusing on "Elizabeth's" vexed response to the horrific image of maternal sexuality, Edelman introduces us to the larger question of female sexuality in Bishop's work as he urges us to hear the "*oh!*" that "emanates from inside the dentist's office, and from inside the waiting room, and from inside the *National Geographic,* and from inside 'In the Waiting Room.' It is a cry that cries out against any attempt to clarify its confusions because it is a female cry—a cry of the female—that recognizes the attempts to clarify it as attempts to put it in its place."[23] That voice of protest, emanating from an epistemological uncertainty, echoes throughout Bishop's work in poems that reengage the mediations between rhetoric and sexual identity. The fall away from awareness of distinctions disrupts the assurance of a constitutive identity, and the restoration of that identity through the intervention of the external is akin to the final stage of the experiential Sublime, wherein the poet's identity, momentarily repressed by a power felt to be greater than and external to it, reemerges. That the experiential Sublime should, in this poem, be so closely linked to the voice of female sexuality and the overthrowing of culturally encoded identities reaffirms the alternative aspect of the psychological Sublime for the woman poet. Gender is at the center of any such aesthetic crisis, and the eroticization of literary categories serves the function of deidealizing the work of the human imagination.

"The Moose" describes a related dynamics of the Sublime wherein separation and fusion, the underlying terms of "Elizabeth's" crisis, are associated with a phenomenon that simultaneously evades and incorporates conventionally disparate categories, for the appearance of the moose—unknown, mysterious—affirms in the passengers' response the unifying effect of joy. Yet that joy itself is located in a question that underscores less the sensation experienced than its totalizing impact:

> Why, why do we feel
> (we all feel) this sweet
> sensation of joy?

Here the issue of communal identity again surfaces only to be called into question as "Elizabeth's" ontological doubt reappears. In the face of the wondrous, the strange, the otherwordly, these passengers' joy is less compelling than the interrogatory form in which it is cast. Bishop's question, if it does not detract from that joy, certainly redirects the reader's attention to forms of response. That the answer goes without saying provides a clue to the ontological ambiguity of the moment (reflected in the moose's own anomalous status). "Towering, antlerless, / high as a church, / homely as a house / (or, safe as houses)," the moose combines the domestic with the sacred, female identity with animal nature.[24] A majestic presence from another world, she appears beyond our expectations, an utterly unanticipated presence escaping the pre-dictability of human experience. Her function as "surprise" (an effect both Bishop and Emerson regarded as among the highest forms of aesthetic achievement) works on another level, for it not only catches us off guard but also challenges our notions of a verifiable, ordered universe.[25] The moose thus embodies a female strangeness that constitutes an inherently subversive notion of the Sublime, and the joy "we all" experience is a joy related to the very interruption of the continuum of expectation, hence predictive consciousness. That a female creature is the occasion for a saving disruption of the normative is itself not unexpected; such a gesture participates in the reaffirmation of mater-nal power that is at once otherworldly and wholly present.

Yet the epistemic displacements of "In the Waiting Room" and "The Moose" create their own anxieties as Bishop pays a price for choosing to work in the liminal space between land and water, the domestic and the strange, eros and art. Against the dangers of exile, Bishop searches for the redemptive possibili-ties of home. Bishop's late poem, "The End of March," most fully articulates her understanding of the relationship between the geography of the imagination and the homeground magisterially domesticated by Emerson, Whitman, and Stevens, the major voices of the American Sublime. Here the speaker's foot-steps follow the tracks of monumental beachcombers who had sought signs of selfhood on their native shores. The poem opens with the inhospitable char-acter of place and weather; it is not a good day to take a walk. "It was cold and windy, scarcely the day / to take a walk on that long beach. / Everything was withdrawn as far as possible, / indrawn." Offering no welcome, the beach grants no access. The bad weather itself, however, makes it possible for the speaker to walk freed from the glaring sun or the night sky's brilliant auroras, so long celebrated as indices of the American Sublime. In the face of such immediately austere conditions, indeed drawn forward by them, the speaker sees "dog-prints (so big / they were more like lion-prints)," which lead to "lengths and lengths, endless, of wet white string, / looping up to the tide-line, down to the water, / over and over."[26] This "line" lures her to

> a thick white snarl, man-size, awash,
> rising on every wave, a sodden ghost,
> falling back, sodden, giving up the ghost. . . .
> A kite string?—But no kite.

The man who has been there before her has vanished into this snarl, his presence become an absence, a ghost who has given up the ghost. Haunted by this absence, the speaker continues her walk, her goal the "crooked box" that would be her "crypto-dream-house" where she imagines a bliss of solitude, a place for desultory reading, and a "lovely diaphanous blue flame," "A light to read by—perfect! But—impossible." Having to turn back because "the wind was much too cold / even to get that far, / and of course the house was boarded up," she cannot remain in this place or find her home on this worn shore. The scene belongs to the Whitman of "Out of the Cradle" and "As I Ebb'd," the dream of habitation to the Stevens of "The Auroras of Autumn":

> Farewell to an idea . . . A cabin stands,
> Deserted, on a beach. It is white,
> As by a custom or according to
>
> An ancestral theme or as a consequence
> Of an infinite course . . .
>
> ....
>
> The season changes. A cold wind chills the beach.
> The long lines of it grow longer, emptier,
> A darkness gathers though its does not fall
>
> And the whiteness grows less vivid on the wall.
> The man who is walking turns blankly on the sand.
> He observes how the north is always enlarging the change,
>
> With its frigid brilliances, its blue-red sweeps
> And gusts of great enkindlings, its polar green,
> The color of ice and fire and solitude.

The "Farewell to an Idea" of "Auroras" must be the speaker's rejection as well, for the possibility of domestic warmth remains an illusion. Seeking her "proto-dream house," the speaker is denied entry, prevented from participating in the Stevensian Sublime of solitude, illumination, and terror. Here is Stevens:

> . . . He opens the door of his house
> On flames. The scholar of one candle sees
> An Arctic effulgence flaring on the frame
> Of everything he is. And he feels afraid.

This is the Sublime fear of external power threatening to overwhelm the solitary scholar; it is the fear that lies at the heart of the experiential Sublime as it bears witness to the forces that lie beyond the self.

Barred from that afflatus of terror, the speaker turns back from her journey, never reaching the house that, of course, is already "boarded up." Instead of the auroras that so powerfully move her precursors, she observes the sun's diminishment as the stones throw out "long shadows, individual shadows, then pull(ed) them in again." Thus Bishop evades the terror of the Whitmanian sublime when it becomes, as it will always become for Whitman, an equivalent anxiety of demand: "Dazzling and tremendous, how quick it could kill me, / If I could not now and always send sunrise out of me."[27] Bishop resists Whitman's defiance by herself noting the sun's fall into the western sky. The sun that formerly walked along the beach trailing his kite string, "making those big, majestic paw-prints, / who perhaps had batted a kite out of the sky to play with," the playful, huge beast of light, fades into the shadows and leaves the poet alone. By abandoning the shore to its ghosts, the poem achieves its own solar flare of momentary brilliance as "the sun came out for just a minute. / For just a minute, set in their bezels of sand, / the drab, damp, scattered stones / were multi-colored, / and all those high enough threw out long shadows, / individual shadows, then pulled them in again." At the poem's close, the sun reappears as a gigantic, playful lion, whose absence leaves a trace of paw prints (and perhaps a bit of lost kite string). This simultaneous expansion and diminution preserves the aura of cosmic power as it calls into play, through its parodic troping, the powers it would cast aside. Thus "The End of March," like "In the Waiting Room" and "The Moose," presents a moment of experiential discontinuity that questions the reaffirmation following loss, a reaffirmation that would announce the resolution of the Sublime. Through such a rhetorical subversion of the major trope of American Sublimity, Bishop wins a distance from her precursor poets, and it is within this difference that she inscribes a geography disdaining the radical solipsism that has for so long marked the American poetic enterprise. What distinguishes Bishop's work from the dominant tradition of the American Sublime might be understood as a loss equivalent to restitution, the enactment of Bishop's "I" as the eye of the traveler or the child that only apparently evades issues of sexuality and gender. Bishop's poems inscribe a map of language where the limitations of sexuality yield before a dis-engendered, highly eroticized imagination. In her revisionary conceptualization of an eros that escapes such categorization, Bishop subtly evades the strife between Emerson and his agonistic disciples. The poems' prevailing absence of overt sexuality—indeed, their very dismissal of binary oppositions—recalls, moreover, Rich's exclusion of the "male" as a way to reestablish women's access to the world and the word. Despite their vast differences, Rich and Bishop both respond to the American tradition's denial of the woman as poet by reasserting their divergence from the scripts of heterosexist culture.

Bishop's poem "Sonnet" (published posthumously in *The New Yorker* in 1979) enacts a rebellion against that script through its rhetorical manipulations of that most traditionally conservative form. The poem engages the tension between sexual freedom and the confines of existing structures:

> Caught—the bubble
> in the spirit-level,
> a creature divided;
> and the compass needle
> wobbling and wavering,
> undecided.
> Freed—the broken
> thermometer's mercury

running away;
and the rainbow-bird
from the narrow bevel
of the empty mirror,
flying wherever
it feels like, gay![28]

From the opening "caught" to the final "gay," "Sonnet" traces the experience of a "creature divided" (one recalls the tense, bifurcated personae of the early poems: "The Gentleman of Shalott," *Cirque d'Hiver*," "From the Country to the City," "The Man-Moth"). "Caught," "wobbling and wavering," "undecided": elements intended to balance are trapped.[29] When, however, the thermometer breaks, its mercury takes flight, for surely "Sonnet" is as much about the spirit's flight upward into a new freedom as it is about the categories that bifurcate and bind our lives.

Formally, the sonnet inverts the Petrarchan paradigm by reversing the positions of the sextet and the octave, a rhetorical shift that mirrors Bishop's play of trope. With the sextet's close, the image changes from the spirit level to the mercury "running away" as it escapes to a sphere beyond measurement where the false determinacy of empiricism loses its meaning in the exuberance of flight. Such freedom bestows shape upon spirit; the conversion of mercury into a "rainbow-bird" transforms the previously entrapped substance into a dazzling presence. If the bird in Shelley's "To a Skylark" sings its ravishing song in a world full of color, the translucent "rainbow-bird" in "Sonnet" embodies this array. By breaking the confines of linearity, moreover, the bead of mercury escapes its identity as sign to be read. Thus, like Shelley's skylark soaring among "rainbow clouds," "Sonnet" describes an exuberance beyond mortal limits, a "joy" (Shelley's word) or gaiety that finds its origins in a release not simply from mortality but also from the specific, articulable divisions associated with measurement and balance. From the first, Bishop's poems have imagined a world of which the rainbow bird is only the last, most beautiful synecdoche. Like Santarém, this is a sacred ground where the differences of literary interpretation fall away before the more sublime possibility of a freedom that rises above distinctions, where the mind, escaping the boundaries of preconception, discovers in its sexual, poetic, and epistemic quests an escape from the mirror of history. It is to this region that Bishop's sexual poetics carries us, to an experiential Sublime that assumes a form freed from the ascriptions of gender. The poetic voice that speaks to and from that region is marked by an authoritative clarity that promises not the transcendence of the body but a redefinition of the body's relation to language. Finally, the rainbow bird's gaiety recalls the power of Bishop's own imagination as it breaks through the inherited codifications of naming to achieve the exuberant stature of an American Counter-Sublime.

7

PLATH'S BODILY EGO

Restaging the Sublime

> . . . despite the insistence of whole traditions
> of poetry and of Romanticism in particular—
> poems are not given *by* pleasure, but by the
> unpleasure of a dangerous situation, the
> situation of anxiety of which the grief of in-
> fluence forms so large a part.
>
> —Harold Bloom[1]

Of no poet is Bloom's observation more true than of Sylvia Plath, whose sense of abiding danger stems from a conflict between her desire to achieve access to the powers of the Romantic imagination (the great tradition whose voices her earlier work so faithfully echoes) and her equally intense determination to bear witness to the alternative situation of the woman poet who refuses to dis-engender herself for art. Thus, the question Plath's poetry engages is how, ←— precisely, to inscribe sexual identity in poems, how to write a revisionary myth of poetic origins.

From her earliest poems, Plath reveals not only a characteristic prescience, but also the distinctive self-knowledge that marks her project of revisionist mythmaking. Among her juvenilia, the poem "Aerialist" most starkly bears witness to Plath's recognition of the dangers that haunt her reconceptualization of the poetic Family Romance. Here Plath identifies a version of psychic activity wherein a young woman confronts the aggression both of those who surround her and of an adversarial world in which she must fight to survive. If one reads this description of physical performance as analogous to the performative paradigm of composition, then writing becomes for Plath an activity simulta-neously designed to arouse and to placate external aggression. Here perform-ance courts as it defends against its powerful enemies in a "tightrope acrobat-ics" that seeks to protect but finally cannot rescue the performer from the risks of her own success. Indeed, the self as aerialist is always a self at risk, punished for its ability to please male authority. If, in her final poems, Plath wins a release from the precarious practice of such psychic tightrope walking (a release that culminates in the final free flight of "Aerial," "Lady Lazarus," and "Fever 103°"), her earliest lessons (like our own) are never completely unlearned and must be defied with an energy that proves self-consuming.

From its opening stanza, "Aerialist" establishes the flight up to the high wire as an imaginative flight:

> Each night, this adroit young lady
> Lies among sheets
> Shredded fine as snowflakes
> Until dream takes her body
> From bed to strict tryouts
> In tightrope acrobatics.

Here, the work of the unconscious takes the body out of itself and performs both outside and within the sleeping subject.[2] Plath becomes an observer of her own performance, with a dreamer's uncanny awareness. Yet if the aerialist performs a dance of the unconscious, the unconscious itself is dominated by masculine control:

> Nightly she balances
> Cat-clever on perilous wire
> In a gigantic hall,
> Footing her delicate dances
> To whipcrack and roar
> Which speak her maestro's will.

But the height of performance is not high enough to escape the weights that fall upon her, for the aerialist performs in an enclosed space, within a "gigantic hall" that encompasses still higher dangers:

> Gilded, coming correct
> Across that sultry air,
> She steps, halts, hung
> In dead center of her act
> As great weights drop all about her
> And commence to swing.

Not only must the aerialist balance between height and depth, she must also maintain her poise against hostile, horizontal forces in an adversarial struggle that, no matter how tortuous for the performer, wins strong audience approval:

> Lessoned thus, the girl
> Parries the lunge and menace
> Of every pendulum;
> By deft duck and twirl
> She draws applause; bright harness
> Bites keen into each brave limb

In this high-wire duel, the aerialist wears the harness that inflicts new pain with each self-protective gesture. If her acrobatic strength is joined by a skill requisite for victory, her power does not deny but itself reinforces a danger associated with femininity—the danger of becoming the object of menacing male desire, the performance as self-perpetuating tease. Whether in performance or in the daily life to which she must return, this "outrageous nimble queen" remains a victim, always on guard against those who punish her for success:

> Now as penalty for her skill,
> By day she must walk in dread
> Steel gauntlets of traffic, terror-struck
> Lest, out of spite, the whole
> Elaborate scaffold of sky overhead
> Fall racketing finale on her luck.

Hers is the luck of the unlucky, a luck that derives what satisfaction it can from warding off a paranoid world constituted of its own alienated desires.

Spatially, the threat of the aerialist's world is that the sphere beyond performance will become contaminated by the threat that exists within, that performance in the "gigantic hall" accurately represents everything beyond it, a performance from which there is no escape in a life led under the "elaborate scaffold of sky."[3] The delusion that one can will the performance of the unconscious is crippling—matched, moreover, by the persecutory pressures created by male observers' lust for revenge. Ironically, Plath's pornographic self-caricature guarantees its own punishment. The extremity of this scenario—the exaggeration with which it depicts both the performative imagination and its dangers—foreshadows Plath's attempts throughout her career to free herself from the "harness" of this grotesquely theatricalized and victimized version of the feminine.[4] Rather than shun by abandoning the risks "Aerialist" so graphically describes, Plath engages the very origins that determine her self-described psychic peril as she explores the sources of her own poetic authority, the sensations of a woman who seeks reciprocity with nature, whose imagination takes as its primary subject its own psychogenesis.[5]

In her desire to establish a relation with the world and in her use of a language of sensation to achieve that reciprocity, Plath follows in the tradition of the Whitmanian American Sublime. Yet the methodological resemblance between Whitman and Plath reveals a major difference, for whereas Whitman achieves intermittent ecstasy within and through his bodily identifications, Plath achieves her sublime moments by the effacement *either* of self or of world, by soaring beyond the pleasure principle into the numinous pursuit of death. Consequently, Plath's is an antinatural Sublime that defies human limitation through its quest for a purification that would rid the imagination of the perils of the body, a body that paradoxically serves as the major tropological source of her art. Plath's poems work against themselves in a series of thrilling, self-destructing performances. The challenge for Plath is to embrace a process of image-making already foredoomed by the prescriptiveness of literary tradition, a tradition she had so arduously labored to inherit. The corporeal power of Plath's poetics (related as it is to Whitman's self-sustaining discourse), when reinscribed by the images of the female body, becomes a form of sacrifice. That this sacrifice may be matched by poetic triumph has not escaped the notice of Plath's most insightful critics. Lynda Bundtzen, for example, notes that "the ideal of woman as vessel for the man's creative seed is replaced in 'Lady Lazarus' by woman as arbitress of her own fate, and perhaps most important as a theme of Plath's late poetry, the ideal of woman as presiding genius of her own body. . . ."[6] Bundtzen, Sandra Gilbert, Susan Van Dyne, and Paula Bennett are among the most persuasive and acute of Plath's readers to interpret the interworkings of gender and poetics as fundamentally empowering. While I would not for a moment wish to deny the experimental brilliance, associational daring, or rhetorical control of Plath's strongest poems, my emphasis here is on the somewhat more problematic tension I perceive building throughout her poetry between the rhetorical opportunities Plath discovers in her gender-identified imagination, on the one hand, and the alienation precipitated by this identification, on the other.

In order to clarify Plath's construction (and subsequent deconstruction) of the corporeal, I want to invoke Freud's concept of the bodily ego, a concept about which he himself has very little to say. In *The Ego and The Id,* Freud offers this brief description: "The ego is first and foremost a bodily ego," and although Freud does not go on to explore the implications of his initial observation, the "bodily ego" is an idea elaborated upon by other psychoanalytic theoreticians, among them Richard Wollheim, whose description proves especially telling in regard to Plath.[7] Wollheim's interpretation of the "bodily ego" emphasizes the ways in which corporeal consciousness engages physical phenomena, investing the physical with feelings that originate in the mind. According to Wollheim, the bodily ego becomes a corporeal "representation" that "extends from phantasy to the figure in the environment who occurs in the phantasy: and given that the phantasy is represented as a bodily process, the figure is represented as the kind of thing that the bodily process would be directed upon." Wollheim immediately acknowledges the solipsistic dangers of the projection he describes: "psychic cannibalism, in other words, consumes a person."[8] Rather than read Plath's poems either as an overly literal transcription of experience or as a highly elaborated rhetorical expression of feeling, the concept of the bodily ego allows us to contextualize both sexual and poetic identity.[9] As Harold Bloom persuasively argues, the history of the psyche can be understood as figured in rhetorical forms that parallel Freud's "concepts of defense." Provisionally, I would suggest that we extend Bloom's insight so that the history of the psyche may be conveyed by the *bodily ego as trope.* Assuredly, Plath is by no means unique in *writing the "bodily ego"* and, as assuredly, the interrelation between such imaginary projections of internal phantasies of the body, the interworkings of the bodily ego and the world, must be understood (in psychoanalytic terms) as a major project of the Romantic imagination.[10] The preeminence of the "bodily ego" for Whitmanian poetics, moreover, can be understood as the distinguishing characteristic of the American Sublime, with its insistence upon an elision of sexual and poetic identities. By invoking the concept of the bodily ego as trope in reading Plath, I strive to evade the double traps of literalization and theatricalization, thereby re-placing Plath's poetics both within and against the male-identified tradition of the Romantic Sublime.

Before I begin this process, however, I wish to clarify my use of the "bodily ego" by distinguishing it from "writing the body," the *écriture feminine* of Hélène Cixous and other French feminist critics.[11] As I conceptualize it, the difference between the bodily ego and "writing the body" is a crucial one. What I am interested in is the way style (primarily tropological constellations) appropriates the language of the body and thereby figuratively reenacts the formative experiences of the authorial psyche. In this method of reading, style becomes a rhetorical and thereby revisionary reenactment of primal experience. My interest in examining Plath's tropes in a psychoanalytic light is *not* to perform an analysis of a psyche only partially elaborated by the poems—such a project seems both audacious and doomed to inaccuracy. What I propose instead is a reading that specifically (although not exclusively) attends to the poetic figurations that arise from projections of the unconscious, that retains the traces of the psyche's earliest memories.

In terms of the poetic tradition, Plath creates a poetics that carries important and disturbing implications for women poets who inherit the dual legacy of a gender-identified Romanticism and the difference of female sexuality. Plath's work stands as a bold warning to future women poets, for the poems envision a freedom achieved only by transcending the inherited categories of patriarchal discourse while remaining wholly within those categories. Plath's poems present, therefore, a Sublime of devastation purchased at the price of the linguistically constructed self. If, in her final poems, Plath imagines a transcendence that depends upon purification, a shedding of the very body upon which her poetics depends, the death and resurrection of the bodily ego associates language with a signifying impurity that itself must be overcome. Plath's sense of her own "impurity" results from the process that seeks to evade it. By appropriating the creative mythos identified with the male poet's authority while reengendering language, Plath places herself in the position of potentially violating the codes by which she has sought to write. Thus, a lethal mix of poetic competition and sexual conflict overdetermines Plath's crisis, for the poet as poet paradoxically depends upon as she simultaneously must destroy an authority that derives from the gender-linked phantasmatic of the Romantic imagination. By imagining herself a Romantic quester while simultaneously inscribing maternal and distinctively female experiences in her work, Plath ties her double bind.[12] Inevitably, the events of a woman's life tell a different story from that of male poets (different as the men's individual stories may be). The woman poet's divergence from the myth of male Romanticism, moreover, creates an ineluctable conflict between traditional notions of poetic authority and the autonomous authority of the woman's voice. By situating herself within male Romantic discourse while speaking from the experience of the woman,

Plath creates an engendered bodily ego reinscribed by and through the scars of poetic figuration. Her strongest poems are works of great experimental brilliance, even as they serve to warn against the potential self-victimization imposed upon the woman who reimagines herself within the Romantic tradition.

Toward the close of "About Chinese Women," Julia Kristeva searches for a means by which to conceptualize the possibility of a woman's voice that escapes what she terms "an impossible dialectic" between "time and its 'truth,' identity and its loss, history and that which produces it: that which remains extraphenomenal, outside the sign, beyond time." She concludes by invoking the suicides of three women writers: Virginia Woolf, Maria Tsvetaeva, and Sylvia Plath. Kristeva argues that suicide is not an exceptional response to imaginative women's predicament in our culture:

> For a woman, the call of the mother is not only a call from beyond time, or beyond the socio-political battle. With family and history at an impasse, this call troubles the word: it generates hallucinations, voices, "madness." After the superego, the ego founders and sinks. . . . Suicide without a cause, or sacrifice without fuss for an apparent cause which, in our age, is usually political: a woman can carry off such things without tragedy, even without drama, without the feeling that she is fleeing a well-fortified front, but rather as though it were simply a matter of making an inevitable, irresistible and self-evident transition.[13]

Kristeva goes on to identify Plath as "another of those women disillusioned with meanings and words, who took refuge in lights, rhythms and sounds: a refuge that already announces, for those who know how to read her, her silent departure from life." Whereas Kristeva would argue for the woman poet's inevitable disavowal of the power of meaning and language, a return to "lights, rhythms and sounds," inchoate forms of perceptual expression, I would suggest that Plath's poetics demand that such perceptions be articulated by and through a deliberate, often painstakingly elaborated artfulness. Plath's final work merges a triumph of articulation with a stunning indictment of the opportunities offered an imagination that struggles to escape the traditional strictures of gender identity.

Before considering Plath's always intermittent rejection of the word, I return to the dangers incurred by the aerialist in order to gauge not only the risks encountered by the engendered imagination but the implications for that imagination as it surveys all that lies beyond it. If Plath's aerialist articulates the dangers that await the female artist always obedient to the demands of others, the alternative possibility, a poetry that speaks directly from its own as yet unrecognized desires, carries an equivalent danger, for neither stance is free of the burdens of marginalization that accompany displacement from cultural and sexual norms. I speak of marginalization in the second instance as well as the first, because for a woman to write from a position of desire is to deny herself the phantasmatic position as "other" bestowed by literary tradition. One notes in this regard how few of Plath's poems describe the pleasures of heterosexual desire. While the reasons for such a choice are necessarily linked to the work of an individuated psyche, Plath's choice has resonant cultural echoes as well. When, in an early poem, Plath does assume the voice of the female lover, when she describes her male "object of desire," she identifies him through a reassertion of cultural hierarchies that would surely undermine any claim to her own poetic authority. In "Ode for Ted," Plath's description of "her man" is not only proprietary but also borders, in its excessive adulation, on the parodic. He owns the world in which he moves and names its creatures.

> Ringdoves roost well within his wood,
> shirr songs to suit which mood
> he saunters in; how but most glad
> could be this adam's woman
> when all earth his words do summon
> leaps to laud such man's blood!

Sandra Gilbert, among others, has discussed the interworkings of competition and eros in Plath's relationship with Ted Hughes.[14] One might extend her observations to ask whether the choice of Hughes as husband does not in and of itself signal Plath's passionate desire for access to poetic power and her eroticization of poetic activity. That the workings of poetic influence should themselves parallel that of romantic love has not escaped the notice of the leading theoretician of influence relations, Harold Bloom, nor should it come as any surprise to those who accept a deidealized notion of the imagination. Although this is not the moment to embark upon a discussion of the interrelation of poetics and eros, one cannot evade recognizing the near impossibility of Plath's claim to a heterosexual, erotic, lyric voice as she herself defines it. The origins of this "impossibility" are linked to the politics that underlie Plath's version of eros, which, if unrevised, stifle the woman speaker's capacity for autonomous poetic authority. Plath turns her back upon an erotic lyricism, choosing instead to speak with an incantatory, oracular voice that explores alternative sources of poetic authority. Plath founds this bid for authority upon the sensations of woman, upon a bodily ego that seeks an always denied reciprocity with nature.

II

To clarify Plath's divergence from the dominant mode of the Romantic Sublime, it may be useful briefly to read her work in the company of her most magisterial and formidable British and American precursors, Wordsworth and Whitman. The question to be asked is the hauntingly elusive question: How does the lens of gender affect the self's relation to nature and to itself? One need only recall the power Whitman ascribes to himself in order to register the bleak contrast between his myth of the bodily ego and Plath's related, yet poignantly distinct, conception.[15] Here is Whitman enjoying a celebratory moment of reciprocity:

A show of the summer softness—a contact of something unseen
  —an amour of the light and air,
I am jealous and overwhelm'd with friendliness,
And will go gallivant with the light and air myself.

                                              ("The Sleepers," 7, 1–3)

Although Whitman is not everywhere so joyous, although he, too, suffers the anguish that inevitably accompanies acute sensibility, the articulation of both the pleasure and pain of experience depends upon his acceptance of a fundamental relation between the world and the body, a body he imagistically represents as the locus of poetic as well as physical sensation. Such physical awareness, as I have earlier asserted, remains at the very heart of Whitman's sexualized poetics, the immanent manifestation of erotic desire translated into the power of speech. Whitman's verbal authority, rather than being purchased at the price of the body, finds its origin in a physicality that enacts the projections of fantasy; his is a poetics that draws for its authority upon the entire history of Western literary culture with its deeply inscribed identification of male sexuality and poetic power. What is so moving about Whitman's affirming bodily ego is a tenderness that does not evacuate but rather confirms a capacity for nurturance. Consider the breathtaking aura of assurance with which Whitman ends "The Sleepers," an affirmation of faith in mutuality as well as in the salvific power of acceptance.

Why should I be afraid to trust myself to you?
I am not afraid, I have been well brought forward by you,
I love the rich running day, but I do not desert her in whom I lay
  so long,
I know not how I came of you and I know not where I go with
  you, but I know I came well and shall go well.

                                              (179–82)

That this faith should be uttered among the shadows of anxiety only deepens its poignancy, as at the moment of departure, Whitman does not abandon the sleepers but renews his faith in a reaffirmation that overcomes fear of departure through trust. Such amorous generosity ensures continuity, a power that directly counters the anxiety associated with all leave-takings. Yet for all his self-proclaimed radicalism and his overt claims to poetic "originality," Whitman cannot evade the gifts of the tradition he would deny. Indeed, his very insistence upon a masculine bodily ego, an imagination embodied by virile presence, allows Whitman to don the cultural authority he elsewhere would cast aside. By embodying poetic priority and employing the corporeal as trope for the life-giving imagination, Whitman deploys sensation in the service of the projective bodily ego, thereby achieving the characteristic guise of assurance that pervades his descriptions of the self in the world.

If equally intense and all-consuming, Plath's version of the bodily ego is everywhere marked by signs of radical discontinuity. Reading Plath's "I Am

Vertical" with the voice of Whitman still echoing in our ears is to experience more intensely the pathos of Plath's experiential exclusion. Here the sustained, explicit comparison between self and nature tears at the self as it simultaneously dismantles the Romantic project of figuring selfhood in natural terms. Plath envisions a nature so exclusionary that only in death can she hope to receive attention.

> I Am Vertical
> But I would rather be horizontal.
> I am not a tree with my root in the soil
> Sucking up minerals and motherly love
> So that each March I may gleam into leaf,
> Nor am I the beauty of a garden bed
> Attracting my share of Ahs and spectacularly painted,
> Unknowing I must soon unpetal
> Compared with me, a tree is immortal
> And a flower-head not tall, but more startling,
> And I want the one's longevity and the other's daring.

Like the Whitman of "The Sleepers," Plath, too, is a night wanderer, keenly aware both of her solitude and the seductive powers of nature. Yet if sensation offers Whitman the opportunity of engaging with the natural world, whether in joy or suffering, Plath's experience overwhelmingly marks the distance that bars her from the figural and the psychological reciprocity she craves.

> Tonight, in the infinitesimal light of the stars,
> The trees and flowers have been strewing their cool odors.
> I walk among them, but none of them are noticing.
> Sometimes I think that when I am sleeping
> I must most perfectly resemble them—

The possibility of resemblance comes with the fading of consciousness; open converse as mutual acceptance follows but cannot precede death. Present in these lines as well is the cruel belief that affection depends upon "use," a belief intensified by the realization expressed in the poem's final line that only in death can the neglected daughter receive the desired reassurance of touch. This profound awareness of separation stirs the ground tone of loss at the center of Plath's proliferating myths of conflict and victimization.

The overwhelming fear in Plath's early poems develops from a terror of absence associated with her profound sense of exclusion, a blankness that meets the eye. To redeem that vast emptiness, Plath initially awaits an inspiration conceived in terms of annunciation; she assumes the passivity of expectation. To conceptualize poetic inspiration in terms of the Annunciation is to remain within the Judeo-Christian framework of sexual identifications.[16] If Plath later reconceptualizes the process of inspiration to be initiated by and through her own imagination, the abandonment of the passive position marks a break with tradition. Interestingly, what replaces the Annunciation in Plath's revisionary myth of poetic transcendence is not the miracle of the Assumption, "the bodily taking up of the Virgin Mary into heaven," but either complicity in the male-identified paradigm of burial and resurrection (see "Lady Lazarus") or a transgressive, inherently self-destructive journey upward that, while moving with stunning verticality, recorporealizes the Assumption by insisting upon a conflagratory purification that anticipates transcendence. Before reaching these alternatives, however, the first, reinstating the feminine within the masculine script, and the second, reinscribing (through violence) the oppression associated with being a woman within that script, Plath investigates the more conservative possibilities within the canonical paradigm of female creativity. When, in the old way, inspiration does occur, it releases consciousness from an ordinariness experienced as devoid of meaning or purpose.

> Out of kitchen table or chair
> As if a celestial burning took
> Possession of the most obtuse objects now and then—
> Thus hallowing an interval
> Otherwise inconsequent
>
> By bestowing largesse, honor,
> One might say love. At any rate, I now walk
> Wary (for it could happen
> Even in this dull, ruinous landscape); skeptical,
> Yet politic; ignorant
>
> Of whatever angel may choose to flare
> Suddenly at my elbow.
>   ("Black Rook in Rainy Weather")

The hope held out by such a descent depends upon the workings of the miraculous. Conjoined with the passivity of awaiting a miracle, however, is an effortful resistance that has nothing to do with grace.

> . . . I only know that a rook
> Ordering its black feathers can so shine
> As to seize my senses, haul
> My eyelids up, and grant
>
> A brief respite from fear
> Of total neutrality.
>   ("Black Rook in Rainy Weather")

"Seize" and "haul," the verbs that Plath chooses to characterize the moment of Sublime intervention, convey the rook's effect upon her as they suggest a resistance on her part, a passivity that must be broken through. When this resistance combines with dread, Plath envisions a world that will not break into moments of radiance but yields only absence, an absence synonymous with a world untransformed by an imaginative power envisioned as having been created by forces beyond the self.

> . . . With luck,
> Trekking stubborn through this season
> Of fatigue, I shall
> Patch together a content
>
> Of sorts. Miracles occur,
> If you care to call those spasmodic
> Tricks of radiance miracles. The wait's begun again,
> The long wait for the angel,
> For that rare, random descent.
> ("Black Rook in Rainy Weather")

The passivity associated with Plath's early understanding of imaginative creativity would later be replaced by a conception of creative powers that originate from within. Such self-reliance, however, depends upon a release from the early poems' fabric of identifications, where the inspiratory powers of the imagination and the voice of poetic authority are both linked to forces external to the self: to the male poet or to an aversive, hostile nature.

Only by reengendering the terms of these initial identifications can Plath escape the equation of poetic inspiration as annunciation and the passivity it entails. But before we can gauge the consequences of a fusion between poetic and gender identities, the creation of a gender-inflected poetics, we need to observe the stark universe Plath envisions when she relies upon the inherited dynamics of the traditional Romantic Sublime.

To trace the origins as well as the persecutory difference that marks Plath's early work, I turn to a passage from *The Prelude*, Book V (Wordsworth's dream of the Arab), wherein the young Wordsworth explores the origins of his faith in works of the mind to endure beyond the ravages of human time, a passage that, in its imagistic associations and recollected urgency, uncannily anticipates Plath's "Hardcastle Crags," a poem of failed consolation and the defeat of instruction.

With its emphasis on dreamlike processes of condensation, displacement, and the symbolic, with its recognition of the possible inclusion of madness in the will to reconcile the human mind with the natural world, this passage is among the most severe of Wordsworth's explorations of the saving powers of the human imagination. What marks its significance in terms of Plath's "Hardcastle Crags" is not only the similarity between physical and psychic circumstances, a related crisis, but also her overt refusal to accept the troubled, profoundly self-aware, and provisional version of Wordsworthian acceptance. For even in Wordsworth's darkest vision of an imagination in flight—deluded and fully cognizant of the potential futility of its gestures—Plath discovers a vision too hopeful, an activity impossible to commence, let alone conclude. Plath's bleak poem denies the very power Wordsworth discovers in the phantasmagoric apparition of his childhood imagination. In a rhetorical inversion of the Wordsworthian moment of awakened vocation and poetic self-renewal, Plath transforms his hope into a brittle testament to her own profound sense of a displacement bordering on despair.

Against the Wordsworthian confirmation of the imagination's powers, "Hardcastle Crags" articulates the effects of a mutuality of resistance, an obdurate world that provokes a corollary blankness within the perceiving self. Plath's poem describes a journey from a "stone-built town," a harsh street of violence where "flintlike, her feet struck / Such a racket of echoes . . ." Here the woman walks in a rage of tension beyond the town walls into a moonlit landscape as burdened with anger as the town from which she fled. Hers is a failed attempt to reach beyond the claustrophobia of rage and find relief in nature. But nothing breaks through to succor the tormented self, as the terms of this failure themselves cruelly recall the restorative tropes of the Wordsworthian dream that instructs the young mind confronting an equally apocalyptic vision in the enduring capacities of the human imagination.

Here is Wordsworth lamenting the limitations of nature as he plangently expresses the need for something that will survive the ravages of time. Against a landscape of catastrophic earthquake and scorching fire, a

> . . . fire come down from far
> to scorch
> Her pleasant habitations, and dry up
> Old Ocean, in his bed left singed and
> bare, . . .
> (*The Prelude,* Book V, ll.31–33)

Frustrated by the ephemeral aspect of the artifacts created by the mind, Wordsworth asks,

> . . . Oh! why hath not
> the Mind
> Some element to stamp her image on
> In nature somewhat nearer to her own?
> Why, gifted with such powers to send abroad
> Her spirit, must it lodge in shrines so frail?
> (*The Prelude,* Book V, ll.44–48)

In response to his youthful question, the mature Wordsworth offers the dream of the quixotic Arab, which, in its evocation of the geographic catastrophes of ravaging flood and fire and its aural transmission of the words of instruction, finds its echoes in Plath's necessarily belated and gender-inflected crisis-poem.

Both Wordsworth and Plath invoke the oneiric powers of the imagination to stave off the bleak, cataclysmic knowledge of temporal destruction. While Plath invokes only to dismiss the salvific potency of dream, it is this power that transforms the Wordsworthian catastrophe into a reaffirmation of the imagination's will. Here is Plath's allusive dismissal:

> . . . Once past
> The dream-peopled village, her eyes entertained no dream,
> And the sandman's dust
>
> Lost lustre under her footsoles.
>
>   ("Hardcastle Crags")

Crucial to the Wordsworthian scene of instruction are the discovery of a guide who would shield him from the imaginary dangers that threaten to engulf the land and the realization that books themselves (as sublimating entities) can potentially stave off the external destruction associated with repressed desires against which the psyche otherwise could not defend. This doubly salutary recognition culminates in the moment of transference of power when the young Wordsworth holds a shell to his ear and hears

> . . . that instant in an unknown tongue,
> Which yet I understood, articulate sounds,
> A loud prophetic blast of harmony;
> An Ode, in passion uttered, which foretold
> Destruction to the children of the earth
> By deluge, now at hand. . . .
>   (*The Prelude,* Book V, ll.93–98)

If in *The Prelude,* the auditory is the means of transferring this knowledge, in "Hardcastle Crags," sound, first as a "racket" of self-created echoes and then as a "burdened whistle," enters the "whorl of [her] ear" only to expand its vacancy. Rather than convey a message of prophetic power that taps the origins of anxiety and expresses the requisite need for art, the wind in Plath's poem "returns" no gift beyond isolation. Seeking relief from rage, Plath pursues her doomed journey in a landscape as "black and void" as *The Prelude*'s dream-scape. Both the dream voyager and the desperate woman experience danger as they confront the possibility of another presence. If Wordsworth recalls his "distress and fear . . . when at [his] side . . . an uncouth shape appeared," Plath conjures up a phantasmatic, ghostly shape only to have it dematerialize before our eyes:

> . . . Though a mist-wraith wound
> Up from the fissured valley and hung shoulder-high
> Ahead, it fattened
>
> To no family-featured ghost,
> Nor did any word body with a name
> The blank mood she walked in. . . .
>   ("Hardcastle Crags")

Whereas the appearance of the Arab initiates Wordsworth into the mysteries of the untranslatable truth beyond words, the language of the unconscious, Plath's persona, deprived of the apparition, hears no such saving language. What

Wordsworth learns, when he holds the shell to his ear, is indeed remarkable. Itself an object of beauty, the shell utters what the young Wordsworth yearns to understand:

> . . . so beautiful in shape,
> In colour so resplendent, with command
> That I should hold it to my ear. I did so,
> And heard that instant in an unknown tongue,
> Which yet I understood, articulate sounds,
> A loud prophetic blast of harmony;
> An Ode, in passion uttered, which foretold
> Destruction to the children of the earth
> By deluge, now at hand. . . .
>
> (*The Prelude,* Book V, ll.90–98)

If, in the moment of crisis, Wordsworth hears a warning that is at once harmonious and prophetic, this is because he both understands what he hears and is in the presence of someone who can simultaneously interpret and offer advice.[17] Yearning for belief, the Plathian woman, as we have seen, produces no such dream-induced vision. As in the defeated conjuring of the "mist-wraith," Plath once again introduces a Wordsworthian possibility only to dismiss it, for not only is the dream made present by the articulation of its absence, but also the experiential self is reduced to a "pinch of flame" to whom the wind speaks—through the ear—conveying its meaningless message:

> The long wind, paring her person down
> To a pinch of flame, blew its burdened whistle
> In the whorl of her ear, and like a scooped-out pumpkin crown
> Her head cupped the babel.
>
> ("Hardcastle Crags")

Moreover, the stones that metamorphose into books in *The Prelude* now relentlessly refuse to bear any symbolic meaning. And whereas, guided by the forces of the irrational, Wordsworth learns to master his anxiety, an anxiety that can be converted into the compensation of poetic activity, in "Hardcastle Crags" the imagination remains a victim of the scene, not its redemptive transcriber:

> . . . The whole landscape
> Loomed absolute as the antique world was
> Once, in its earliest sway of lymph and sap,
> Unaltered by eyes,
>
> Enough to snuff the quick
> Of her small heat out, but before the weight
> Of stones and hills of stones could break
> Her down to mere quartz grit in that stony light
> She turned back.
>
> ("Hardcastle Crags")

This is a world bled of life that threatens to stifle and crush the self both by its omnipresent resistance and its aversive impenetrability. Although Wordsworth's dream ends with the deluded, terrified Arab urging the boy to flee the "waters of a drowning world / In chase of him," the interpretation of the dream evades its manifest content, for its sustaining value stems from Wordsworth's reverence for the Arab's redemptive task. Already on fire, herself a flame, Plath most assuredly would welcome the engulfing waters the mad Arab knows he must flee.[18] The possibility of gaining access to that water (transported in Wordsworth's passage through the medium of the shell) remains decidedly absent from Plath's scorched vision.

In his study on genitality, Sandor Ferenczi discusses dreams of rescues from drowning. Referring to Freud's *Interpretation of Dreams,* Ferenczi writes: "It is very frequently the case that we cannot explain the dream image or the dream experience of the *rescue of a person from water* otherwise than as the symbolic equating of birth with rescue from water. In the dreams of people, too, who are in great difficulties or who are suffering from an anxiety state, rescue from water may occur as a wish-fulfilling deliverance."[19] Following Ferenczi, we might interpret the Wordsworthian Arab's delusion as articulating the power books assume to ward off the primal fear of confronting one's own birth. Thus, writing would represent a coming to safe ground, an escape from being engulfed by an anxiety caused by recognition of the birth trauma, and hence recognition of one's mortality. Literature, as Wordsworth elsewhere imagines it, serves to displace the original birth trauma through its reinscription of the mind's capacity (hence recuperative power) to interpret and thereby master experience. By contrast, the dessication that threatens Plath proves no saving ground either as landscape or as image. Neither biological birth nor intellectual sublimation will assuage Plath's anxiety. Disquieting though it may be, we need to go farther into this arid land before we can attempt to discover why neither the voice of the sea nor the promise of dry land offers Plath consolation.

In her early poem "The Thin People," Plath anatomizes the aridity of "Hardcastle Crags" into an even deadlier dessication. With the finality of desperation, Plath writes,

> We own no wildernesses rich and deep enough
> For stronghold against their stiff
>
> Battalions. See, how the tree boles flatten
> And lose their good browns
>
> If the thin people simply stand in the forest,
> Making the world go thin as a wasp's nest
>
> And grayer; not even moving their bones.

The fear of the death of the imagination—its silences—becomes an ubiquitous stimulus against which no resource proves adequate, for mnemonic power destroys rather than enhances nature's restorative capacities. Through the personification of danger, by means of the spectral "thin people" of memory, Plath converts absence into aggression, into an alien otherness whose very indifference must be overcome. Whether writing of the abandonment of divination from the land (see, for example, "On the Difficulty of Conjuring Up a Dryad") or testifying to the oppression caused by an overwhelming abundance of magical spirits, Plath perceives an atmosphere of oppression. Whether regarding nature with a "threadbare eye" or viewing it with too fecund a vision, the self that quests for a relation with reality fails before the exclusionary self-sufficiency of the material world. Plath's quest is for a poetics that will resist the profane silence that threatens to stifle the fires of the purifying imagination. Exiled from the mediating process of Romanticism, faced with a nature perceived as retreating from the self, Plath focuses upon her own body as the source of nature's rejection. Plath, moreover, repeatedly seizes upon the fact of her sexual identity as the source of her exclusion from the consolations of a tradition she identifies with male power and masculine authority.[20] In response to this recognition, Plath locates her poetry in that very difference: in the re-creation of a gender-inflected bodily ego that marks her exclusion from the continuities as well as the encoded identities that have long marked the landscape of the Romantic Sublime.

III

If one observes the bodily ego as it emerges in the poems from the early and middle stages of Plath's career, one notes the predominance of the conflict between a desire for a nurturant love and an abiding anxiety regarding the hold that any "other," person or object, might exercise over her. Repeatedly, Plath describes the risks run by a self with a fragile sense of boundaries.[21] When, for example, Plath describes a scenario of nurturance in "Virgin in a Tree," the "nipple-flowers" are "shrouded to suckle darkness." Consuming and being consumed, the terrors of orality remain a constant threat, for Plath perceives interdependence as fundamentally fatal. Whether describing the false and true selves of "In Plaster" or the horror of the intermittent caused by separation (see "Mirror"), Plath returns to issues surrounding a split identity and the risk of merger. Such horrific or morbid dependency, as Plath articulates it, is related to the guilt of the daughter, a guilt awakened by the thought that, through her illicit desires, she has caused her father's death and that she can never adequately compensate for her mother's self-sacrifice.[22]

In an attempt to escape this daughterly double burden, Plath turns to the possibilities of a womanhood associated with biological fertility.[23] Yet, inevitably, the promise of fertility awakens a recapitulation of anxieties associated with separation and autonomy. The fertility so richly celebrated by the First Voice of *Three Women*, a fertility that would rescue the self from a world of male "flatness," is countered by the attractions of isolation: "It is so beautiful to have no attachments! I am solitary as grass. What is it I miss?" Barrenness as threat and possibility finds a reciprocal danger in what lies beyond it, for the world, in its unself-conscious natural fecundity, does not, as we have seen, serve Plath as a source of potential solace but threatens to torture the barren self. Here is Plath's prototypical moon-mother:

> The moon, also, is merciless: she would drag me
> Cruelly, being barren.
> Her radiance scathes me. . . .
>
> ("Elm")

Whether fearing her own barrenness, mourning a stillborn child, or seeking revenge upon the severed, "perfected self," the voice that speaks throughout these poems expresses the conflicts associated with maternal relationships.[24] If several of Plath's poems about her children offer a respite from the dark, charged world of conflict that dominates her work, it is in part because children offer the hope of clarity, the innocence of the eye that promises a release from what must surely have seemed to Plath an increasingly rigidified and terroristic vision. The cleansing aspect of the "child" poems, where the child is described as "right, like a well-done sum. / A clean slate, with your own face on" ("You're") is deconstructed by surrounding poems, for surely, despite her desires, Plath was not so naive as to imagine that motherhood would not implicate her in the conflicts she experienced as a daughter. Indeed, "Child" itself is the lament of all mothers who recognize that they cannot return to their children the idealized innocence they experience through them. As her child's mirror, Plath witnesses her maternal opacities:

> Your clear eye is the one absolutely beautiful thing.
> I want to fill it with color and ducks,
> The zoo of the new
>
> Whose names you meditate—
> April snowdrop, Indian pipe,
> Little
>
> Stalk without wrinkle,
> Pool in which images
> Should be grand and classical
>
> Not this troublous
> Wringing of hands, this dark
> Ceiling without a star.

Wherever Plath looks, she is "hooked" by the otherness of beings or world. Wherever she ventures, she sees "a snag . . . lifting a valedictory, pale hand" ("Crossing the Water"). If "Poppies in July," those "little hell flames," cannot ignite her into feeling, if they assume a naturalistic projection of the bodily ego "flickering like that, wrinkly and clear red, like the skin of a mouth. / A mouth just bloodied," they become, in their very suffering, objects of envy: "If my mouth could marry a hurt like that!" Victim of her own projections, Plath is trapped in a world that replicates the unresolved conflicts of her bodily ego.

> O my God, what am I
> That these late mouths should cry open
> In a forest of frost, in a dawn of cornflowers.
> ("Poppies in October")

Absorption, incorporation, and engulfment everywhere define relationships in a universe that threatens to suck Plath dry. Nowhere is the tension between Plath's yearning for solidity (a haven of maternal affection) and her perception of universal danger more overt than in "Nick and the Candlestick," where the speaker as "miner" attempts to penetrate and survive the dangers of the cave in order to create a "cave with roses" for her son. But the cave as synecdochic body of the world defines the properties against which she must struggle, a world inhabited by internal conflicts:

> I am a miner. The light burns blue.
> Waxy stalactites
> Dry and thicken, tears
>
> The earthen womb
> Exudes from its dead boredom.
> Black bat airs
>
> Wrap me, raggy shawls,
> Cold homicides.
> They weld to me like plums.
>
> Old cave of calcium
> Icicles, old echoer.
> Even the newts are white,
>
> Those holy Joes.
> And the fish, the fish—
> Christ! they are panes of ice,
>
> A vice of knives,
> A piranha
> Religion, drinking
>
> Its first communion out of my live toes. . . .

Against this "piranha religion," Plath invests her faith in the infant Nicholas, the illusion of new life: "The blood blooms clean / In you, ruby." In a vertiginous world where "mercuric / Atoms that cripple drip / Into the terrible well," "You are the one / Solid the spaces lean on, envious. / You are the baby in the barn." Yet the symbiotic mother-child passion upon which Plath would found her faith inevitably falters, for such an omnivorous need cannot be met by any child. Such symbiotic compulsion as that articulated in "Totem" conveys the compulsive self-absorption that defines Plath's poetic imagination, substituting as it does a mechanical for a bodily image, while containing within it a related image of the devouring other:

> The engine is killing the track, the track is silver,
> It stretches into the distance. It will be eaten nevertheless.

The self's destruction of the very thing it requires emerges from the unrelenting compulsion of engine-killing-track, a drama that, despite the apparent shift in tropological systems from the bodily to the mechanical, a change in what Plath elsewhere would name the "old whore petticoats" of language, cannot alter the structures of the imagination through which all relationships are inevitably mediated:

> The world is blood-hot and personal
>
> Dawn says, with its blood-flush.
> There is no terminus, only suitcases
>
> Out of which the same self unfolds like a suit
> Bald and shiny, with pockets of wishes,
>
> Notions and tickets, short circuits and folding mirrors.
> I am mad, calls the spider, waving its many arms.

Here, as elsewhere, Plath envisions the doomed voyage of the entrapped body confined by destiny. Only a shedding of identity in a flight upward and beyond the existing structures of the imagination, beyond self-conceptions and sociocultural identities, will provide release. Whether as mother, daughter, barren woman, or widow, the tentacles of Plath's engendered identity retain their hold and will not release her. The "sun's poultice" drawing "on" her "inflammation" ("Berck-Plage," section 1) is the inverse of the bruise that so clearly signifies the vulnerability of the bodily ego wounded by a heedlessly needy world:

> Color floods to the spot, dull purple.
> The rest of the body is all washed out,
> The color of pearl.
>
> In a pit of rock
> The sea sucks obsessively,
> One hollow the whole sea's pivot.
>
> The size of a fly,
> The doom mark
> Crawls down the wall.

> The heart shuts,
> The sea slides back,
> The mirrors are sheeted.
>   ("Contusion")

It is here that figuration stops and mourning begins. Yet this coming to an end is not so much a chronological or sequential process as a repetition and intensification of a perception constant throughout Plath's poems, a fear that the world's evasions and nature's silence will foredoom her own—"Tongues are strange, / Signs say nothing" ("Incommunicado").[25] Conversely, words, with all their potentially definitional capacities, threaten to stifle their very articulation: "The word, defining, muzzles" ("Poems, Potatoes").

Such a problematic view of the relation between word and world, a problematics we have already charted in Emerson, Whitman, Dickinson, Moore, and Bishop, acquires a specific shape in Plath, as linguistic anxieties are relentlessly associated with surgical procedures, shock treatments, and bodily injury. With brutal, phantasmatic facticity Plath appropriates her personal history to define the conditions of human and literary experience. The delineation of the relationship between self and world in terms of physical trauma makes sensation a primary subject.

> Abrading my lid, the small grain burns:
> Red cinder around which I myself,
> Horses, planets and spires revolve.
>   ("The Eye-mote")

The severe alternations of consciousness and the disrupting of perception caused by trauma constitute the aftershock this poem recalls; the final stanza speaks in a post-traumatic voice, wishing for what can never reappear:

> What I want back is what I was
> Before the bed, before the knife,
> Before the brooch-pin and the salve
> Fixed me in this parenthesis:
> Horses fluent in the wind,
> A place, a time gone out of mind.
>   ("The Eye-mote")

The empowering literality of physical trauma articulates the strength of Plath's desire to reclaim this place. Against the irretrievable status of surgical procedures and the incidents that signify psychic victimization (as well as the overwhelmingly conflictual associations surrounding fertility and motherhood), Plath explores the recuperative possibilities of a liminal relationship with nature. It is only on the border, in ceremonies that incorporate as they preserve a saving distance, in her abiding obsession with boundaries, mirrors, and surfaces, that Plath can discover an enabling poetic space. Such liminal ceremonies are best illustrated by the "bee poems," which testify to the function of ritual to preserve contact with nature and retain a requisite control over life beyond the self.

In her fine study of Plath's manuscripts for the bee poems, Susan Van Dyne demonstrates how Plath incorporates explicitly biographical experience into the poems to achieve a sense of mastery. Van Dyne notes, "The bee poems represent a pivotal moment in Plath's career, when she attempted to articulate who she was in terms of her emotional and artistic past and to imagine who she would become."[26] In the midst of personal betrayal (Ted Hughes's affair) and on the eve of her thirtieth birthday, Plath attempts to win poetic freedom from her perennial conflict between self and other, to acquire power over the victimized role in which she had so often cast herself. This search for a triumphant self, however, proves only temporary, for even if, as Van Dyne suggests, the ceremonies of beekeeping permit Plath to experiment with alternative sex roles, with "issues of control, ownership, and power," as Plath "tries to imagine . . . an autonomous potent identity as a poet" (p. 156), they fail to banish the deeply troubling persecutory feelings they seek to vent. Van Dyne wisely notes the psychodynamics enacted and controlled in Plath's reworking of the manuscripts: "Just as the keeper manipulates the queen's productivity, the poet sought to exploit the queen as metaphor for her troubled questions about authorship. Repeatedly in the sequence, the powers of creation represented by the bees threaten to become agents of destruction. The speaker's conscious control over this transformation is alternately asserted and denied" (p. 161). In terms of Plath's unresolved conflicts relating to the anxiety of authorship and the tenuous vulnerability of the bodily ego, these drafts reveal the dangers that the final versions repress. Despite the triumph of the queen in the published version of "Wintering," the first handwritten draft of the poem's closing stanza bespeaks the continuation of doubt: a failure, despite the achievement of this poetic sequence, to win through to a resolution of Plath's sense of disempowerment, a failure to resolve these doubts or to check her fury:

> Will the hive survive, will the gladiolas
> Succeed in banking their fires
> to enter another year?
> What will they taste (like) of the Christmas roses?
> Snow water? Corpses? (Thin, sweet Spring.)
> (A sweet Spring?) Spring?
> (Impossible spring?)
> (What sort of spring?)
> (O God, let them taste of spring.)[27]

That final, desperate hope, "O God, let them taste of spring," becomes the *willed* triumph of the poem, but a triumph won within a context that simultaneously personifies the bees as it robs them of any redeeming subjectivity.

> The bees are all women,
> Maids and the long royal lady.
> They have got rid of the men,

> The blunt, clumsy stumblers, the boors.
> Winter is for women—
> The woman, still at her knitting,
> At the cradle of Spanish walnut,
> Her body a bulb in the cold and too dumb to think.

Neither the male nor the female bees, the clumsy stumblers nor the "bulb . . . too dumb to think," escapes Plath's contempt. If "Wintering" announces the end of Plath's belief in the imaginative powers of maternity, if here she strains the restorative ties she had elsewhere established between maternal identity and human affection, "Stings" reveals a similar embodiment that exposes the limits of analogizing between the creaturely and the imaginary, for it preserves the tension between an exceptional self and female "others," as well as the conflict between the distrusted male with whom the female must enact an exchange and the queen who would purchase her private resurrection at the price of others' lives.

> It is almost over.
> I am in control.
> Here is my honey-machine,
> It will work without thinking,
> Opening, in spring, like an industrious virgin
>
> To scour the creaming crests
> As the moon, for its ivory powders, scours the sea.

In language of fiery transcendence, "Stings" closes by asserting the speaker's defiant ambition to recover the queen:

> They thought death was worth it, but I
> Have a self to recover, a queen.
> Is she dead, is she sleeping?
> Where has she been,
> With her lion-red body, her wings of glass?
>
> Now she is flying
> More terrible than she ever was, red
> Scar in the sky, red comet
> Over the engine that killed her—
> The mausoleum, the wax house.

Despite their ceremonial balance and willed triumph, the bee poems do not, finally, alleviate Plath's psychic entrapment, for borderline ceremonies and the analogical investment of self into natural process fail to resolve the sense of overwhelming insufficiency: "I am myself. That is not enough" ("The Jailer").

IV

> Indeterminate criminal,
> I die with variety—
> Hung, starved, burned, hooked.
>
> ("The Jailer")

In a world predicated upon dependency, it is hardly surprising that the possibility of personal freedom threatens everything beyond the self, for symbiosis allows neither party freedom of choice.

> That being free. What would the dark
> Do without fevers to eat?
> What would the light
> Do without eyes to knife, what would he
> Do, do, do without me?
>
> ("The Jailer")

The victim's appeal to the welfare of the victimizer as sufficient reason for preserving the status quo signals the total dependence of a self foredoomed by the role assigned her by the other as oppressor. The consequences of conceptualizing the self as victim grow increasingly severe and Plath's work relentlessly claustrophobic, as poems ostensibly describing opposed states of feeling return to fixed imagistic structures. Written two days apart, "Morning Song" and "Barren Woman" (19 February 1961 and 21 February 1961) reflect Plath's passionate response to motherhood. "Morning Song" describes the early cries of the infant celebrated by his joyous mother, whereas "Barren Woman" expresses the grief of infertility. Yet both poems share an aura of emptiness and a single scenario—the blankness of a museum of the mind that reifies life and has turned away from everything and everyone. The mechanistic, always threatening to break through in Plath's poems, here takes over as the relation between self and other becomes merely reflexive, exposing the solitude of the self and the denial of all relationality. Is there any substantive difference between the emotional dynamic of the mother who greets her child as a "New statue. / In a drafty museum," whose "nakedness / Shadows our safety" and the thoughts of the barren woman, who, in her own emptiness, becomes a "museum without statues, grand with pillars, porticoes, rotundas"? In the more optimistic "Morning Song," maternity itself is defined not as the creation of a new duality, but as the mirroring of disappearance:

> I'm no more your mother
> Than the cloud that distills a mirror to reflect its own slow
> Effacement at the wind's hand.

In its destruction of the hope of reciprocity, this negative maternal mirroring might be interpreted as an even darker vision than that of the barren woman, who has herself become a museum that echoes in and through her emptiness. If in "Morning Song," the infant is alive, its breathing assumes a nonhuman quality that aestheticizes and so diminishes its unique, human vitality: "All night your moth-breath / Flickers among the flat pink roses." Waking "to listen," Plath witnesses a disturbingly intimate distance: "A far sea moves in my ear." Note also the syntactic parallel between the lines describing the baby's breathing in "Morning Song" and the barren woman's description of the lifelessness that decorates her museum self: "Marble lilies / Exhale their pallor like scent," an inversion of Plath's earlier dehumanization of her child's breath. Even within "Morning Song," the benign is converted into a dehumanizing echo as Plath frames the nursing infant against a "window square" that "whitens and swallows its dull stars." The image chains of "Morning Song" and "Barren Woman" do, however, finally diverge when, in the earlier poem, the infant's voice breaks through the mother's negations: "And now you try / Your handful of notes; / The clear vowels rise like balloons." In the child's cry, Plath combines the hopeful-ness of clarity with the distinctly eerie, liminal balloons that appear in her work as phenomena of suspended animation covered by a thin skin that can be perforated at any moment. In "Barren Woman," however, the child's "handful of notes" is replaced by the moon's hand, the moon as "blank-faced" mother who offers no solace for wounds inflicted by the dead. Whereas the "clear vowels" in "Morning Song" escape Plath's museum of psychic emptiness, "Barren Woman," while employing a similarly aural trope, ends in silence, the moon "mum as a nurse."

If maternity (witness "Lesbos" and "Stopped Dead") fails to offer Plath the requisite relief from conflict, marriage reinscribes the victimization we have already witnessed. Indeed, familial intimacy reawakens Plath's feelings of per-secution. Employing an image that recalls the Binswangerian *versteiglichkeit* that haunts "Aerialist" and from which Plath's "Ariel" will, at least momentarily, escape, "The Jailer" speaks from the position of one who feels herself not only trapped but fallen, and in that fall destroyed.

> Something is gone.
> My sleeping capsule, my red and blue zeppelin
> Drops me from a terrible altitude.
> Carapace smashed,
> I spread to the beaks of birds.[28]

The prepositional "to" conveys not only self-destruction but also a willed open-ing up to the reenactment of the birds' sexual aggression, with its combined phallic and oral associations. The starving victim distorts the perceptual world in some essential but unidentified way. That the jailer should retain his capacity to inflict injury in the face of his patent inauthenticity only reinforces the impres-sion conveyed by his sexual and social positions. What comes to his defense is the very "armor of fakery, / His high cold masks of amnesia." Her crime unknown even to herself, a prisoner of drugged consciousness, the victim nevertheless continues to perform with the "variety" we have come to expect of the Plathian victim as performer, whether in "Daddy" or "Lady Lazarus," a variety that cloaks repetition in the appearance of difference. This "victim" remains imprisoned by the jailer's dependence as the woman protects him from recognition of his own impotence:

> I imagine him
> Impotent as distant thunder,
> In whose shadow I have eaten my ghost ration.
> I wish him dead or away.
> That, it seems, is the impossibility.
>
> That being free. What would the dark
> Do without fevers to eat?
> What would the light
> Do without eyes to knife, what would he
> Do, do, do without me?

As in Plath's other poems of performative victimization, here verbal repetition ("do . . . do, do, do") underscores the process of entrapment, victimization, and the compulsion to repeat. It is not until the final poems of "Ariel," and there only intermittently, that this closed system of language breaks down in the face of a double recognition: first, that no resolution of rage or distress can be discovered beyond the confines of the gender-inflected script in which Plath has so passionately invested, and second, that the capacity to write poems is intimately connected with both her rage and her need to discover a poetic voice that will keep anger intact as it permits its evacuation.

Before that double recognition can be enacted, Plath describes her need for escape with an austere clarity. Thus, the huge, horizontal form in "Gulliver" is urged to break free of "the spider-men" that "have caught" him:

> Step off seven leagues, like those distances
>
> That revolve in Crivelli, untouchable.
> Let this eye be an eagle,
> The shadow of this lip, an abyss.

It is within this vertical space, between the eye of the eagle and the shadow of a lip, that the abyss opens from which Plath writes her final poems, shattering the "stasis of darkness" to achieve an upward flight. "Insane for the destination" ("Getting There"), Plath leaves a world that defines her as "Adam's side" to enact a purification of language, a sacrifice of the metaphor of the body to speech. That, in the end, the "bodily ego" enacts a metamorphosis into nonbeing should come as no surprise, given Plath's deeply ambivalent representation of the site of language and of an identity that cannot evade its own destructive representations. Only through the transfiguration of the body as trope can Plath find a voice through which to speak, a voice that despite its weariness resounds with stunning, oracular power.

V

It is the triumphant irony of Plath's final poems that they should describe the desire to transcend the body while using the "bodily ego" to articulate the very process of transcendence. Hence the literal desire to escape bodily articulation conflicts with the metaphorical necessity of the corporeal. Bloom's meditation upon Freud's "concepts of defense and the poetic will" illuminates the tensions between the demands of Plath's psychic life and her means of verbal figuration. Writing on the relation between thanatos and eros, between figural discourse and mental processes, Bloom describes the crisis for the poet when sadomasochism is divested of trope:

> Freud concluded "that the death drives are by their nature mute and that the clamour of life proceeds for the most part from Eros." Can we interpret this as meaning that wounded narcissism becomes physical aggression because the loss of self-esteem is also a loss in the language of Eros? Wounded narcissism is at the origins of poetry also, but in poetry the blow to self-esteem strengthens the language of Eros, which defends the poetic will through all the resources of troping. Lacking poetry, the sado-masochistic yields to the literalism of the death-drive precisely out of a rage against literal meaning. When figuration and sado-masochism are identified, as in Swinburne or Robinson Jeffers, then we find always the obsession with poetic *belatedness* risen to a terrible intensity that plays out the poetic will's revenge against time by the unhappy substitution of the body, another body or one's own, *for* time. Raging against time, the sado-masochist over-literalizes his revenge and so yields to the death-drive.[29]

Plath's poetic will had more to revenge itself upon than time, and, if she "over-literalizes revenge" and yields to the "death-drive," she does so only after exploring the limits of metaphorization of the "bodily ego." Plath's obsession, moreover, is less with poetic belatedness than with the haunting implications for metaphoricity as it relates to her primary trope, the engendered body. Purification, which becomes the means of escape, also threatens to destroy the body through which it speaks. Having created a poetics based upon the metaphorical interdependence of biological fertility and poetics and having aligned herself with the culturally inscribed definitions of the feminine, Plath, in her late poems, describes the breakdown of that relationship, the inevitable failure of an over-literalization of figuration. Words turn against her with an all-too-familiar violence:

> Axes
> After whose stroke the wood rings,
> And the echoes!
> Echoes traveling
> Off from the center like horses.
>
> The sap
> Wells like tears, like the

> Water striving
> To re-establish its mirror
> Over the rock
>
> That drops and turns,
> A white skull,
> Eaten by weedy greens.
> Years later I
> Encounter them on the road—
>
> Words dry and riderless,
> The indefatigable hoof-taps.
> While
> From the bottom of the pool, fixed stars
> Govern a life.
> ("Words," 1 February 1963)[30]

Here Plath does not abandon the "bodily ego" but returns to a dessicated physicality to prophecy the death of figuration. In this conflict between fate and the body, one may discern not simply resignation but also a challenge to the efficacy of poetic figurations to stave off despair. Once the process of mirroring is effaced, Plath can discover no recourse in the realm of nature to create the poetic correspondence that the natural world hitherto had offered. Hence these final poems, so rich in figuration, describe the approach of a deadly literalization, a purification through defiguration that erases differences between self and object as it dissolves the mediating distance between the imagination and the world by denying that such reciprocity can rescue one from one's fate.

In their vatic urgency and passion for transcendence, Plath's final poems rediscover themselves at the center of the Romantic Sublime. What marks Plath's difference from that Sublime is neither her apocalyptic vision nor her intensity, but the explicit identification of Romantic agony with the female-identified bodily ego. Surely, the brilliance of these final poems might be said to reside in Plath's capacity to retain a Romantic intensity while overtly replacing the male subject with a female-embodied presence, yet that brilliance contains its own tragedy. Like Whitman, Plath envisions a poetics grounded in sensation and self-divination, a poetics that depends upon an unrelenting and continuous testing of one's powers. Yet if Whitman can proffer consolation to all he meets, retaining for himself the confidence that he understands their dreams and assures their rest, Plath finds no commensurate reassurance:

> Ousted from that warm bed
> We are a dream they dream.
> Their eyelids keep the shade.
> No harm can come to them.
> We cast our skins and slide
> Into another time.
> ("The Sleepers")

If the unnamed sleepers are themselves protected while they dream, "we" have become their text, and their protection offers no consolation for the fantasy we embody.

By reinscribing herself as daugher and mother, Plath has consistently hoped to discover not poetic defeat but an "original" authority. And if Plath's final poems attest to her belief that language has failed her, it is a belief belied by the poems themselves. Rather than accept psychic defeat, Plath pushes the bodily ego to its metaphoric limits. Faced with the imperative to speak from the position of woman, yet unable to resolve the conflicts arising from her biological, cultural, and literary identities, Plath centers her poetry in the body and its desire to escape from those identities upon which she previously had drawn.[31]

Sloughing off the bee poems' analogical ceremonies, "Fever 103°"and "Ariel" return us to the end of "Stings," where the speaker achieves a revenge of flight, an escape now predicated upon her recognition that to live in the world is, of necessity, to live in pain:

> I am too pure for you or anyone.
> Your body
> Hurts me as the world hurts God. . . .
> ("Fever 103°")

The desire for escape links pain to power, preserving Plath's omnipotence, for to be hurt "as the world hurts God" is to become the source of life through victimization, the center of creation by injury. Refusing to endure such pain, the speaker would become incandescent, "a lantern" that in its self-illumination could escape the images thrown upon it by all external sources. Moreover, this self-generated power is intimately linked to a sexual pleasure akin to the Whitmanian trope of masturbation as poetic activity.

> Does not my heat astound you. And my light.
> All by myself I am a huge camellia
> Glowing and coming and going, flush on flush.
>
> I think I am going up,
> I think I may rise—
> ("Fever 103°")

This transcendence through self-initiated sexual activity frees the subject from the injurious need for the other as it simultaneously subverts by recalling the traditional apparatus of Christian resurrection. Female reerection carries the speaker beyond all dependence in an autoerotic flight that secures power over words that might otherwise ensnare her in the nets of heterosexual love. By placing herself at the center of her own language-making and by asserting the potency of such autoeroticism, Plath momentarily resolves the poetic crisis that had for so long defied attempts at resolution. This flight upward, moreover, brings with it a purity that all naming by others takes away.

> . . . and I, love, I
>
> Am a pure acetylene
> Virgin
> Attended by roses,
>
> By kisses, by cherubim,
> By whatever these pink things mean
> Not you, nor him,
>
> Not him, nor him
> (My selves dissolving, old whore petticoats)—
> To Paradise.
>
> ("Fever 103°")

Unlike Dickinson, who writes most formidably of such transcendence, Plath recalls as she repudiates the presence of another being, for the voice burns through to a purification of the male-defined and -defiled. To achieve such purification through desire, the speaker must relinquish life, for hers is a poetics based upon the traditional forms of naming, whether in myth, Freudian psychology, or Romantic poetics.

If Plath reengenders the Romantic Sublime in order to speak with a voice of impassioned authority, the words that voice utters and the story it tells in these late poems announce that hers is an endgame of the Romantic Sublime for women poets. Unless a woman can reimagine her position vis-à-vis the Romantic Sublime, she will be forced either to redefine her sexuality or to evade it. To redefine identity, Plath must forget, a forgetting that threatens her authority over signification. The "old whore petticoats" of identity that fall away in "Fever 103°" are like the lost memories of Plath's amnesiac: "old happenings / Peel from his skin." Rather than accept the identity of victim, the amnesiac finds freedom in forgetfulness:

> O sister, mother, wife,
> Sweet Lethe is my life.
> I am never, never, never coming home!
>
> ("Amnesiac")

Here, the male patient is implicated in a stultifying net of associations. Domesticity smothers both him and his "little toy wife," as all recedes to the size of the "minute doctor," externality yielding before a fantasy of union with the "red headed sister he never dared to touch," a fantasy that breaks the incest taboo and with it the cultural law of the Father upon which familial and cultural institutions are based. As the flight of the male amnesiac marks a turn to fantasy (the breaking through to the freedom of fantasy accompanied by a total loss of memory), so in "Fever 103°" incendiary destruction accompanies transcendence. This desire to escape and the passion for transcendence converge in "Ariel," which enacts a release from the false garments of the self into a purification intimately related to self-destruction.

Like the poem it uncannily resembles, Dickinson's "Because I could not stop for Death," "Ariel" projects a voyage beyond death, past the identifications of premortuary history. In its violence, rapidity, and purposive action, "Ariel" differs from Dickinson's solemn, sedate recognition. Yet in their imaginary journeys beyond the ending, both Dickinson and Plath attempt to wrest from death the power of speech. Crucially, Plath not only describes her mad rush toward transcendence but also assumes mastery over it. Whereas Dickinson's persona only slowly "surmises" that the horses' heads are "toward Eternity," Plath is both horse and rider, embodying the power from which she had heretofore felt excluded: she commandeers her flight.

Through with the "berries" that "cast dark hooks," the oppressive nature of the immanent, oral, sucking, draining world, the "black sweet blood mouthfuls," Plath silences that world. Denuded of the material substance of life, she is reborn into a daring symbol of sexuality, into the pride of self-possession:

> White
> Godiva, I unpeel—
> Dead hands, dead stringencies.

The escape from the body brings with it an animal potency that for Plath signifies freedom:

> And now I
> Foam to wheat, a glitter of seas.
> The child's cry
>
> Melts in the wall.

To flee the child's cry, which, in its need, represents her final hold on life, the "I" hurls herself into unrestricted liberty:

> And I
> Am the arrow,
>
> The dew that flies
> Suicidal, at one with the drive
> Into the red
>
> Eye, the cauldron of morning
> (27 October 1962)

Simultaneously to be the arrow (purposive agent of freedom) and the dew (suicidal, for it will evaporate in the cauldron of morning), to assume both male and female identities, is surely to win through to freedom. Such an apocalyptic accomplishment constitutes both the courage and the tragedy of Plath's stunning poems: "All the gods know is destinations" ("Getting There"), a teleological imperative that assumes increasing authority in Plath's late work as she envisions a violent rush toward a purification of the bodily ego that would fulfill her consummate ambition.

The freedom of "Ariel" is not simply the freedom of flight but also the need for conflagration. The risks involved in the woman poet's desire for ascension are intensified both because of Plath's individual psychosexual conflicts and her recognition of the violative implications imposed upon the woman poet by the Romantic imagination, for Plath knows where, traditionally, female sexuality should reside: in the muse, in the object of desire, but not *as* the willing subject of desire itself. Yet such a disfiguring of body and word leaves Plath no alternative but a transgressive flight upward. The need to slough off the "old whore petticoats" of sexual identity coincides with a related need to break free of the traces of a language whose capacity for metaphorization has hooked, sucked, shrouded her as woman and as poet. Plath's symbiotic or, as Aurelia Plath called it, "osmotic" relationship with her mother informs the poet's interpretation of the reciprocal interplay between self and world as inherently aggressive and devouring. Stifled by these psychic formulations and her internalized notions of gender, Plath sought a poetics of transfiguration, a flight beyond language itself. Yet such transfiguration, with its erasure of the "profane" identities inscribed upon the body of language (and the reinscription of language by the body), necessitates a relinquishment of that codified body upon which representation depends.

Whether Plath's search to discover a sustaining poetics would have yielded an alternative course, we will never know. Yet the terms of this conflict carry implications beyond Plath's individual work, testifying to the austere anatomy lessons of the Romantic imagination. Having initially learned to await the annunication, the muse's descendental flight, Plath later actively strives to pursue poetic power. That she refuses to subordinate her sexual identity to the poet's quest is a sign of her courage. That the price she pays for preserving sexual identity is a divestiture of the figural language that empowers her poems is a stark commentary upon the burden difference creates for women poets of the American Sublime.

8

"OF WOMAN BORN"

Adrienne Rich and the Feminist Sublime

> Every age has its characteristic faults, its typical temptation to overemphasize some virtue at the expense of others, and the typical danger for poets in our age is, perhaps, the desire to be "original." This is natural, for who in his daydreams does not prefer to see himself as a leader rather than a follower, an explorer rather than a cultivator and a settler? Unfortunately, the possibility of realizing such a dream is limited, not only by talent but also by time, and even a superior gift cannot cancel historical priority; he who today climbs the Matterhorn, though he be the greatest climber who ever lived, must tread in Whymper's footsteps.
>
> Radical changes and significant novelty in artistic style can only occur when there has been a radical change in human sensibility to require them. The spectacular events of the present time must not blind us to the fact that we are living not at the beginning but in the middle of a historical epoch; they are not novel but repetitions on a vastly enlarged scale and at a violently accelerated tempo of events which took place long since.
>
> —W. H. Auden, "Foreword" to Adrienne Rich's A Change of World (1951)[1]

The "radical change in human sensibility" W. H. Auden finds essential to poetic originality is at once documented and created in the overarching shape of Adrienne Rich's poetic career. That career may best be summarized as a move away from painstaking imitation, through encoded representations of women's experience, to a radical poetics that seeks to reimagine the relationship among writing, eros, and sexual identity.[2] In its devotion to both Whitman and Dickinson (as well as to the American literary tradition more generally), Rich's work enacts the revisionary project of merging Whitmanian power with the legacy of Dickinson's alternative Sublime. The interplay between Rich's sources underlies the discussion that follows, an evaluation of Rich's attempt to construct a single-sex, feminist poetics and her subsequent repudiation of the exclusionary aspects of that poetics in favor of a more inclusive yet specifically female-identified vision.[3] I begin with *The Dream of a Common Language,* for it is in this volume that Rich most fully elaborates a gender-based poetics. And it is here as well that Rich describes the dream of finding a language with the capacity to release itself from its own history, the power to escape the lengthening shadows of the patriarchal poetic tradition. That such a vision carries with it a risk—the danger of silencing the poetic or linguistic imagination—is neither surprising nor new, for the woman poet's need to find her own language in order to assume the prerogatives of an originating voice has been the central challenge facing all ambitious nineteenth- and twentieth-century women poets. In the wake of the Romantics' self-conscious identification of the male poet as quester and poetry as the language of desire, women who wish to write repeatedly strive for ways to appropriate language, to claim it for female experience. If the title of Rich's volume acknowledges the visionary character of such an enterprise, it also names its audience, for what Rich hopes to discover is a language that, while freeing itself from the exclusionary dominance of patriarchy, establishes a new, antithetical commonality of readers, a language spoken by and for other women. Rich's title contains an allusion to Virginia Woolf's sense of commonality as Woolf described it in her introductory essay to *The Common Reader.* Here Woolf quotes a sentence from Dr. Johnson's "Life of Gray": ". . . I rejoice to concur with the common reader; for by the common sense of readers, uncorrupted by literary prejudices, after all the refinements of subtlety and the dogmatism of learning, must be finally decided all claim to poetical honours."[4] Rich makes clear that she shares with Woolf the desire to speak not to an exclusive, educated audience but to those who share the concerns, desires, and burdens that define them as being excluded from the tradition of patriarchy, the lineage of male writers that has dominated literature in the West. Rich aims, moreover, to reach beyond the "exceptional" women who have developed an awareness of their situation, and who have the means to articulate their burden, to reach those deprived of such opportunities. It is from her sense of audience and the politics that determines such a sense that the literary method of her poems develops. The desire to convert ordinariness into a new mythos leads Rich to explore the conversational aspects of a language close to speech, in which secrets are laid open and wishes, too long silent, find their voice.

How can woman, that perpetual "other" of male consciousness, his object of desire, create either the linguistic and/or social conditions that establish *her* not as the mediator of inspiration, the maculate whore-mother-muse of tradition, but as the predominant, shaping consciousness, inventor of relationships that inform art? Although Rich's major nineteenth-century predecessors, Elizabeth

Barrett Browning, Christina Rossetti, and Emily Dickinson, did find ways of breaking through the male dominance of language to discover new possibilities for the word, the difficulty of their search for imaginative priority does not, of course, fade with time. There can be no "final solution" for a woman who faces the cumulative force of a tradition that has its origins in the Homeric voice and echoes with renewed strength in our post-Miltonic assumptions about the nature of language and the patriarchal perceptions of image-making itself.[5] It is just this need to find a way of piercing the web of traditional discourse to open and extend her dialogue with the predominant culture that Rich explores. Her search for a shared mythology becomes a means of reclaiming a communal experience for women that takes them into history, on an archaeological dig for lost possibilities of metaphor. In an essay on Levertov, Rich, and Rukeyser, Rachel Blau DuPlessis remarks on this remythologizing process in Rich's "Diving into the Wreck":

> In this poem of journey and transformation Rich is tapping the energies and plots of myth, while re-envisioning the content. While there is a hero, a quest, and a buried treasure, the hero is a woman; the quest is a critique of old myths; the treasure is knowledge: the whole buried knowledge of the personal and cultural foundering of the relations between the sexes, and a self-knowledge that can be won only through the act of criticism.[6]

The opening poem in *The Dream of a Common Language* describes a similar revision of myth—again, the hero is a woman, and the treasure is not simply scientific knowledge but also knowledge of self, as the poet describes an attempt to reach into the earth for the sources of woman's distinctive power.[7] Rich first combs through the earth deposits of "our" (female) experience of history to discover the amber bottle with its bogus palliative that will not ease the pain "for living on this earth   in the winters of this climate." The second gesture of the poem is toward a text and model: the story of Marie Curie, a woman who seeks a "cure," denying that the "element she had purified" causes her fatal illness. Her refusal to confront the crippling force of her success and recognize the deadly implications of original discovery enables Curie to continue her work at the cost of her life. Denying the reality of the flesh, "the cracked and suppurating skin   of her finger-ends," she presses on to death:

> She died   a famous woman   denying
> her wounds
> denying
> her wounds   came   from the same source as her power

Here, in the poem's closing lines, Rich uses physical space and the absence of punctuation (an extension of Dickinson's use of dashes) to loosen the deliberate, syntactic connections between words and thus introduces ambiguities that disrupt normative forms. The separation between words determines through the movement of the reader's eye—the movement past the "wounds" where it had rested the first time—the emphasis on the activity of denial and its necessary violation. The second "denying" carries the reader past the initial negativity of a woman's denying self-destruction by extending the phrase "denying her wounds" into "denying her wounds came from the same source as her power." Denial is an essential precondition for the woman inventor's continuing to succeed; what she is denying, of course, is the inevitable sacrifice of self in work as well as the knowledge that her power and her wounds share a common source. Like Curie, this book's later poems inform us, the woman poet must recognize a similar repression of her knowledge that what she is doing involves a deliberate rejection of the borrowed power of the tradition, the necessity of incurring the self-inflicted wounds that mark the birth of an individuated poetic voice.

Why should the process of image-making, using language for one's own ends, be, in Rich's words, "mined with risks" for women?[8] And how are these pressures different from those confronting men? The poems respond directly to these issues and suggest that women are not only secondary in status but also latecomers to a patriarchal world of images. In a culture where words are formed and assigned their dominant associations by men, women, in order to speak at all, either must subvert their own speech by using the patriarchal tongue or seek for themselves experiences available only to women—what it means to be a daughter, the emotions of a lesbian relationship, the process of childbirth—experiences that would serve to free women poets through their choice of subject from the history of patriarchal associations. Thus Rich insists upon the authority of, as well as the necessity for, solely female experience.[9] Other women poets, of course (Sylvia Plath, Ann Sexton, and their contemporaries), have written of this need and described it. Each, in her own way, asserts that the power of language depends upon the originary capacity of the woman poet, her ability to create a linguistic context freed from the prescriptive tradition of male-dominated images. Rich's "Phantasia for Elvira Shatayev," for example, attempts to replace the received image of the male adventurer, the rugged masculinity of the climber, with the woman hero. In this poem, which speaks through the voice of the leader of a women's climbing team whose members died in a storm on Lenin Peak, Rich provides a narrative that supports the need to climb to a fresh place, to discover a ground where emotions stifled for years can be expressed. Describing an experience customarily associated with men and showing instead the physical courage of women demonstrates how female consciousness can transgress and repossess male territory. The newness of the possibility for free expression depends upon an isolation complete and uncompromised, a quest that demands the sacrifice of life itself to reach it. In the courageous spirit of Dickinson's "If your Nerve, deny you—Go above your Nerve—" the climbers adjust to a cold matched only by the blood's will to turn still colder. In a dream, Elvira Shatayev voices her intent—to speak not as an individual but with a language shared by this team of women climbers, a voice that achieves authority through the heroic and fatal struggle to the summit. But what these women learn transcends (thus calling into question) the power of language itself. Leaving behind the separation that exists between women on the earth below, the climbers discover that

> What we were to learn   was simply   what we had
> up here   as out of all words   that *yes*   gathered
> its forces   fused itself   and only just in time
> to meet a   *No* of no degrees
> the black hole   sucking the world in

Only through a rejection of tainted or "grounded" language, in this will to confront physical challenge, can the "yes" be fulfilled. Although the voice we hear is triumphant in its achieved independence, it is that of a dead woman. Yet even after death, Shatayev guards against her husband's powers of appropriation as he pursues the team to discover their fate. If in the past, his wife has trailed him through the Caucasus, she escapes this secondariness in death:

> Now I am further
> ahead than either of us dreamed   anyone would be

Her "self" merges with the land:

> I have become
> the white snow packed like asphalt by the wind

And death completes the commonality of the climbers:

> the women I love   lightly flung   against the mountain
> that blue sky
> our frozen eyes unribboned   through the storm
> we could have stitched that blueness   together   like a quilt

After her husband finds the bodies and tells his story, Shatayev insists that the women's experience does not end; their death engenders a physical metamorphosis into the world's being that continues the internal transformation of their climb. But this union of mind and spirit, this sharing of love, grows only as the women leave the world; in the diary, which must be "torn" from the dead climber's fingers (as if, even in death, she were still insisting that the words belonged to her alone), Shatayev had written:

> *What does love mean*
> *what does it mean   "to survive"*
> *A cable of blue fire ropes our bodies*
> *burning together in the snow   We will not live*
> *to settle for less   We have dreamed of this*
> *all of our lives*

The burning, ice-blue cable of connection holds the climbers, enforcing as it symbolizes the symbiotic relationship among the women and between life and death as well. These women who "will not live to settle for less" lose their lives in the attempt to reach new possibilities for living. Here Rich asserts the belief (echoed throughout these poems) that what women seek, this new ground, is a space where love and language find meanings that transgress the rules of society and supercede the tradition of a male-dominated discourse. Like Marie Curie in "Power," achievement depends upon the sacrifice of one's life. In the face of such a sacrifice, Rich keeps asking, can we achieve this requisite freedom and survive?

If the climate in which women live proves stultifying, if our language has become too tainted to trust, can we find a world more congenial to an imagination that seeks a reawakening of the powers of language and a field for its own intelligence? What determines the success or failure of this enterprise for Rich is whether she can stake out a territory freed from traditional identities and associations; she cannot forget the history of poetry because it is not hers. As outsider, Rich seeks a way to reappropriate language, to find a means of forcing language to free itself from its patriarchal origins; yet Rich embarks on this search not in innocence, but with the knowledge that such a pursuit will necessarily require her to banish, repress, or "consign to oblivion" the impossibility of establishing an alternative language capable of reaching beyond male experience into exclusive relationships between women. Although love between women becomes a way of discovering fresh ground, of defining a world that will and can only be described by women, the play of desire and the formal character of language cannot, of course, simply be destroyed. Nevertheless, asserting the priority of experience, Rich turns to address the woman who seeks to map a territory for such a language and faces the problem of conceiving a poetics based on transgression, a violation of societal expectation. The desire to make things whole, to love "for once with all [her] intelligence,"[10] becomes a move to cast out the relation of male self and female/male other, to reassert mother-daughter intimacy and thus validate the emotional self-sufficiency of women. Placing woman-woman relationships at the center of poetic attention may establish the experiential basis for a figurative discourse no longer dependent upon the traditional patterns of heterosexual romance.

Rich's poetics of transgression becomes a source of "truth" in her twenty-one love poems. In the center of the book she enacts the poetic theories she had asserted in the volume's beginning and the assertions she will return to at its close. Here Rich attempts to make a poetry that refuses to succumb to the lies she must utter when living within the confines of a heterosexist culture. These poems demonstrate the difficulties of fusing a poetics out of politics, for they raise a question fundamental to Rich's project: If women have been stifled by a society they reject, can a rejection of that society's mores in and of itself free the poet, and thus restore to her the power of an "original" language? On this subject, Rich remarks, "Heterosexuality as an institution has also drowned in silence the erotic feelings between women. I myself lived half a lifetime in the lie of that denial. That silence makes us all, to some degree, into liars."[11] To express, openly and without hesitation, her feelings as they develop in a lesbian relationship becomes a way of escaping the "silence and lies" that heretofore governed "women's love for women." Out of this assertion of truthfulness, Rich discovers, on her own terms, new possibilities for "truth": "When a woman tells the truth she is creating the possibility for truth around her."[12] The relation of a lesbian ontology to poetic praxis is not, however, so direct as Rich would have us believe. Merely to eliminate an overt stigma, to reject the veil of obfuscation, will not of itself produce effective poetry, no matter how liberating a gesture for the poet's psyche. What this lesbian relationship, as a ground of experience, does offer the woman poet is the possibility of escaping the anxieties of male-dominated poetic influence. Ideally, Rich can thus draw on both female and male precursors while maintaining the authority that comes from a description of life that taps the more generally recognized emotions associated with eros, while simultaneously centering the poetry in a relationship that excludes male consciousness—hence, the male poet.[13] Helpful as sexual truth-telling may be, however, it does not resolve the problem these poems so starkly articulate: the difficulty of reinventing names for experience, of placing the female self at the center of the mimetic process.

In her essay, "When We Dead Awaken: Writing as Re-Vision," Rich discusses the relationship between woman's survival in this world and man's authority as the one who names what we experience:

> And this drive to self-knowledge, for women, is more than a search for identity: it is part of our refusal of the self-destructiveness of male-dominated society. A radical critique of literature, feminist in its impulse, would take the work first of all as a clue to how we live, how we have been living, how we have been led to imagine ourselves, how our language has trapped as well as liberated us, how the very act of naming has been till now a male prerogative, and how we can begin to see and name—and therefore live—afresh.[14]

In *The Dream of a Common Language,* the politics of experience becomes a question of style, for the poems either assert in a strong rhetorical voice or enact in a more muted conversational manner the distinction between gender-based differences in language. As Rich herself states, "Poetry is, among other things, a criticism of language."[15] More specifically in "Twenty-One Love Poems," Rich proceeds to make a myth out of the dailiness of her experience, because, as she asserts, "No one has imagined us." The female poet can, as Adam in the Garden, name rather than rename the world around her. This transference allows the woman to be both subject and object of consciousness, the agent of desire and its aim. The poem sequence's language, with its attempts to bear witness to the individual, private quality of an intimate relationship, moves between tones of understatement and forthright assertion of the difficulty of sustaining such a poetry in the face of a tradition of silence, in the face of "centuries of books unwritten piled behind these shelves" (V). These poems seek to combine a self-consciousness associated with establishing an alternative poetic ground based on a lesbian relationship, a world without men, and an attempt to convert a specific intimacy into a paradigm that maps the possibilities of such a relationship for a radically alternative poetics. Rich confronts the inherent problem of combining these aims as she questions the mythopoetic enterprise itself—the conversion of private experience into an alternative program: "What kind of beast would turn its life into words? / What atonement is this all about?" (VII). But Rich also sees this attempt as a kind of evasion of the even more disruptive goal of centering the female self and making that self the origin for naming all that stands outside it:

> And how have I used rivers, how have I used wars
> to escape writing the worst thing of all—
> not the crimes of others, not even our own death,
> but the failure to want our freedom passionately enough
> so that blighted elms, sick rivers, massacres would seem
> mere emblems of that desecration of ourselves?
>
> (VII)

The question of renaming the world is crucial because Rich understands the necessity of escaping the boundaries of convention to make a new world "by women outside the law" (XIII). Moreover, these poems mirror the conviction that only by choosing one's own life freely and converting one's choice into language can a woman poet begin to redefine poetry by appropriating the power of naming. The love poems close with Rich's assertion of the autonomy she seeks and the corollary mythos she would create:

> I choose to be a figure in that light,
> half-blotted by darkness, something moving
> across that space, the color of stone
> greeting the moon, yet more than stone:
> a woman. I choose to walk here. And to draw this circle.
>
> (XXI)

Echoing Aurora Leigh's decision, "I choose to walk at all risks," Rich shares her choice; the tradition reaffirmed continues.[16]

Yet such exclusionary tactics as Rich employs in the twenty-one love poems do not necessarily release the poet from her own linguistic anxieties; the word can never free itself of its accrued meanings as emotion here strives to do. If the woman poet discards traditional images, where will she discover her First Idea? Power inheres in the word; it cannot rid itself of centuries of connotation. Knowing this, Rich turns away from the outspoken word, the power of voice, to advocate a language that borders on silence. Thus the gesture of isolation, the exclusionary act itself, may, Rich speculates, provide an untainted source of female power. Consequently, the poems in this volume in various ways address the need to minimize language, to divest the word of its accretions of power by replacing it with actions identified as preserving and sustaining a woman's

integrity. Rich most powerfully resolves the difficulties of her apparently con-
tradictory poetic aspirations in "Paula Becker to Clara Westhoff" and "A Woman
Dead in Her Forties," for both poems achieve the balance between intimacy and
assertion toward which Rich strives throughout this volume. In both poems, the
speaker's words are shadowed by death; in the earlier poem, Becker writes to
Westhoff, and her "letter" acquires for us a sorrowful resonance as her mingled
hopes for her work combine with her sense of bewildered regret as she
unwittingly prophecies her death in childbirth. As in the twenty-one love poems,
we are readers who overhear—only now the imaginative reconstruction of the
letter Becker writes creates a further distance. Through this double distancing
and tone of intimacy, Rich is able simultaneously to use her words in a
conversational, muted way and to give her language dramatic force, for the
letter itself is not a private document, but becomes through our reading a public
performance. This same sense of violated yet shared intimacy controls "A
Woman Dead in Her Forties," only here the survivor speaks of all she could
never say while her friend was still alive. Again death endows her words with
renewed pathos, and the difficulty of speech, the price for honoring the taboo of
silence, is measured by the irrevocable silence of death itself. Once more, we
overhear words meant for another, and this act of overhearing enables the
poem to mediate successfully between a conversational language (the intimate
voice) and the power to transform this language into performance, into the
language of poetry.

Yet such poems, although they do balance, can only provisionally resolve the
underlying linguistic questions to which Rich returns throughout her work. If the
poet cannot even trust the words she writes, her voice must be relegated to
silence, but if silence will not suffice, the problem remains: how to control
distrust of the very language the woman poet must invoke. The claims to be
made for silence, its capacity for interrupting the repetition-compulsion of
naming, the danger either of echoing or antithetically mimicking the patriarchal
voice, achieve an eloquent expression of their own:

> Silence can be a plan
> rigorously executed
>
> the blueprint to a life
>
> It is a presence
> it has a history   a form
>
> Do not confuse it
> with any kind of absence[17]

But the power of silence casts its own shadow, for the refusal to speak may not
be a simple desire to escape the strictures of conventional discourse but may
signify, in the absence of any interpretative gesture, the negative act of willful
withholding. The tension between these possibilities cannot be resolved within
silence but must seek its resolution in the margins of discourse; by margins, I

mean the outermost edges where Rich can best mediate between the desire for speech and her need to respect the communicative force of silence. The margins of discourse become for Rich the thoughts that precede or follow conversations, momentary impressions, the internalized voice to which she returns throughout the volume.

In "Cartographies of Silence," a mapping of the possibilities and dangers of the word, the poet expresses her longing for a language that would itself be a "pure" imaging forth; she desires an impossible linguistic form that would transcend discourse through its own originating presence:

> The Silence that strips bare:
> In Dreyer's *Passion of Joan*
>
> Falconetti's face, hair shorn, a great geography
> mutely surveyed by the camera
>
> If there were a poetry where this could happen
> not as blank spaces or as words
>
> stretched like a skin over meanings
> but as silence falls at the end
>
> of a night through which two people
> have talked till dawn[18]

In this linguistic utopia, poetry would win freedom from voicing either by the signifying power of physical presence (the camera's moving in silently to survey Falconetti's face) or by the mutual plenum of meaning created by a night of intimate conversation. In both instances, a temporary resolution is achieved. The ultimate irresolution of the character of silence, however, does not allow Rich to evade the more precise demands of speech. In her earlier poems—one thinks particularly of "Shooting Script"—Rich attempted to apply cinematic techniques (splicing, close-ups, fade-outs) to writing, but in her most recent work, she insists upon the distinctions between the two media.[19] Despite her occasional envy of "the pure annunciations to the eye," what Rich keeps choosing "are these words, these whispers, conversations / from which time after time the truth breaks moist and green." These words, at the close of "Cartographies of Silence," complete the equation between the act of renaming the world and the power of speech. Like those celebrants of the Eleusinian rites, the woman poet celebrates her choice: "these words, these whispers, con-servations" that will bring, as did the goddess worshipped by the hierophants, a return of spring to the world.[20] The woman poet through her very presence becomes, as in the myth of Demeter and Kore, the regenerative life force. Although Rich is drawn to silence, her poems refuse to relinquish the life-giving possibilities of an eloquence based upon the vocative powers of the word, the truth-telling capacities of the woman poet who defies convention to redefine the very nature of performative language.

The central paradox of this volume resides in the poems' assertion of this move toward a new mode of writing, toward a gentle poetics antithetical to the aggressions of the patriarchal tradition of Western poetry, while at the same time claiming the bold, heroic nature of this enterprise. Consequently, Rich shifts from the intimate voice of inner conversation to the rhetorical formulations of the need for an alternative form of power. Although the reader may initially be puzzled by this disjunction as she moves from poem to poem, the two modes are interdependent, for the apparently heterogeneous voices cohere around a common purpose—to strive toward overcoming the delimiting properties of language itself. The "radical change in sensibility" Rich at once explores and articulates depends in part upon the appropriation of Whitmanian expansiveness for women; she is here to experience, as *only a woman can,* "the rainbow laboring to extend herself / where neither men nor cattle understand."[21] She envisions woman as explorer—a miner whose headlamp, as we by now might expect, casts a ray: "a weight like death." Despite the lethal dangers revealed by the woman poet's light, she alone can enter sacred ground. We hear Rich invoking the Whitman of "The Sleepers," with all his confidence in the prepotent self, as she describes a woman's solitary voyage:

> The cage drops into the dark,
> the routine of life goes on:
>
> a woman turns a doorknob, but so slowly
> so quietly, that no one wakes
>
> and it is she alone who gazes
> into the dark of bedrooms, ascertains
>
> how they sleep, who needs her touch
> what window blows the ice of February
>
> into the room and who must be protected:
> It is only she who sees; who was trained to see

She wanders all night in her vision, and her freedom draws upon the power Whitman had claimed for himself. Note how close Whitman comes to this assertion of universal consciousness as he appropriates the metaphor of birth to inform his return to the world of night, dreams, and death:

> I will duly pass the day O my mother and duly return to you;
> Not you will yield forth the dawn again more surely
>   than you will yield forth me again,
> Not the womb yields the babe in its time more surely than
>   I shall be yielded from you in my time.[22]

This is the voice of the divinating American poet—Emerson, the father; Whitman, the son—members of the descendental tradition of a powerful patriarchy that claims for itself the possibility of an awful knowledge, a universal transparency that enables men to see and know the dreams of their mothers and daughters. Women confront such a company, each of whom asserts that he is "the man who would dare to know us." In response, Rich creates experiences that exclude men; she envisions a world of women, a kind of love in which men play no part.

From this renewed ground of being, what kind of poetry? In lieu of aggressive consciousness, the powerful men of imagination, what possibility? Or to ask these questions in another way, can language survive if we divest it of its appropriative power over the world of things? This is the heart of the problem, and like other originating tensions, its power lies in its capacity to resist solutions. In the final passages of "Natural Resources," the poem that earlier made Whitmanian claims for the female imagination, Rich turns to gentleness and a conserving stoicism as ways of combating aggression without diminishing the capacity for verbalization. "These scraps, turned into patchwork, . . . a universe of humble things"—what options do these offer?[23] Women must, Rich asserts, strive against the assaults of both life and language; she must seek to save; but the burden is in the labor, the bringing forth. Returning to the rainbow that *labors* to extend itself, the natural work only a woman can understand, Rich closes this poem with her counterclaim against the male tradition:

> The women who first knew themselves
> miners, are dead. The rainbow flies
>
> like a flying buttress from the walls
> of cloud, the silver-and-green vein
>
> awaits the battering of the pick
> the dark lode weeps for light
>
> My heart is moved by all I cannot save:
> so much has been destroyed
>
> I have to cast my lot with those
> who age after age, perversely,
>
> with no extraordinary power,
> reconstitute the world.

But can such stoic gentleness, or biological capacity, create an individuating language? Or is the very act of finding words and sending them out of oneself, an activity that must imply violation, a gesture of trespass against the world? Here Rich faces her most severe challenge: at once to speak of the place without violating its presence and to find a common language that repudiates the mode of aggression in favor of a discourse of conservancy:

> if I could know
> in what language to address
> the spirits that claim a place
> beneath these low and simple ceilings,
> tenants that neither speak nor stir
> Yet dwell in mute insistence
> till I can feel utterly ghosted in this house.

The poet searches for a spider thread that will lead her back to the origins of discovery, the answers that will inform her historical moment.[24] Seeking a "directive" that will lead her home, Rich turns to housewifely duties—"brushing the thread of the spider aside," a thread she earlier hoped might lead her to the source of lucid understanding, a thread that now she must sever rather than spin in order, paradoxically, to reform the thread of poetic continuity. Merely to preserve appearances is not to save them.

Yet if the gentle occupations of the housewife of language will not suffice, what alternatives remain for the woman poet? Rich explicitly rejects the American Romantics' belief in the poem as performative act:

> And we're not performers, like Liszt, competing
> against the world for speed and brilliance
> (the 79-year-old pianist said, when I asked her
> *What makes a virtuoso?—Competitiveness.*)
> The longer I live the more I mistrust
> theatricality, the false glamour cast
> by performance, the more I know its poverty beside
> the truths we are salvaging from
> the splitting-open of our lives.[25]

To deny a language of competition, to reject performance—"cut the wires, / find ourselves in free-fall"—is to incur a risk akin to that of living in a world where conventional self-other relations are redefined, where the solace of precedent ceases to exist, where the tradition casts the word into a void:

> No one who survives to speak
> new language, has avoided this:
> the cutting-away of an old force that held her
> rooted to an old ground[26]

What that new poetry will depend upon are the origins of the poet's vision, and in the final lines of this volume's final poem, "Transcendental Etude," Rich shows us her vision through an extended simile:

> Vision begins to happen in such a life
> as if a woman quietly walked away
> from the argument and jargon in a room
> and sitting down in the kitchen, began turning in her lap
> bits of yarn, calico and velvet scraps,
> laying them out absently on the scrubbed boards
> in the lamplight, with small rainbow-colored shells
> sent in cotton-wool from somewhere far away,
> and skeins of milkweed from the nearest meadow—
> original domestic silk, the finest findings—[27]

This would be a poetry of what is close, precious through personal association, and drawn from the domestic landscape.[28] Such a poetry would pull "the tenets of a life together / with no mere will to mastery, / only care for the many-lived unending / forms in which she finds herself." The woman, in a return to a kind of "negative capability" that results in imagistic poetry, would find herself

> becoming now the sherd of broken glass
> slicing light in a corner, dangerous
> to flesh, now the plentiful, soft leaf
> that wrapped round the throbbing finger, soothes the wound;
> and now the stone foundation, rockshelf further
> forming underneath everything that grows.[29]

It is she who protects by becoming, who re-creates by combining into the form of art the foundations of life, a life not of argument or jargon (a life of intellectual displacement), but a life so close to its sources, so open to experience, that it provides the foundations for a new home and a new world. The woman becomes this foundation as she creates her language out of what she knows, the acceptance of the common, the life-sustaining forces that allow her to grow and to write.

II

> It is important to me to know that, through most of her life, Bishop was critically and consciously trying to explore marginality, power and powerlessness, often in poetry of great beauty and sensuous power. That not all these poems are fully realized or satisfying simply means that the living who care that art should embody these questions have still more work to do.
> —Adrienne Rich, "The Eye of the Outsider: The Poetry of Elizabeth Bishop"

To examine Rich's comments on Elizabeth Bishop is not only to learn what Rich values in her formidable predecessor but also to discover Rich's aspirations for her own work. If *The Dream of a Common Language* offers an alternative poetics based upon gender, Rich's most recent poems return with "still more work to do," testing and expanding the possibilities of a gender-based poetics as they reach deep into the pain of the body and far into the historical and social events that shape contemporary life. The audacity of Rich's 1986 book commences with its title, for in naming this collection *Your Native Land, Your Life,* Rich asserts an authority over the reader's experience as she invents a patriotism that locates its origins in Whitman's audacious claims for the poet as not merely representative, but also himself the embodiment of America in all its diversity and difference. Despite this wildly ambitious, thoroughly native assertion, however, Rich's more recent work preserves her earlier conversational, explicitly "nonperformative" diction; only now Rich is willing to confront the long-suppressed memories of husband and father, the men who also shaped her life. In this resurgence of openness, Rich returns to heterosexual as well as homoerotic experience, delving into her fund of recollection to address a "you" neither exclusively female-identified nor overtly adversarial. The dream of a common language has been extended to include the reimagining of a past that recognizes rather than rejects the sources of personal as well as cultural history; Rich incorporates the most threatening aspects of her past without subordinating her feminist sense of difference. What Rich asks of us is that we reexamine the relationship between ethics and poetics, between the conduct of our lives and the forms of its expression. That the relationship between the conduct of life and the praxis of art has not gone unexamined by American poets is a fact clarified by our poetic history. Yet with its incantatory power and its huge Whitmanian claims, *Your Native Land, Your Life* pursues this awareness from a position of marginalization that nevertheless asserts its authority to representation. Moreover, Rich's gender-inflected subjectivity is balanced by her deployment of the word as cultural sign and as expression of a distinctly decentered imagination. Thus, Rich works toward a feminist discourse that is at once inclusive and humane, that in exploring the rhetorical possibilities of its own gender-inflected identity registers the presence of others while acknowledging the figural powers of the natural world: the enunciation of a woman-centered Counter-Sublime.

Focusing on the experiential aspects of women's lives, these poems, while overtly asserting no special claim to rhetorical power, nevertheless betray mastery of a distinctive style of reading as well as writing. Surely, in the creation of the sustained illusion of conversation and the never obtrusive yet deftly figurative use of the natural, Rich displays the achievement of her craft. Technical skill does its work through pacing, line breaks, and subtle, often elusive rhymes. Interestingly, for one who explicitly disavows Whitman's overt will to power, Rich's language, with its imperative force and didactic assurance, may at times resemble his own. In "You who think I find words for everything" ("Contradictions: Tracking Poems," 29, p. 111) Rich opens with the readerly "you's" suppositions concerning the speaker and responds by challenging herself to break free from the words she herself writes. In a Whitmanian gesture that echoes the assertion, " he most honors my style who learns under it to destroy the teacher" ("Song of Myself," section 47, l.1236), Rich advocates a commensurate self-reliance that depends for its authority not on the body's individuating strength, but upon its shared, inherent vulnerability. The reality of pain becomes not an isolating reality but a force for relation beyond the suffering self.[30] Rich accomplishes what Whitman as nurse and wound-dresser had achieved before her—a deeply empathic sense of the other arising from that apparently least communicative of sources, the body in pain. What serves to isolate each of us, the inherently incommunicable experience of pain, Rich renders with a specificity that not only strives to articulate individuated suffering but also makes of that pain a relational phenomenon. The danger (one that Rich herself recognizes) is the possibility that personal and social suffering may become confused. Always alert to this danger, Rich writes of bodily pain as a way of working against the self's desire to close itself off, its yearning for definitive boundaries, for "clear edges." Instead, pain may offer a way of merging but not blurring identities, of restoring the connection between individual and social experience. As a result, the reality of pain becomes not an isolating condition but a force for feeling beyond the self.

> You who think I find words for everything
> this is enough for now
> cut it short   cut loose from my words
>
> You for whom I write this
> in the night hours when the wrecked cartilage
> sifts round the mystical jointure of the bones
> when the insect of detritus crawls
> from shoulder to elbow to wristbone
> remember: the body's pain and the pain on the streets
> are not the same   but you can learn
> from the edges that blur   O you who love clear edges
> more than anything   watch the edges that blur
>   ("Contradictions: Tracking Poems," 29, p. 111)

Here Rich addresses someone with a distinct aesthetic preference for clarity, yet the poem also speaks to the more generalized human need for distinctions, delimitations, and boundaries. Indeed, the repetition of the "you" in the poem's opening lines suggests the distinction between the immediate addressee and a more collective audience. Against this desire, Rich assumes the burden of connections as she strives to retrieve past experience:

> how can I show you what I'm barely
> coming into possession of, invisible luggage
> of more than fifty years, looking at first
> glance like everyone else's, turning up
> at the airport carousel
> and waiting for it, knowing what nobody
> would steal must eventually come round—
> feeling obsessed, peculiar, longing?
>   ("Contradictions: Tracking Poems," 15, p. 97)

This luggage—common, not distinguished—is nevertheless valuable because unique. The insouciance of the carousel watcher, like the Whitmanian insouciance in "Crossing Brooklyn Ferry," defends as it accepts its own anxious history. The anxiety of the carousel watcher is, moreover, an adult anxiety that has little to do with childhood pleasures. The assurance that nobody "would steal" the luggage guarantees that it "must eventually come round": absence of overt value ensures its being found. The quality of the unexceptional, the value assigned to the ordinary, identifies this luggage and endows it with meaning. But the apparent tedium of airport rituals elsewhere yields to Rich's focus upon the representational possibilities of individual suffering.

In another "Tracking Poem," Rich explores the tension between the pain of individual suffering and the reclamation of communal life wherein pain is made to serve a social vision. Discharged from the hospital after what has euphemistically come to be called "elective surgery" (a phrase more reminiscent of a Calvinist than a contemporary notion of the body), the poem connects post operative suffering with the "pain on the streets." Here physical suffering becomes a way of knowing, an empowering experience that does not, as it so often seems to do, isolate self from world, but permits the individual to bridge the inviolable boundaries of otherness. If this poem opens with the characterization of the self as other, objectified as the "woman" being watched, by its close that division has been dissolved into the unitary subject speaking for and out of her own consciousness of pain.

> I came out of the hospital like a woman
> who'd watched a massacre
> not knowing how to tell
> my adhesions   the lingering infections
> from the pain on the streets
> In my room on Yom Kippur they took me off morphine
> I saw shadows on the wall   the dying and the dead
> They said Christian Phalangists did it
> Then Kol Nidre on the radio   and my own
> unhoused spirit   trying to find a home
> Was it then or another day
> in what order did it happen
> I thought   *They call this elective surgery*
> *but we all have died of this.*
>
> ("Tracking Poem":11)

Introspection does not so much delineate the imagination's refashioning of life as record the realities of what it can neither control nor evade, thus converting victimization into a potentially communal vision. Hallucinations on the wall (recalling, perhaps, "H. D."'s Corfu visions) do not symbolize an individuating prophecy so much as a means whereby the poet can experience and speak for others' political and social suffering. Here and elsewhere, Rich uses the data of physical sensation to imagine and inhabit other lives. This desire to incorporate otherness, to extend the self through the imagination's empathic powers, corresponds to a similar process within the self as the dialogic movement of self and other becomes internalized when Rich attempts to heal her own crippling divisions. If Dickinson boldly asserts, "I like a look of Agony, / Because I know it's true—," Rich views her pain as providing an inclusive vision that does not so much test the authenticity of external experience as deploy the personal as a universalizing agent. But the situation is more complicated, for pain may (as in this poem) cause "adhesion," a dangerous rather than beneficial blurring of boundaries that creates confusion between the subjective self and social reality. The aftereffects of the morphine induce the sensation of feeling "unhoused," opening a continuum of memory though which private experience connects with various kinds of suffering that span both time and space.

The question for the empathic imagination is how to sustain compassion for experience beyond one's own without relinquishing the self's boundaries or an awareness of the *difference* between physical pain and political oppression. Rich knows that resemblance does not equal identity, for she confronts the risks involved in any simple equation of private suffering and social injustice. Although Rich's commitment to issues of class, race, and gender is not a new phenomenon, what she now explicitly engages is the univocal position of the exile. Recognizing the authority that exists in the position of marginalization, she draws upon this power to speak for and to other victims of oppression. Rich investigates and reimagines (as she had in her earlier work) historical women and delineates the relationship between their lives and her own in poems of praise and sympathy. Yet in terms of Rich's own poetic evolution, the most revealing poems in "Sources" may be those that explore her relationships with her father and her dead husband. In choosing now to converse with them through her poetry, Rich clarifies and extends her quest for a woman's poetic authority. In *The Dream of a Common Language,* Rich described a newly imagined commonality defined by gender and based upon a rejection of men as both readers and lovers. The poems in "Sources" do not so much relinquish as extend that search for a distinctive, personally valid aesthetic and moral vision. In *Your Native Land, Your Life,* however, Rich explores the possibilities of an individuating poetics while at the same time revealing an openness toward prior experience. This revisionary work of introspection yields a freedom from the need for others to serve as sources of rejection. Rich lets go of a poetics based upon selectivity or the creation of difference as the source of victimization to fashion a "new" language that acknowledges difference as a necessary and enabling fact that affords generous authority.

"Sources" investigates the question of strength, both moral and poetic, and how Rich might discover such strength within her experience. It might, therefore, be read as the "career of the woman poet" in its careful delineation of the eventfulness of a woman's life and its articulation of how these events, both literary and personal, inform a mature, aesthetic vision that supercedes Rich's former, exclusionary stance. What emerges from Rich's reclamation of her Jewish and heterosexual origins is a stronger and more deeply empowered poetics based not on defense but upon what Emerson, in an evocative phrase, described as the "flames and generosities of the heart" (Whicher, "Circles," p. 178).

III

Writing from the conditions of her life, Rich explores the origins of this strength, discovering once again that her power depends upon firsthand experience. Although this self-reliance does not negate the importance of others, it nevertheless insists upon the edge between self and other necessary for any truly communal vision. Implicit in Rich's mapping the career of a woman is an inherent rejection of the cultural myths of heterosexual romance predicated upon the notion that completion of self depends upon a desired other, that each of us is perceived as fragmented, a system in which the male/female needs the other for a transcendent union. Like Whitman, Rich grounds the work of her empathic imagination in a homoeroticism that confirms the power of bodily sensation. Whitman's homoeroticism functions analogously to Rich's lesbianism, for they both share a sensibility alive to sensation and an imaginative endurance that enables them to endow pain with meaning. Here, in cadences that echo Whitman's characteristic tones of willful assurance, Rich writes of pain and advancing age, the *écriture feminine* of "real life."

> I refuse to become a seeker for cures.
> Everything that has ever
> helped me has come through what already
> lay stored in me.   Old things, diffuse, unnamed, lie strong
> across my heart.
>   This is from where
> my strength comes, even when I miss my strength
> even when it turns on me
> like a violent master.
>
> ("Sources," II, p. 4)

The origins of that strength and its familial, political, and aesthetic sources continue to govern Rich's work. Again, Rich echoes Whitman asking his usual questions of origin and affiliation, and like Whitman, Rich insists upon the wanderings of her own imagination as she relinquishes the certainty of solitude for the reader's trust.

> *With whom do you believe your lot is cast?*
> *From where does your strength come?*
>
> I think somehow, somewhere
> every poem of mine must repeat those questions
>
> which are not the same.   There is a *whom*, a *where*
> that is not chosen   that is given   and sometimes falsely given
>
> in the beginning we grasp whatever we can
> to survive
>
> ("Sources," IV, p. 6)

The poems that follow hold open to inquiry the conceptions that have frequently informed Rich's past; the genetic, social, and historical presuppositions that resist the capacities of reason. They include the myth of inhabiting a "special destiny" (V, p. 7), the conviction that she was one of a "chosen people," and a belief in the value of performance as a way to combat alienation. Rather than viewing these myths with anger or resentment, Rich acknowledges their capacity for personal injury as she faces their origins in human frailty and the instinct for survival; Rich has learned to forgive. Of her father, she observes,

> I saw my father building
> his rootless ideology
>
> his private castle in air
>
> in that most dangerous place, the family home
> we were the chosen people
>
> In the beginning we grasp whatever we can
> ("Sources," VI, p. 8)

In the prose poem that follows (VII), Rich recounts her persistent struggle with her father but with a compassion that frees her from that conflict and allows her to view it with the maturity of one who herself has come to terms with suffering. It is this enabling capacity that Rich identifies with gender: "It is only now, under a powerful, womanly lens, that I can decipher your suffering and deny no part of my own" (VII, p. 9).

Rich identifies what must be lived through before she can achieve this freedom, the process that intervenes between her more recent poems and her earlier, more explicitly polemical phase:

> After your death I met you again as the face of patriarchy, could name at last precisely the principle you embodied, there was an ideology at last which let me dispose of you, identify the suffering you caused, hate you righteously as part of a system, the kingdom of the fathers. I saw the power and arrogance of the male as your true watermark; I did not see beneath it the suffering of the Jew, the alien stamp you bore, because you had deliberately arranged that it should be invisible to me. . . .
> ("Sources," VII, p. 9)

What now renders that suffering visible and so frees her from its tyranny is the "womanly lens" that clarifies experiences of marginalization and the pain of misunderstanding. Geography and home mark a search for beginnings, the scenes of initial compassion. Note Rich's description of the idea of "destiny," with its accompanying dangers:

> It's an oldfashioned, an outrageous thing
> to believe one has a "destiny"
>
> —a thought often peculiar to those
> who possess privilege—
>
> but there is something else: the faith
> of those despised and endangered
>
> that they are not merely the sum
> of damages done to them:
>
> have kept beyond violence the knowledge
> arranged in patterns like kente-cloth

unexpected as in batik
recurrent as bitter herbs and unleavened bread

of being a connective link
in a long, continuous way

of ordering hunger, weather, death, desire
and the nearness of chaos.
                    ("Sources," XV, p. 17)

The ritualistic Seder plate, the bitter herbs, and unleavened bread—the "fabulous" rituals of remembrance that celebrate the continuity of sympathy over against the individual and cultural traumas of dislocation and suffering—gesture toward the ordering power of language itself, the patterns of linguistic meaning that ensure personal as well as cultural survival. Even those links we seek to deny remain present within us. What one has excluded or ignored may survive and participate in the colloquies of the forgiving imagination. Rich warily approaches the subject of her dead husband by "talking" about him with her father. By not immediately identifying the mutual topic of conversation, Rich achieves an objectivity made possible only by triangulation: "But there is also the other Jew. The one you most feared, the one from the *shtetl*, from Brooklyn, from the wrong part of history, the wrong accent, the wrong class. The one I left you for. . . ." ("Sources," XVII, p. 19). Rich constructs the story of these two men in terms of the daughter's betrayal, recognizing, retrospectively, the underlying similarities between the two men, yet refusing to dismiss these similarities as a mere consequence of category. Instead, she imagines their resemblances as founded upon their shared cultural and personal alienation. Within this conversational context, Rich describes her husband, allowing us to "overhear" words addressed to her father:

> . . . The one both like and unlike you, who explained you to me for years, who could not explain himself.   The one who said, as if he had memorized the formula, *There's nothing left now but the food and the humor.*   The one who, like you, ended isolate, who had tried to move in the floating world of the assimilated who know and deny they will always be aliens.   Who drove to Vermont in a rented car at dawn and shot himself.   For so many years I had thought you and he were in opposition. I needed your unlikeness then; now it's your likeness that stares me in the face.   There is something more than food, humor, a turn of phrase, a gesture of the hands: there is something more.
>
> ("Sources," XVII, p. 19)

Surely, in the phrase, "now it's your likeness that stares me in the face," one notes not only the resemblance between the two men, but also between daughter and father. From this recognition of the link between father and husband comes Rich's refusal to acquiesce to the bankruptcy of her father's exclusivity or to the despair of her husband's suicide.

Breaking through the silence of decades, Rich later addresses her husband in the voice of premonitory urgency that one associates with the completion of a psychic task. In its colloquial accuracy, this passage assumes the power of portraiture, and it is all the more moving for its rejection of either idealization or abstraction. Rich's verbal modesty here proliferates into a fecundity that reawakens both long-forgotten pleasure and the recognition of that pleasure's final insufficiency. Aware of the danger of violation, the risk of exploiting another's death, Rich writes: "But, you, I've had a sense of protecting your existence, not using it merely as a theme for poetry or tragic musings; letting you dwell in the minds of those who have reason to miss you, in your way, or their way, not mine. The living, writers especially, are terrible projectionists. I hate the way they use the dead" ("Sources," XXII, p. 25). Having confronted these dangers, Rich no longer can evade the formerly unmentionable subject, for she recognizes the obligation to speak the truth about her "sources," converting the danger of exploitation into a greater imaginative reciprocity. Once again, Rich admits her husband into her life by invoking a tactile and aural immediacy that implies what is never fully articulated—the extent to which she herself participated in his life. Returning to the insufficiency of her husband's strategies for survival, Rich addresses his suffering: "You knew there was more to life than food and humor. Even as you said that in 1953 I knew it was a formula you had found, to stand between you and pain" ("Sources," XXII, p. 25).

To resist that pain, Rich argues for a confrontive empathy: "That's why I want to speak to you now. To say: no person, trying to take responsibility for her or his identity, should have to be so alone. There must be those among whom we can sit down and weep, and still be counted as warriors. (I make up this strange, angry packet for you, threaded with love)" ("Sources," XXII, p. 25). No longer banished from her writing, her husband has been transformed into a muse of loss, an occasion for verbal expression to perform salutary explorations into new modes of life.

In taking up the challenge of delineating an alternative existence, Rich strives to construct a world predicated upon a community that offers support beyond purely private forms of solace. Thus, Rich converts her husband's loss into an occasion for envisioning a more generous view of self and others: "I think you thought there was no such place for you, and perhaps there was none then, and perhaps there is none now; but we will have to make it, we who want an end to suffering, who want to change the laws of history, if we are not to *give ourselves away*" ("Sources," XXII, p. 25). This "we" blends the voice of Rich, her husband, and ourselves in an appeal so intimate that it assumes the quality of an affectionate polemics.

Moving from this most empathic of ambitions, Rich gestures beyond the self into geography with a Whitmanian expansiveness complicated by her awareness of her own alienation from dominant national values. Dislocation haunts her desire for identification with the land, a dislocation she seeks to transform into acceptance. Confronting her desire to find consolation in natural facts, Rich realizes the impossibility of finding solace in reification: "I have wished I could rest among the beautiful and common weeds I cán name, both here and in

other tracts of the globe. But there is no finite knowing, no such rest"
("Sources," XXIII, p. 27). For Rich, "an end to suffering" does not mean "an-
esthesia." Instead, what she wills to choose is a knowledge of the world that
includes awareness of estrangement, and the pain of the survivor—a suffering
born of loss. Rich envisions herself as a survivor who can empower her life
through the deliberateness of choice: "I mean knowing the world, and my place
in it, not in order to stare with bitterness or detachment, but as a powerful and
womanly series of choices: and here I write the words, in their fullness:
powerful;   womanly" ("Sources," XXIII, p. 27).

If here the polemical and aesthetic coincide in their assertive refusal to flinch
before the obdurate conditions of life, elsewhere in Rich's work power resides in
the more modulated cadences of speech. In its insistence upon the fun-
damental importance of individual history, the significance of an historically
engaged imagination, and poetry's capacity to establish a continuum between
the self and the world, Rich's work most closely resembles Robert Lowell's.
What distinguishes Rich from Lowell, however, is her fusion of introspection
with a radically alternative understanding of the politics of experience based
upon the distinctive events of a woman's life. Rich, furthermore, revises that
experience to create a gender-inflected interpretation of history, one that de-
lineates a response to experience centered in female identity. This constitutive
female, poetic selfhood turns away from the exceptional, from insisting upon
differences among women to stressing the commonality of their lives. Rich's
poetic voice is most responsive to her intellectual project when it fuses intimacy
with passion, the polemical with the personal. Surely the sustained illusion of
ongoing colloquy, the reader's listening in on or overhearing a conversation,
creates the *illusion* of intimacy between the poem and its readers that marks
these poems' particular strength.

In a conversation between the poet and a historical, reimagined woman, Rich
reveals the power such an imaginative colloquy may assume:

> I try to conjure the kind of joy
> you tracked through the wildwoods where the tribes
> had set up their poles   what brought you
> how by boat, water, wind, you found
> yourself facing the one great art
> of your native land, your life
>
> ("Emily Carr," p. 64)

Yet this reimagining of the nineteenth-century American artist Emily Carr is not
without its own risk, for what marks this as well as other poems in *Your Native
Land, Your Life* is the explicit acknowledgment of the difficulty of trying to write
such poems, of trying to change, of trying to imagine. If Rich strives toward an
integrity of experience, that integrity is based upon achieving a balance between
voice and sensibility, a refusal to lose one's way in one's own subjectivity, a
rejection of the solipsistic temptations of the American Sublime. Rich's poetry,
therefore, works toward an integration between self and world that keeps

demanding the presence of others who literally may be absent but whose imaginative presence must not be suppressed. This transpersonal selfhood, so reminiscent of Whitman's ideal, quests for a relationship between the poet and the other, most often a woman whose isolation lends Rich courage as she pursues her own work. With a distinctively American sense of the organic, Rich allows errors of consciousness to stand, using these misapprehensions to modulate and render spontaneous her more clarified vision:

> *Wait for me, I have waited so long for you*
> But you never said that   I
> am ashamed to have thought it
> You had no personal leanings
> You brushed in the final storm-blue stroke
> and gave it its name: *Skidegate Pole*
>   ("Emily Carr," pp. 64–65)

Through a process of imaginative self-correction, Rich brings Emily Carr's vision into greater relief as the poem describes Rich's expressed "shame" as well as her ability to perceive difference. When such interpretative "errors" or assumptions appear only to be modified, they create the illusion of immediacy, of a voice that controls its own will to power and thereby achieves it.

Read as a whole, the poems of *Your Native Land, Your Life* are about what is recoverable, what can be salvaged for an imagination that takes cognizance of the sociohistorical realities of injustice, brutality, and terror. How does one accommodate human suffering without suppressing the desire to praise the ahistorical natural world, the world of the kingfisher, the lupines, the Pacific shore? How can one mediate between the imagination's aversion to what is cruel, to what is painful? How does one meet, in Elaine Scarry's words, "the rhetorical challenge of finding a language that will at once communicate the torture of an other human being's unknown suffering to someone who would rather avoid it but who is needed to help alleviate the very thing she would prefer to forget?" (Elaine Scarry, *The Body In Pain*).

What can be saved for poetry when the words themselves, once written, no longer remain the same, but are overnight transformed by the social conditions in which we live?

Envisioning a utopia of fulfilled needs, "Poetry: III" describes an ordered existence freed from the obligations, enslavement, and guilt of life as we know it. Would such a utopia, the falling away of resistance and illusion, release the act of writing from the burden of guilt?

> would we give ourselves
> more calmly over   feel less criminal joy
> when the thing comes   as it does come
> clarifying grammar
> and the fixed and mutable stars—?

To be "fixed" and "mutable" is simultaneously to be immune to the workings of the poetic imagination and susceptible to poetic transformation. Unable to erase the cruelty of the world in a blaze of language, Rich continuously returns to the difficulties of writing poetry in late-twentieth-century America in the face of personal loss and extreme violence. "Blue Rock" bears the fullest exploration of this conflict, as a piece of lapis lazuli "shoots its stain / blue into the wineglass on the table."

> This is a chunk of your world, a piece of its heart:
> split from the rest, does it suffer?

This is the situation of poetry at the present time:

> At the end of the twentieth century
> cardiac graphs of torture reply to poetry
>
> line by line: in North America
> the strokes of the stylus continue
>
> the figures of terror are reinvented
> all night, after I turn the lamp off, blotting
>
> wineglass, rock and roses, leaving pages
> like this scrawled with mistakes and love,
>
> falling asleep; but the stylus does not sleep,
> cruelly the drum revolves, cruelty writes its name.

According to Rich, this has not always been the situation of the poet or her language but represents a distinct response to the horror of contemporary life. Even in terms of her own career, Rich can chart a historical change in consciousness:

> Once when I wrote poems they did not change
> left overnight on the page
>
> they stayed as they were and daylight broke
> on the lines, as on the clotheslines in the yard
>
> heavy with clothes forgotten or left out
> for a better sun next day
>
> but now I know what happens while I sleep
> and when I wake the poem has changed:
>
> the facts have dilated it, or cancelled it;
> and in every morning's light, your rock is there.
>   1985

If external circumstances can alter a poem's words, how much greater a loss whose origins reside in the mind's own failing powers?

> Someone said to me: *It's just that we don't*
> *know how to cope with the loss of memory.*
> *When your own grandfather doesn't know you*
> *when your mother thinks you're somebody else*
> *it's a terrible thing.*
> ("Contradictions: Tracking Poems," 24, p. 106)

What happens when the insignia of our individualities are effaced, when each of us and her words are no longer remembered? The next poem in the sequence extends this personal loss to the historical memory of the holocaust: the anonymity of the dead, the realization that this horror has for millions of us already occurred.

The final poem of the volume, with its conversational quietness, description of physical pain, and yearning for closure, teaches what can be learned from "the edges that blur," the coincidence of bodily and social afflictions.

> You who think I find words for everything
> this is enough for now
> cut it short   cut loose from my words
>
> You for whom I write this
> in the night hours when the wrecked cartilage
> sifts round the mystical jointure of the bones
> when the insect of detritus crawls
> from shoulder to elbow to wristbone
> remember: the body's pain and the pain on the streets
> are not the same   but you can learn
> from the edges that blur   O you who love clear edges
> more than anything   watch the edges that blur
> ("Contradictions: Tracking Poems," 29, p. 111)

Only by acknowledging the blurring of edges can poetry continue to make connections between the personal and the public, between self and world. With her Whitmanian, vocative "you," Rich sends the reader forward. Cut free from her words and her pain, we are admonished to learn through observation, through the synthesizing powers of the imagination. Not by confusing personal and historical pain, but by learning to experience the contiguities of private and public experience can we discover the courage to make choices: the will to change.

Rich writes with the ardor of someone constructing a world from memory rather than repression, who chooses to celebrate the capacities of an imagination informed by the experiences of gender, race, and class. This regenerative voice serves to encourage contemporary women poets to write without sacrificing either their marginality or their authority. Like Dickinson, Rich seeks to "have it out at last on her own premises," but those premises have extended beyond Dickinson's necessarily restrictive, nineteenth-century terrain.[31] Thus Dickinson's consciousness of competition falls away before Rich's hope of mutuality, as Rich's "plaine style" emerges from the complexities of Dickinson's encoded poetics.[32] For surely, Rich participates in the ongoing project of twentieth-century women writers who have begun to delineate a feminist poetics that flourishes on the margins imposed by the male-identified American Sublime.

NOTES

1. From Emerson to Whitman

1. Ralph Waldo Emerson, "The Poet," *Selections from Ralph Waldo Emerson,* edited by Stephen E. Whicher (Boston: Houghton Mifflin, 1960), p. 233.

2. For a discussion of Emerson in relation to the Romantic tradition, see R. A. Yoder, *Emerson and the Orphic Poet in America* (Berkeley: University of California Press, 1978). Yoder asserts Emerson's centrality: "Because America has always had great expectations of a sublime and philosophical literature, its poets have accepted the tradition that Orpheus, the first poet, was the Whole or Universal Man, and they have tried to live up to Emerson's magnificent fable of the Orphic poet that promises freedom, revolution, and transcendence" p. 173. It is the aim of my work to interrogate the effects of this masculine-identified "magnificent fable."

3. See Bruce Clarke, "Sublimation and Sublimity in Home at Grasmere," *Studies in Romanticism* 19:3 (Fall 1980).

4. The terms in which the eighteenth-century critic John Dennis describes the Sublime reveal its erotic associations. Dennis remarks that it "does not so properly persuade us, as it ravishes and transports us, . . . it gives a noble Vigour to a Discourse, an invincible Force, which commits a pleasing Rape upon the very Soul of the Reader; that whenever it breaks out where it ought to do, like the Artillery of Jove, it thunders, blazes, and strikes at once, and shews all the united Force of a Writer." The discourse of passion is symptomatic of the context in which the tradition of the Sublime develops; the pleasing "rape upon the very Soul of the Reader" is foreshadowed by the experience of the poet who, submitting to a force greater than her/himself, in a condition of transport, experiences the Sublime moment. John Dennis, *Works,* II, "Grounds of Criticism," cited in Samuel H. Monk's *The Sublime: A Study of Critical Theories in VIII-Century England* (Ann Arbor: The University of Michigan Press, 1960).

5. Thomas Weiskel, *The Romantic Sublime* (Baltimore: The Johns Hopkins University Press, 1976), p. 93.

6. Weiskel, p. 99.

7. For a discussion of "the physiognomy of the ordinary" and its relation to the Sublime, see Stanley Cavell, *The Senses of Walden,* Expanded Edition (San Francisco: North Point Press, 1981), p. 149–50.

8. Emerson, "The American Scholar," p. 78.

9. Emerson, "Self-Reliance," p. 150.

10. See David Van Leer on Emerson's quest for solitude. Of Emerson's "famous renunciation of family relations," Van Leer remarks, "The passage is not a dramatic decision to be the truth's, but a sadder realization that man cannot live phenomenally 'after appearances.' The preference for proximities over covenants seems more fated than willful, a translation of Humean contiguity into the moral sphere. Recalling the early function of 'essaying,' the insistence that 'I must be myself' states less who he must be than merely that he himself must be. Existence is not a group activity." *Emerson's Epistemology: The Argument of the Essays* (Cambridge: Cambridge University Press, 1986), p. 139.

11. Emerson, "Experience," p. 269.

12. Emerson, "The Poet," p. 231–32.

13. For an analysis of Emerson in relation to gender, see Eric Cheyfitz, *The Trans-Parent: Sexual Politics in the Language of Emerson* (Baltimore and London: The Johns Hopkins University Press, 1981). Cheyfitz notes the "masculine bias of Emerson's work aligned to his vision of power, with the presence of the Mother enacting an ironic function that questions the Father's power" (see Cheyfitz, "Preface," p. xiv).

14. Emerson, "Experience," p. 270.

15. As B. L. Packer notes, ". . . the chief difficulty with Emerson's theory of poetry is not the obsolescence to which it dooms the poem but the intolerable strain to which it subjects the poet. The poet must be a prophet; a healer, who 'repairs the decays of things'; the 'true and only doctor,' who, by his revelation that the material universe is in essence symbolic, invites his fellow men 'into the science of the real.' His only way of 'sharing the path or circuit of things through forms, and so making them translucid to others,' is to surrender himself 'at all risks' to 'the divine *aura* which breathes through things' and experience in himself the flowing metamorphosis he is to describe. And his chief merit as a practicing poet will be his ability simply to keep going, to endure this *ecstasis* as long as possible and hence to suggest, through his ceaseless proliferation of tropes, the 'splendor of meaning that plays over the visible world.' " B. L. Packer, *Emerson's Fall: A New Interpretation of the Major Essays* (New York: Continuum, 1982), p. 195.

16. "Woman," *The Complete Works of Ralph Waldo Emerson,* Centenary Edition, ed. Edward Waldo Emerson, 12 vols. (Boston and New York: Houghton Mifflin Co., 1903–04), vol. 11, p. 405.

17. See "Woman," pp. 407, 410, 412, 413, 426, and passim.

18. Christina Zwarg argues for Emerson's feminist position. She reads his speech before the Woman's Rights Convention held in Boston in 1855 as a major statement on the power of women to transform culture. She writes, "Emerson's 1855 lecture on 'Woman' challenges the critical assumptions underlying the dominant trends of literary history, including the first strains of feminist criticism emerging from that history." Contextualizing Emerson's lecture, Zwarg continues that what "distinguishes him from Derrida and Nietzsche is Margaret Fuller's intervention." Emerson, as Zwarg interprets him, places his confidence in "conversation," by which "he truly means an oracular voice come among us. . . ." She concludes that "women are finally 'poets who believe their own poetry' and it is their conversational realm of the home, released from the false seductions of 'truth' yet cognizant of an undecidable responsibility toward it, that he finds attractive." Christina Zwarg, "Emerson's 'Scene' Before the Women: The Feminist Poetics of Paraphernalia," *Social Text: Theory/Culture/Ideology* (Winter 1987–88), pp. 133, 141, and passim, p. 129–44. Although I find Zwarg's apocalyptically hopeful view of Emerson's essay intriguing, I would balance this with the more restrictive aspects of women's experience as Emerson describes it.

19. Emerson, "Heroism," *Essays: First Series,* p. 259–60.

20. Emerson, "The Poet," p. 239–40.

21. Emerson, "The Poet," p. 241.

22. Casting the progression from Emerson to Whitman in oedipal terms, Harold Bloom sums up the central difference between the Emersonian and Whitmanian Sublime: "Whitman's ego, in his most Sublime transformations, wholly absorbs and thus pragmatically forgets the fathering force, and presents instead the force of the son, of his own self or, in Whitman's case, perhaps we should say of his own selves. Where Emerson *urges* forgetfulness of anteriority, Whitman more strenuously *does* forget it, though at a considerable cost. Emerson says: '*I and the Abyss*'; Whitman says: '*The Abyss of My Self.*' The second statement is necessarily more Sublime and, alas, even more American" (see Bloom, "Emerson and Whitman: The American Sublime," *Poetry and Repression: Revisionism from Blake to Stevens* [New Haven: Yale University Press, 1976], p. 266).

23. Bloom, in his essay "Whitman's Image of Voice: To the Tally of My Soul," *Agon: Towards a Theory of Revisionism* (New York: Oxford University Press, 1982), asserts that "Whitman . . . *is* the American Sublime," p. 182. In the essay, Bloom develops the idea of writing as voice and delineates a version of the Whitmanian Sublime that traces a progression from listening that "regresses to touch," and concludes with "both orgasm and poetic release through a Sublime yet quite literal masturbation," p. 188.

24. All references to Whitman's poems will be included in the text by poem title,

section, line number, and page. The text cited throughout is *Walt Whitman, Leaves of Grass: Comprehensive Reader's Edition,* ed. Harold W. Blodgett and Sculley Bradley (New York: W. W. Norton & Co., 1965). See 19.316–322, p. 335.

25. Stephen A. Black, *Whitman's Journeys into Chaos: A Psychoanalytic Study of the Poetic Process* (Princeton: Princeton University Press, 1975), discusses "Poem of Many in One" ("By Blue Ontario's Shore") in relation to Whitman's psychological development. He notes that this poem is "one of the strongest and most direct of Whitman's poems about his poetic processes," p. 143. For an analysis of the poem, see Black, p. 143–57.

26. M. Wynn Thomas, *The Lunar Light of Whitman's Poetry* (Cambridge: Harvard University Press, 1987), recalls the history of the composition of "By Blue Ontario's Shore" and Whitman's decision "not to alter the whole tenor of the piece, but to announce this at the outset by providing an introduction which makes it appear as if the whole work had originated in—had even been irresistibly dictated by—the war," p. 259–62.

27. A fragment from Whitman's notebooks suggests his interest in disentagling himself from mediatory social reality and reestablishing a sense of origination and psychic isolation. Here are the instructions for a Whitmanian preparatory meditation:

> First of all prepare for study by the following self-teaching exercises. Abstract yourself from this book; realize where you are at present located, the point you stand that is now to you the centre of all. Look up overhead, think of space stretching out, think of all the unnumbered orbs wheeling safely there, invisible to us by day, some visible by night. . . . Spend some minutes faithfully in this exercise. Then again realize yourself upon the earth, at the particular point you now occupy. Which way stretches the north, and what countries, seas, etc.? Which way the south? Which way the east? Which way the west? Seize these firmly in your mind, pass freely over immense distances. Turn your face a moment thither. Fix the direction and the idea of the distances of separate sections of your own country, also of England, the Mediterranean Sea, Cape Horn, the North Pole, and such like distant places.

Walt Whitman, *Notes and Fragments,* ed. Richard M. Bucke (London: privately printed, 1899), cited in Roger Asselineau, *The Evolution of Walt Whitman* (Cambridge: Harvard University Press, Belknap Press 1962), 2:101–2.

28. See Jerome Loving, *Emerson, Whitman, and the American Muse* (Chapel Hill: University of North Carolina Press, 1982), p. 97.

29. As Whitman once remarked to Emerson, cutting sex out of *Leaves of Grass* would be the same as "castrating a virile man." See Loving, p. 150, who cites for this quotation *With Walt Whitman in Camden,* ed. Horace Traubel, six volumes, vol. 3:32 (New York: Mitchell Kennerly, 1914–15).

30. See Whitman's letter to Emerson, Brooklyn, August 1856 *(Leaves of Grass),* p. 734, line 68.

31. Of Whitman's literary eroticism, Eve Kosofsky Sedgwick writes, "The ravishing and peculiar eros in *Leaves of Grass* resisted translation as insistently as it demanded it. The slippage back and forth between the masturbatory and the homosexual, for instance, or the suppleness and rapidity with which the reader personally is enfolded in a drama of domination with the speaker, made a transposition into physical terms, much less into programmatic ones, necessarily a distortion and, oddly, a desexualization of the original. Early Whitman's unrelenting emphasis in the poetry and in the biography on *incarnating* a phallic erethism—his erectness, his eternally rosy skin, his injections of life and health into scenes of death and wounds—had, again, at least a double effect. Put schematically, rather than having a phallus, he enacted one. Seeming at first to invite a naively celebratory, male-exalting afflatus of phallic worship, the deeper glamor of this

pose lay in the drama (called *Leaves of Absence?*) of shame, concealment, and exhibition; of engorgement (related to shame) and vacancy; of boastful inadequacy; of being like a woman, since to have to enact rather than possess a phallus is (in this system) a feminine condition; of being always only everything or nothing, and the hilarious bravado of asserting a mere human personality or desire in the face of that." See Eve Kosovsky Sedgwick, *Between Men: English Literature and Male Homosocial Desire* (New York: Columbia University Press, 1985), p. 205. I am particularly interested in Sedgwick's analysis of the relation between Whitman's enactment of the possession of the phallus and the implications for a poetics founded upon that enactment.

32. For a discussion of the specific interrelation between tallying and masturbatory activity in Whitman, see Bloom, p. 186.

33. See Justin Kaplan, *Walt Whitman, a Life* (New York: Simon and Schuster, 1980), p. 18.

34. Kaplan, p. 63.

35. See Whitman to Emerson, 1856, p. 739 (Blodgett).

36. See D. H. Lawrence, "Walt Whitman," *Whitman: A Collection of Critical Essays,* ed. Roy Harvey Pearce (Englewood Cliffs, N.J.: Prentice-Hall, Inc., 1962). Repr. from *Studies in Classic American Literature* (New York: 1923), p. 11–22 passim.

37. R. W. B. Lewis, "The New Adam: Whitman," in *Whitman: A Collection of Critical Essays,* p. 116.

38. F. O. Matthiessen, "Only a Language Experiment," in *Whitman: A Collection of Critical Essays,* p. 79.

2. Another Way to See

1. See Cristanne Miller, *Emily Dickinson: A Poet's Grammar* (Cambridge: Harvard University, 1987), for a perceptive analysis of Dickinson's distinctive uses of language to construct "multiplicity of meaning," "indeterminacy of reference," and a "fluctuating tone," p. 18 and passim.

2. All references to Dickinson's poems appear in the text identified by poem number according to the Johnson variorum edition.

3. Vivian R. Pollak notes that Dickinson's "identity crisis was, broadly speaking, a crisis of sexual identity, that her poetry associates love and social power, and that, as the laureate of the dispossessed, Dickinson is also the laureate of sexual despair." See *Dickinson: The Anxiety of Gender* (Ithaca: Cornell University Press, 1984), p. 9 and passim.

4. Sharon Cameron evaluates what she describes as Dickinson's "dialectics of rage." See *Lyric Time* (Baltimore: The Johns Hopkins University Press, 1979), p. 56–90.

5. Shira Wolosky remarks on Dickinson's aggressive poetics: "Privacy and fear are certainly present in Dickinson's work, as are anguish and morbid sensitivity. But their quality is different from that generally presumed. The overwhelming effect of Dickinson's verse is not delicacy. It is ferocity. Dickinson is an assertive and determined poet, as much fury as maiden, whose retirement is a stance of attack, whose timidity is aggressive. Her poetry leaves an impression of defiance rather than detachment, and her poetic is neither helpless nor quaking. It is, rather, one of ironic twists, sudden stabs, and poison. . . ." Introduction, *Emily Dickinson: A Voice of War* (New Haven: Yale University Press, 1984).

6. For an insightful analysis of Dickinson's use of the "daughter" persona, see Barbara Clarke Mossberg, *Emily Dickinson: When a Writer Is a Daughter* (Bloomington: Indiana University Press, 1982).

7. See my essay "Murderous Poetics: Dickinson, the Father, and the Text," in *Daughters and Fathers,* eds. L. Boose, B. S. Flowers (Baltimore: The Johns Hopkins University Press, 1988), for an elaboration on the interrelation of aggression and poetics.

8. Several critics have commented upon Dickinson's creation of a composite figure

and discussed her attitude toward him. See, for example, Nina Baym's "God, Father, and Lover in Emily Dickinson's Poetry," in *Puritan Influences in American Literature,* ed. Emory Elliott (Urbana: University of Illinois Press, 1979), p. 198.

9. Mossberg writes, "What emerges from an analysis of Dickinson's relationship with men is a pattern of behavior that is modeled on her experience as her father's daughter, which results in an attitude toward men that Clark Griffith defines as 'compounded of awe and bitterness, of reverence and fear, all struggling together in one uneasy emotional amalgam.' Dickinson projects this ambivalent attitude onto all concepts which she interprets as authoritarian and which try to exercise power over her," p. 92. Mossberg quotes Griffith, *The Long Shadow: Emily Dickinson's Tragic Poetry* (Princeton: Princeton University Press, 1968). For a more general discussion of Dickinson's presentation of herself as daughter, see Mossberg.

10. For a more extensive reading of this poem, with particular attention paid to the double work of "executor," see my essay " 'Ransom in a Voice': Language as Defense in Dickinson's Poetry," in *Feminist Critics Read Emily Dickinson,* ed. Suzanne Juhasz (Bloomington: Indiana University Press, 1983), p. 161–62.

11. Christopher E. G. Benfey contextualizes "A Word Made Flesh" in terms of Dickinson's ideas of the body. See Benfey, *Emily Dickinson and the Problem of Others* (Amherst: The University of Massachusetts Press, 1984), p. 95–96 and passim.

12. For a discussion of Dickinson's distrust of silence and her skepticism regarding language, see E. Miller Budick, *Emily Dickinson and the Life of Language: A Study in Symbolic Poetics* (Baton Rouge: Louisiana State University Press, 1985), p. 165–67.

13. See Sigmund Freud, "The Theme of the Three Caskets," in *On Creativity and The Unconscious: Papers on the Psychology of Art, Literature, Love, Religion,* sel. Benjamin Nelson (New York: Harper Colophon Books, 1958).

14. In her reading of "Because I could not stop for Death—," Jane Donahue Eberwein comments on the "decidedly imaginary person" who is the poem's speaker. She continues: "Indeed, Death does not launch the persona of this poem into another world. . . . Instead Death leaves his date buried within the margin of the circuit, in a 'House' that she can maintain like one of those 'Alabaster Chambers' (p. 216) in which numb corpses lie but which are designed and built of elegant materials still gratifying to the circuit-locked mentality. A quester for circumference would greet Death more enthusiastically, and would both value and cultivate Death's ties to Immortality. For such a quester, the destination of the journey might prove more wondrous," p. 216–19. While I would not disagree with Eberwin's assertion that the "I" here is a persona, I would suggest that the tensions among expectations, language, and the promise of immortality are central to Dickinson's experience, that the poignancy of her turn to language in order to voice her despair is among this poem's central concerns. *Dickinson's Strategies of Limitation* (Amherst: The University of Massachusetts Press, 1985).

15. See Harold Bloom, *A Map of Misreading* (New York: Oxford University Press, 1975), p. 185 and passim.

3. Dickinson, Moore, and the Poetics of Deflection

1. Geoffrey H. Hartman, *Criticism in the Wilderness: The Study of Literature Today* (New Haven: Yale University Press, 1980), p. 124.

2. Bonnie Costello writes, "While Moore follows the tendency in 'feminine realism' to keep an eye on the external object, she is distinctly modern in her awareness of the limits of language to present that object. Moore's 'descriptions' break up the conventions of composition, not to protect the self but to bring language into a more adequate relationship to experience, to discover a new realism which resists the habits of mind and eye. But what such resistance to referential conventions does, finally, is bring us into a closer awareness of the surface of language." Costello, "The 'Feminine' Language of Marianne Moore," *American Poetry 1915–1945,* ed. Harold Bloom (New York: Chelsea House, 1987), p. 218.

3. Ralph Waldo Emerson, "The Divinity School Address," in *Selections from Ralph Waldo Emerson,* ed. Stephen E. Whicher (Boston: Houghton Mifflin, 1957), p. 106.

4. On Crane's relation to Whitman's and Keats's conception of the relative powers of the imagination and nature (specifically passages from "Ave Maria"), Lee Edelman notes that "the tendency to appropriate to the poetic imagination the external light of the sun, and thus an insistent focus on issues of authority or power, seems to serve as the point of intersection for these passages from Whitman and Keats. The gesture of poetic aggrandizement allows both poets to make daringly extravagant claims for the imagination at nature's expense. Just as Keats declares poetry 'the supreme of power,' so Whitman, who begins by acclaiming the creative abilities of a 'nameless' and 'transcendent' presence, ends by internalizing the power of that entity, claiming it as his own." See Lee Edelman, *Transmemberment of Song: Hart Crane's Anatomies of Rhetoric and Desire* (Stanford: Stanford University Press, 1987), p. 202.

5. Robert Lowell, quoted by Elizabeth Bishop in letter to Lowell, 25 June 1961, Lowell Collection, Houghton Library, Harvard University (unpublished).

6. Marie Borroff, *Language and the Poet: Verbal Artistry in Frost, Stevens, and Moore* (Chicago: The University of Chicago Press, 1979), pp. 83, 80–135 passim.

7. Marianne Moore, "Edith Sitwell, Virtuoso," *The Complete Prose of Marianne Moore,* ed. Patricia C. Willis (New York: Viking, Elisabeth Sifton Books, 1986), p. 522.

8. Randall Jarrell, "Her Shield," *Marianne Moore: A Collection of Critical Essays,* ed. Charles Tomlinson (Englewood Cliffs: Prentice Hall, 1969), p. 122.

9. Jarrell, p. 122.

10. Dickinson, poem 744.

11. Dickinson, poem 627.

12. Harold Bloom, *Wallace Stevens, The Poems of Our Climate* (Ithaca and London: Cornell University Press, 1977), see pp. 233, 281–92 and passim.

4. Marianne Moore

1. See Elizabeth Bishop, "Efforts of Affection: A Memoir of Marianne Moore," in *The Collected Prose* (New York: Farrar, Straus, Giroux, 1984), p. 143. Bishop recalls the following exchange:

> I do not remember her ever referring to Emily Dickinson, but on one occasion, when we were walking in Brooklyn on our way to a favored tea shop, I noticed we were on a street associated with the *Brooklyn Eagle,* and I said fatuously, "Marianne, isn't it odd to think of you and Walt Whitman walking this same street over and over?" She exclaimed in her mock-ferocious tone, "Elizabeth, don't speak to me about that man!" So I never did again. (p. 143)

2. Marianne Moore, *The Complete Prose of Marianne Moore* (New York: Elisabeth Sifton Books, Viking, 1986), p. 516.

3. Grace Schulman, *Marianne Moore: The Poetry of Engagement* (Urbana and Chicago: University of Illinois Press, 1986), p. 13.

4. In this regard see especially Taffy Martin, *Marianne Moore: Subversive Modernist* (Austin: University of Texas Press, 1986), and John Slatin, *The Savage's Romance: The Poetry of Marianne Moore* (University Park and London: The Pennsylvania State University Press, 1986). "By versifying prose as varied as Turgenev's *Fathers and Sons* and statements by Dr. E. H. Kellogg of Carlisle's Presbyterian Church, she unified poetry with the language of everyday life and yet preserved the tensions between them." Schulman, *Marianne Moore: The Poetry of Engagement* (Urbana and Chicago: University of Illinois Press, 1986), p. 109.

5. See Martin, p. 139, and passim.

6. On her awareness of isolation, see Marianne Moore, "A Letter to Ezra Pound," in

Marianne Moore: A Collection of Critical Essays, ed. Charles Tomlinson (Englewood Cliffs, N.J.: Prentice-Hall, 1969), p. 17.

7. Harold Bloom, *Wallace Stevens: The Poems of Our Climate* (Ithaca and London: Cornell University Press, 1977), p. 17. Bloom writes, "The connection with Stevens is that he and Dickinson, more than any other Americans, more than any other moderns, labor successfully to make the visible a little hard to see."

8. Of this passage, Harold Bloom writes, "Like nearly every other quotation in this poem, the two lines from Sir Francis Bacon gain nothing for Moore's own text by being restored to their own context. Steel burned by fire does not exactly brighten into a golden bough, so the 'gilt' is in cognitive sequence with 'goldenness' and 'bright,' even if we rightly expect to behold blackened steel." Speaking more generally, Bloom continues, "All who have known marriage (as Moore declined to do) will register an unhappy shudder at the force the Baconian phrases take on when Moore appropriates them. Traditions as treasons become circular, and together with impostures can be read here either as performing many despoilments or as investing many gains of previous despoilments. Either way, it might seem as though an ingenuity avoiding this equivocal enterprise could only be taken as criminal by some dogmatist, whether societal or theological." *Marianne Moore: Modern Critical Views,* ed. Harold Bloom, (New York: Chelsea House, 1987), p. 4–5.

9. Pamela White Hadas, in her extensive discussion of "Marriage," "Fighting Affections," in *Marianne Moore: Poet of Affection* (Syracuse, N.Y.: Syracuse University Press, 1977), notes that "Moore's quotation of Bacon, so aptly placed for rendering the symbol of love into an image of social greed, and the eternal circle into an image of unprogressive self-interest, applies as much to a style of writing and speaking as it does to the life style of prospective husbands and wives. Social mores, ingenious in the enshrinement of the original *felix culpa,* must be fought with ingenuity. What Adam and Eve might think of it is certainly no consolation," p. 143.

10. Of the succeeding passage, Laurence Stapleton (*Marianne Moore: The Poet's Advance* [Princeton: Princeton University Press, 1978]) notes that the quotation that Eve makes her own is from Baxter's *The Saints' Everlasting Rest.* Baxter will also be a source for passages in "An Octopus." Here is the passage to which Stapleton refers:

> "the heart rising
> in its estate of peace
> as a boat rises
> with the rising of the water."
> (quoted by Stapleton, p. 38)

Stapleton notes that "some of the trial lines in Marianne Moore's workbook suggest a different direction for the poem. One rejected passage will show this. It begins 'Adam / I have seen him when he was so handsome that he gave me a start / then he went off / appearing in his true colours / the transition fr. Apollo to Apollyon / being swift like Jack before and after the beanstalk.' As the thinking about Adam's possessiveness and desire for power continues, a conclusion is made: 'this division into masculine and feminine compartments of achievement will not do . . . one feels oneself to be an integer / but one is not one is a particle / in an existence to which Adam and Eve / are incidental to the plot.' But this interior dialogue of the writer with herself while drafting the poem was eventually translated into the impersonal irony of the lines that soon appear in the draft, and begin in the published poem," p. 39. Stapleton's characterization of the shift from an apparently unresolved inner dialogue to the more distanced position of "impersonal irony" is related to Slatin's observations on "Marriage" and to the argument I advance here.

Of interest as well is Moore's use of Baxter in both "Marriage" and "An Octopus," another indication of the poems' initial interrelation. Also suggestive is Moore's use of Greek myth and folk tale as analogs for the Adamic allusion.

11. Of Nessus's short, Bloom writes: "Here the nightingale, perhaps by way of Keats's erotic allusions, becomes an emblem of the female, while the male speaker, ravished by the silences of the emblem, becomes Hercules suicidally aflame with the shirt of Nessus." The associations awakened by Moore's invocation of Nessus's shirt contribute, in the original story's dynamics of love, jealousy, and punishment, to the description of the workings of desire and marriage that Moore's poem takes as its subject. The story is from the myth of Hercules, a strangely evocative figure for Moore. See Bloom, p. 7.

Hercules is a figure with whom Moore elsewhere identifies the burdens and pleasures of being a poet as well as the heroism of maternity. Here the allusion recalls the final episode in Hercules' life, when Deianira, his devoted wife, learning that Hercules is infatuated by Iole, the captive princess, anoints Hercules with a robe charmed by the blood of the Centaur Nessus, a magical garment that could be used if Hercules ever loved another woman more than her. As Edith Hamilton writes, when Hercules dons the robe its effect is "the same as that of the robe Medea had sent her rival whom Jason was about to marry." In great anguish, but himself unable to die, he plots his own death. Deianira, when she learns the consequences of her gift, kills herself. Plagued by a burning fire he cannot control, Hercules has a pyre built on Mount Oeta and is placed upon it. Philoctetes torches the fire, and Hercules goes to heaven, where he is "reconciled to Hera" and marries her daughter Hebe. Thus, jealousy avenges itself in death. See Edith Hamilton, *Mythology* (New York: A Mentor Book, New American Library, 1942), p. 171–72.

12. For a discussion of oral desires and their relation to fear, see Hadas, p. 162–64. Invoking Kenneth Burke's argument in "Freud and the Analysis of Poetry," Hadas concludes: "The psychoanalytic coordinates of the passage just discussed, and perhaps the whole poem 'Marriage,' would seem to be on one hand the desire to be satisfied, to be 'fed' and treated royally, as if one had power; on the other hand, we have the coordinate of fear of betrayal, enslavement, and physical injury to which any intimacy with another human being makes one vulnerable. It is summed up in 'the spiked hand / that has an affection for one / and proves it to the bone.' The 'displacement' of this desire and this fear is, as is characteristic in Moore's poetry, raised to the level of art—the Old Testament, the Elizabethan play, and the western tea ceremony—and to the level of occasions where people get especially dressed up and speak in carefully calculated phrases which invariably mean something other than they seem to mean. Sublime Sublimation." Hadas, p. 164. The specific passage to which Hadas refers is reproduced below, from the Manikin edition of "Marriage." The brackets, taken from Hadas's printing, indicate lines or phrases excised in other versions of the poem:

> [When do we feed?]
> We Occidentals are so unemotional,
> [we quarrel as we feed;
> one's] self [love's labor] lost
> the irony preserved
> in "the Ahasuerus tête-à-tête banquet"
> with its small orchids like snakes' tongues,
> with its "good monster lead the way,"
> with little laughter
> and munificence of humor
> in which "four o'clock does not exist,
> but at five o'clock
> the ladies in their imperious humility
> are ready to receive you";
> in which experience attests
> that men have power
> and sometimes one is made to feel it.
>   (Hadas, p. 162–63)

It is interesting to note the presence of the "small orchids like snakes' tongues," image of tantalizing danger, in terms of the appearance of the later excised Calypso orchid—haunting and hidden—in Moore's notebook passages relating to "An Octopus."

13. Hadas underscores the insufficiency of Webster's words: "The summary: 'Liberty and union / now and forever.' / Liberty is not union and now is not forever, but one can say it; it sounds nice and people want to believe it, and they do," p. 175.

14. In a trenchant, illuminating discussion of "Marriage," John Slatin compares Moore's poem to Eliot's "The Waste Land," reading passages from Section II, "A Game of Chess" (Eliot's descriptions of Cleopatra) alongside Moore's passages on Eve. Slatin suggests that if both "The Waste Land" and "Marriage" confront a problematic, post-lapsarian view of sexual relations, Moore situates herself as a woman speaking against the voices of masculine poetic authority. Interestingly, Slatin points out that Moore's lines

> He dares not clap his hands
> to make it go on
> lest it should fly off;
> if he does nothing, it will sleep
> if he cries out, it will not understand.

are quoted from Edward Thomas's *Feminine Influence on the Poets* (1910), "a passage in which Thomas summarizes what he calls 'the central experience' of *The King is Quair.*" Slatin notes, "It is a poignant moment, and it has its poignancy in 'Marriage,' too—but in its context there, it is sharply ironic as well. For although there is no literal prison in Paradise, Adam's paralysis is clearly his own fault, the consequence of his immoderate 'joy' at having 'become an idol.'" Slatin continues, "Like Bluebeard, then, he is imprisoned in the 'tower' of his own self-consciousness," p. 366–67. Slatin interprets Moore's description of marriage as "a *male* experiment . . . with ways out but no way in." Hence, "it must be examined from the outside by a woman fully conscious . . . that she is 'Treading chasms / on the uncertain footing of a spear'," p. 371.

Slatin argues that Moore uses quotations as a means to avoid entrapment by language, a "self-entrapment" that might otherwise destroy her determination to escape the Adamic snare. Yet Slatin is fully cognizant of the trap quotation itself might become for Moore. He describes her subtle deployment of quotations in "dramatic" terms: "The quotations, like the protagonist (if, indeed, the distinction means anything), must seem to be talking past and against one another while the poet's ironic voice runs rapidly from one to the next, explaining, supplying the 'despised . . . connectives. . . .'," p. 374. See John Slatin, unpublished manuscript, p. 361–76.

15. Bonnie Costello interprets "Marriage" as a more dialectically balanced work. She writes of the poem's end, "In her conclusion Moore describes an institution not only ironic and absurd but also dynamic and enticing in its balances of contentions." Bonnie Costello, *Marianne Moore: Imaginary Possessions* (Cambridge: Harvard University Press, 1981), p. 176.

5. The "Piercing, Melting Word"

1. My discussion of "An Octopus" draws upon factual information, notebook passages, and the 1924 version of "An Octopus" included in Patricia Willis's article, "The Road to Paradise: First Notes on Marianne Moore's 'An Octopus,'" in *Twentieth Century Literature*, vol. 30, nos. 2 and 3 (Summer/Fall 1984), p. 247. I am indebted to Patricia Willis for her valuable elaboration of materials relating to the genesis of the poem.

2. "Here," [Willis writes] "the 'octopus of ice' heads a set of phrases used directly in 'Marriage'—'I want to be alone' and 'so handsome you gave me a start'—and in-

directly—'cool,' 'violence,' 'static emotionless.' While not returning to the image of an octopus *per se,* Moore uses the next thirty pages to work over ideas for a poem about Adam, paradise, love, theology, divorce, woman, and hell, while including references to eagles, an impostor, a storm, and a waterfall. The controlling ideas are those expressed in 'Marriage' but images later used in 'An Octopus' are present." *Twentieth Century Literature,* p. 247.

I would add that the passage reveals a nascent conjunction of interrelated concerns wherein the self "reads" the other—the octopus of ice—in silence and perceives that otherness as both static and enterprising, both desirous of being alone and intimidating in its desire; so handsome it startles. This engendered, readerly encounter between the speaker and the masculine octopus of ice would undergo extensive elaboration before resolving itself into the published text of the 1924 "An Octopus" (let alone subsequent revisions). What this notebook passage reveals are the shared origins of both "Marriage" and "An Octopus" in an engendered, vexed attempt to come to terms with what is most tantalizing and forbidding beyond the self.

3. John Slatin, *The Savage's Romance: The Poetry of Marianne Moore* (University Park and London: The Pennsylvania State University Press, 1986), in his discussion of "Virginia Britannia" alluded to Moore's interest in Shelley: "The nature of Moore's interest in Shelley is most clearly indicated by the words of Scofield Thayer, who wrote of Shelley in 1913 that while 'many of the poet's ideals now appear scarcely comprehensible, the integrity of his purpose is not the less patent.' " Slatin notes that Moore copied these phrases from Thayer's essay, "Shelley: or the Poetic Value of Revolutionary Principles," which "had appeared in the *Harvard Monthly* in April 1913; see Rosenbach 1250/5, p. 165–66 (Nov. 1928)," Slatin, n. 273. For the influence of Shelley and the other Romantics on Moore, see Slatin, p. 210–16 (Wordsworth), p. 234–45 (Keats), p. 244–45 (Shelley), and passim. In regard to the subject of influence and Moore's gradually overcoming her deep fear of imitation, see "Advancing Backward in a Circle: The Poet as (Natural) Historian," p. 205–52. Especially useful is Slatin's analysis of Moore's resolution of the conflict between her desire for originality and the lure of imitation, a conflict she often resolves through parody.

4. The imagistic resemblances between "An Octopus" and "Mont Blanc" are striking. One thinks especially of ll, 12–30, the Ravine of Arve passage, with its description of the surrounding trees as children and the image of enclosure as "the strange sleep . . . Which when the voices of the desert fail / Wraps all in its own deep eternity." "An Octopus" similarly conceives of flora as family and the image of envelopment is reenacted in the dangerously enfolding arms of the glacier itself. Here is Shelley:

> Thy giant brood of pines around thee clinging,
> Children of elder time, in whose devotion
> The chainless winds still come and ever came
> To drink their odours, and their mighty swinging
> To hear—an old and solemn harmony:
> Thine earthly rainbows stretched across the sweep
> Of the aethereal waterfall, whose veil
> Robes some unsculptured image; the strange sleep
> Which when the voices of the desert fail
> Wraps all in its own deep eternity;—
>
> (20–29)

The fir trees, shrubbery, waterfall, and imagistic stationing all reappear in Moore's description. Later in "Mont Blanc," Shelley asks the question Moore herself will make the heart of her poem: Can such a predatory scene of destruction possibly be a source of maternal instruction, even if it be the instruction of ruin?

> . . . how hideously
> Its shapes are heaped around! rude, bare, and high,
> Ghastly, and scarred, and riven.—Is this the scene
> Where the old Earthquake-daemon taught her young
> Ruin? Were these their toys? or did a sea
> Of fire envelope once this silent snow?
> None can reply—all seems eternal now.
> (69–75)

5. In *The Romantic Sublime: Studies in the Structure and Psychology of Transcendence* (Baltimore and London: The Johns Hopkins University Press, 1976), Thomas Weiskel describes the detemporalization and depersonalization that occur in these lines:

The passage may strike us as archaic not only in its embrace of traditional ontology but also in its surprising lack of self-consciousness. In the style, for example: the Shakespearean doublets ("the sick sight / And giddy prospect of the raving stream, / The unfettered clouds and region of the Heavens") suggest an amplitude which retards the progress toward climax by detemporalizing it, so that the order of description already subtly leaves the chronicle of experience for the reflective order of Eternity. The climax itself—

> Tumult and peace, the darkness and the light—
> Were all like . . .

—is not revelation, a lifting of the mask, but the merest sliding over the threshold into interpretation. The mounting rhythm of perception is then discharged in the subsequent phrases and the very variety of alternatives they enlist: "workings . . . features . . . blossoms . . . Characters . . . types and symbols. " In a sense, however, the perceptional *gradatio* is illusory, for the interpretative (symbolic) order has already been the aspect of these images: "were all along like" rather than "now suddenly became." In style as well as in thought the "I"—with its characteristic effect of making the progress of the verse the very dramatic progress of a consciousness—has disappeared. Not Wordworth's kind of greatness." (198–99)

This *may* not be Wordsworth's "kind of greatness," but it is very much Moore's. The close of "An Octopus," in its reiteration of the rhetorical processes of detemporalization and depersonalization register the difference between the Wordsworthian Sublime and Moore's.

6. Slatin suggests a reference to William Carlos Williams' phrase in *Kora in Hell:* "suggesting dustbrushes, not trees." Slatin writes, "they also suggest the broom with which Williams (or rather his wife; he is watching her clean house) 'swish(es) from room to room,' digging 'the dust out of every corner' before wrapping 'the house . . . in brown paper' and sending it off 'to a publisher' as a finished 'work of art'," p. 164. But as Slatin goes on to remark, ". . . the debris of 'An Octopus' cannot be swept up: the 'winds . . . tear the snow to bits / and hurl it like a sandblast' at us, just as, in Williams's Coda to the improvisation quoted above, 'the north wind, coming and passing, swelling and dying, lifts the frozen sand (and) drives it arattle against the lidless windows . . .'," Slatin, p. 164.

7. For a discussion of the goat as "at best a debased parody" of Moore's land unicorn in "Sea Unicorns and Land Unicorns" and as a figure that itself calls into question the capacity for naming, see Slatin, p. 168.

8. See Willis, p. 252–53.

9. Willis notes, "In 'An Octopus,' Mrs. Moore is the 'ouzel,' 'with its passion for rapids and high pressured falls.' Marianne is the 'rat, skipping along to its burrow,' a character borrowed from the poet rat in *The Wind in the Willows.* Warner's nickname comes from the same story; in this poem 'when you hear the best wild music of the forest it is sure to

be a badger.' Moore knew full well that the badger-looking creature in the Northwest is actually a marmot, and at some time between submission of the manuscript to *The Dial* and the publication of the poem, she changed badger to 'marmot,' in the interest of accuracy, but with her brother no doubt still in mind," p. 244–45.

10. The Audubon Guide identifies the calypso orchid as "rare"; a "fairy slipper," pink, bilateral flower hangs at the top. Named for the sea nymph Calypso of Homer's *Odyssey*." "Like Calypso, the plant is beautiful and prefers secluded haunts." *The Audubon Society Field Guide to North American Wildflowers* (New York: Alfred A. Knopf, 1985).

11. See Bonnie Costello's discussion of "The Paper Nautilus," in *Marianne Moore: Imaginary Possession*. Costello identifies "maternity" as the subject of the poem. She writes, "We conventionally think of maternal affection as a soft, graceful attitude, and Moore's poetry has been prized (with condescension), for its 'relaxed ease.' But the poem describes the process of nurture as a struggle beneath an apparent gentleness. As always, Moore directly associates these issues of protection and struggle with problems of language and interpretation." Later in her analysis, Costello notes, "The poem describes the creative process as a highly precarious restraint of energy. The health of the eggs somehow depends upon maximum power and maximum restraint" (p. 119).

12. Edith Hamilton describes Hercules: "His intellect was not strong. His emotions were. Nevertheless he had true greatness. Not because he had complete courage based upon overwhelming strength, which is merely a matter of course, but because, by his sorrow for wrongdoing and his willingness to do anything to expiate it, he showed greatness of soul. If only he had had some greatness of mind as well, at least enough to lead him along the ways of reason, he would have been the perfect hero." *Mythology* (A Mentor Book, The New American Library of World Literature, 1942), p. 164.

13. Hamilton, p. 164.

14. Laurence Stapleton quotes a letter of 15 January 1941 in which Moore writes, "I rather favor as a title for my ostrich The One Remaining Rebel as making a nice echo for the conclusion." Stapleton notes, "Although she chose instead a phrase from Lily's *Euphues* for the title 'He "Digesteth Harde Yron,'" the twofold emphasis is clear, the superlative adaptability of the rebel as an antidote to greed." Stapleton, p. 117. In her discussion of "Marriage" and "An Octopus," Stapleton observes that "An Octopus" dispenses with narrative and dialogue. She goes on to consider its composition and its relation to the longer poems, and compares it to Williams' *Paterson* "at its best . . ." (p. 45).

15. The allusion to the arms on the mane of the Parthenon horse may refer to the representation of the combat between the Lapiths and the centaurs.

16. Costello, p. 119.

6. Bishop's Sexual Poetics

1. Elizabeth Bishop to Anne Stevenson, quoted in "Letters from Elizabeth Bishop," by Anne Stevenson, *Times Literary Supplement*, March 1980, p. 261.

2. "Letters from Elizabeth Bishop," p. 261.

3. Bishop's copy of *Leaves of Grass*, ed. Emory Holloway (Garden City, N.Y; Doubleday, Page & Co., 1926), is marked and contains some marginalia. Bishop's signature is in a childlike hand (see the Bishop Collection, The Houghton Library, Harvard University, Cambridge, Mass., for books from Elizabeth Bishop's library). I incorporate Bishop's markings and page references in the text.

4. Commenting on Bishop's poem "Florida," David Kalstone notes the difference between Bishop's mode of description and Whitman's. "A descriptive poem," Kalstone writes, "which in other hands, say Whitman's, appropriates landscapes and objects, here makes us aware just how, just why we are excluded from such appropriations." See

David Kalstone, "Elizabeth Bishop: Questions of Memory, Questions of Travel," in *Five Temperaments* (New York: Oxford University Press, 1977), p. 12–41; repr. *Elizabeth Bishop and Her Art,* ed. Lloyd Schwartz and Sybil P. Estess (Ann Arbor: The University of Michigan Press, 1983), p. 7. Bishop's departure from Whitman depends, as Kalstone suggests, upon her sense of exclusion, a subject I will turn to later in this chapter.

5. "Elizabeth Bishop Speaks about her Poetry," in *New Paper* (Bennington College, vol. IV, no. 3, June 1978).

6. As John Hollander observes, "The very island is an exemplar, a representation; it is a place which stands for the life lived on it as much as it supports that life. Its unique species are emblems of the selfhood that the whole region distills and enforces, and on it, life and word and art are one, and the homemade Dionysus is (rather than blesses from without or within) his votary." See "Elizabeth Bishop's Mappings of Life," in *Parnassus* (Fall 1977), p. 359–66; repr. Schwartz and Estess, p. 250.

7. Marjorie Perloff notes Bishop's procedures of narrative. Although Perloff is describing the narrative technique of "In the Village," her observations are useful when reading "Crusoe In England." Citing Roman Jakobson's study of Pasternak's early prose, Perloff states that "Jakobson argues that unlike Mayakovsky, whose poetic mode is insistently metaphoric, Pasternak follows the path of contiguous relations, metonymically digressing from the plot to the atmosphere and from the characters to the setting in space and time. . . . Like Pasternak, Bishop digresses from actor to setting, from plot to atmosphere." The narrative of contiguity and metonymic relations characterizes "Crusoe In England" as well as "In the Village." See Marjorie Perloff, "Elizabeth Bishop: The Course of a Particular," in *Modern Poetry Studies,* Vol. 8, no. 3 (1977), p. 183.

8. See Alan Williamson, "*A Cold Spring:* The Poet of Feeling," in *Elizabeth Bishop and Her Art,* ed. Lloyd Schwartz and Sybil P. Estess (Ann Arbor: The University of Michigan Press, 1983), p. 103.

9. Jerome Mazzaro comments on Friday's gender: "Friday's being male . . . limits the urge toward futurity that the poem identifies with duty to rude artifacts, since the urge cannot be served in biological propagation. Art thus becomes some kind of adjustment to Necessity." My discussion attempts to consider what kind of adjustment that might be. See Jerome Mazzaro, "The Poetics of Impediment," in *Postmodern American Poetry* (Urbana: University of Illinois Press, 1980); repr. in *Elizabeth Bishop,* ed. Harold Bloom (New York and New Haven: Chelsea House, 1985), p. 34.

10. In *A Conversation with Elizabeth Bishop,* conducted by George Starbuck and originally published in *Ploughshares* 3, nos. 3 & 4 (1977) (reprinted in Schwartz and Estess, p. 312–30), Bishop alludes to reading *Robinson Crusoe:*

GS: What got the Crusoe poem started?
EB: I don't know. I reread the book and discovered how really awful Robinson Crusoe was, which I hadn't realized. I hadn't read it in a long time. And then I was remembering a visit to Aruba—long before it was a developed "resort." I took a trip across the island and it's true that there are small volcanoes all over the place.
GS: I forget the end of *Robinson Crusoe.* Does the poem converge on the book?
EB: No. I've forgotten the facts, there, exactly. I reread it all one night. And I had forgotten it was so moral. All that Christianity. So I think I wanted to re-see it with all that left out.

11. Adrienne Rich, "The Eye of the Outsider: The Poetry of Elizabeth Bishop," in *Boston Review,* April 1983, p. 16.

12. See J. D. McClatchy's essay "One Art" for a discussion of the sources and formal aspects of Bishop's villanelle. J. D. McClatchy, "Some Notes on 'One Art,' " in FIELD: *Contemporary Poetry and Poetics* 31 (Fall 1984), p. 39.

13. Draft ten of "One Art" conveys a much more specific impression of the "you" who may be lost: "But, losing you (eyes of the Azure Aster) / But-you-if I lose you—(eyes of

azure aster) / all that I write is false." Line two is crossed out in this version, and the final "false" is crossed out as well. See the drafts of "One Art," Bishop Collection, Vassar College Library, box XXVII, folder 410.

14. Kalstone comments on the poem's opening: " 'Brazil, January 1, 1502': . . . its first word is the generalizing *Januaries*. No longer the 'here' and 'now' of the uninstructed tourist, the poem fans out into the repeating present of the botanist and the anthropologist," Bloom, p. 64.

15. Willard Spiegelman notes Bishop's exploration of "the clichés of masculine conquest in "Brazil, January 1, 1502" and in the first half of "Roosters." See Willard Spiegelman, "Elizabeth Bishop's 'Natural Heroism,' " in *Centennial Review* (Winter 1978); repr. Bloom, p. 98. Spiegelman compares Bishop's roosters to Stevens's Chief Iffucan and notes their "lunatic, pseudo-heroic fighting swagger," Bloom, p. 99.

16. For a sustained reading of "Roosters" and a study of its compositional origins, see Anne R. Newman, "Elizabeth Bishop's 'Roosters,' " in *Pebble: A Book of Rereadings in Recent American Poetry* (p. 18–20, triple issue), copyright 1979 by Greg Kuzma; repr. Bloom, p. 111–20. Newman comments on the comparison (in the second part of the poem) between "Magdalen's sin and Peter's—hers of the 'flesh alone,' his of the 'spirit.' " Newman notes that "the male-female comparisons are interesting and add a personal dimension to the poem, but they do not take precedence over the concern for all mankind," Bloom, p. 116–17. Here I would differ, suggesting that the comparison between Magdalen's and Peter's sins underscores the prevailing thematics of the poem, of female-to-female intimacy and the dangers of a distinctively masculine betrayal.

17. Focusing on these lines, David Bromwich writes, "Indeed, there is something like self-reproach in a line that begins the final movement of 'Roosters': 'how could the night have come to grief?' By a trick of context, this phrase opens up an ambiguity in the cliché. It warns us that there has been matter for grieving during the night, before the first rooster crowed, at a scene of passion which is also a betrayal." See David Bromwich, "Elizabeth Bishop's Dream-Houses," in *Raritan* 4, no. 1 (Summer 1984); repr. Bloom, 1986, p. 34.

18. On the draft labeled "I.", Bishop wrote "my good dog" above "Pink Dog," the first phrase emphasizing her proprietary relationship with the animal she describes. On an unnumbered typed draft, Bishop has written and then crossed out the phrase, "solution is disguise." See Bishop Manuscript Collection, Vassar College Library, box XXVIII, folder 418.

19. Of the poems in *Geography III* Kalstone notes, "Her 'questions of travel' modulate now, almost imperceptibly, into questions of memory and loss. Attentive still to landscape where one can feel the sweep and violence of encircling and eroding geological powers, poems such as 'Crusoe in England' and 'The Moose' pose their problems retrospectively," Bloom, p. 70.

20. Bonnie Costello observes, "Most of the enclosed places Bishop describes are waiting rooms in one way or another (the most extreme being a wake). Her ports, islands, bights, are not microcosms of, or escapes from, history; they contain the tides of unity and discontinuity, of presence and absence, with much the same incompleteness as any wider experience of flux." See Bonnie Costello, "The Impersonal and the Interrogative in the Poetry of Elizabeth Bishop," in Schwartz and Estess, p. 114.

21. Lee Edelman, "The Geography of Gender: Elizabeth Bishop's 'In the Waiting Room'," in *Contemporary Literature*, vol. 26, no. 2 (Summer 1985), p. 188.

22. Edelman, p. 191.

23. Edelman, p. 196.

24. Helen Vendler draws several interesting distinctions between "The Moose" and Robert Frost's "The Most of It." "There, as in Bishop's poem, a creature emerges from 'the impenetrable wood' and is beheld. But Frost's beast disappoints expectation. The poet had wanted 'counter-love, original response,' but the 'embodiment that crashed' proves to be not 'human,' not 'someone else additional to him,' but rather a large buck,

which disappears as it came." Vendler continues, "Frost's beast is male, Bishop's female; Frost's a symbol of brute force,' Bishop's a creature 'safe as houses'; Frost's a challenge, Bishop's a reassurance." See Helen Vendler, "Domestication, Domesticity, and the Otherworldly," in *Part of Nature, Part of Us* (Cambridge: Harvard University Press, 1980); repr. Schwartz and Estess, p. 46.

25. In an interview with the *Christian Science Monitor* (Thursday, 23 March 1978) conducted by Alexandra Johnson, Bishop comments on the value of surprise: "A final question: What one quality should every poem have?"

"Surprise. The subject and the language which conveys it should surprise you. You should be surprised at seeing something new and strangely alive."

26. Harold Bloom contrasts Stevens's lion with Bishop's: "In Stevens, the lion tends to represent poetry as a destructive force, as the imposition of the poet's will-to-power over reality. . . . Here, I take it, Bishop's affectionate riposte:

> "They could have been teasing the lion sun,
> except that now he was behind them
> —a sun who'd walked the beach the last low tide,
> making those big, majestic paw-prints,
> who perhaps had batted a kite out of the sky to play with.

"A somewhat Stevensian lion sun, clearly, but with something better to do than standing potent in itself. The path away from poetry as a destructive force can only be through play, the play of trope. Within her tradition so securely, Bishop profoundly plays at trope. Dickinson, Moore, and Bishop resemble Emerson, Frost, and Stevens in that tradition, with a difference due not to mere nature or mere ideology but to superb art," Bloom.

Although I share Bloom's conviction that Bishop is "secure" in her tradition and that she profoundly plays with trope, I would insert between his terms "nature" and "mere ideology" the gender-inflected imagination, for surely to evade the role of sexuality in the life of the mind is to play into the hands of those very idealizers of the imagination Bloom himself so sharply criticizes.

27. Whitman, "Song of Myself," in *Leaves of Grass*, section 25, 560–61.

28. Jean Valentine notes, "This short poem, 'Sonnet,' was to be the last poem she would write: one of her most purely joyful poems about 'the size of our abidance'; a redemptive poem for any particular guests on this earth who start out 'caught' and hope to end up 'freed.' In a published manuscript draft, Bishop tries the first line as 'Oh brain, bubble'; in the finished poem, the bubble itself is freed to be more than brain, to be 'creature.' At the end, the mirror is empty, and the creature is not only freed, but lives to tell the story." See Jean Valentine, "Sonnet," in *Elizabeth Bishop: A Symposium, FIELD: Contemporary Poetry and Poetics*, no. 31 (Fall 1984). Although I share Valentine's interest in the move from "brain" to "creature," I would suggest that what "Sonnet" may redeem is not the self-limiting experience "about the size of our abidance," but the vision of a larger world of unrestricted possibility that breaks through the limitations so often probed in Bishop's earlier work.

29. One recalls Bishop's use of "wavering" in "Love Lies Sleeping":

> From the window I see
> an immense city, carefully revealed,
> made delicate by over-workmanship,
> detail upon detail,
> cornice upon facade,
>
> reaching so languidly up into
> a weak white sky, it seems to waver there.

7. Plath's Bodily Ego

1. Harold Bloom, *The Anxiety of Influence* (New York: Oxford University Press, 1973), p. 58.

2. In "Sylvia Plath: The Mythically Fated Self," Paul Breslin notes that "critics such as Jon Rosenblatt and Judith Kroll have tried to correct the exaggerations in the Rosenthal-Alvarez view of Plath by arguing that her poems must be separated to some extent from the life and must not be read as a teleological journey toward her eventual suicide. Kroll quite justly remarks that Plath, unlike Lowell or Sexton, seldom presents autobiography in much literal detail. Rather, she treats the events of her life as the plot of a myth, turning the key persons—herself, her father, her children, and her husband—into archetypal figures, transposing the story into a language of recurring symbols. . . . In Plath—although many narrative details of her mythic system are drawn from her life—the emphasis is more on expressing the structure of her state of being." "But," Breslin continues, "the mythical interpretation of Plath's work can be turned around to confirm the conventional wisdom, since it shows that Plath constructed the posthumous myth herself, within the poems. Her suicide enacts the myth on the literal level, closing the gap between art and life, myth and biography," p. 95–96. For a discussion of the devastating psychic consequences of conceptualizing one's life as myth, see Breslin, p. 96 and passim. (*The Psycho-Political Muse: American Poetry Since the Fifties* [Chicago and London: The University of Chicago Press, 1987.])

3. For the importance of dreams as a sign of imaginative vitality and an occasion for marital competition, see Plath's story "The Wishing Box," in *Johnny Panic and the Bible of Dreams and Other Prose Writings* (London: Faber and Faber Ltd., 1977), p. 54–61. The title story of that collection, "Johnny Panic and the Bible of Dreams," traces the narrator's increasing obsession with the dreams she is employed to record. Here religious devotion, the power of dreams, and the value of the imagination merge into an experience worshipped by the narrator. "Psyche-doctors" (p. 32) are perceived as the enemy who would rob the mind of its imaginative powers and reason for being. See, in this regard, Plath's description of her flight down the mountain while skiing in *The Bell Jar* (New York: Harper & Row, Publishers, 1971), p. 79.

4. The theatricalization of the self and its consequent conversion into a valuable commodity find mature expression in "Lady Lazarus." The rage that accompanies recognition of the commodification of the self informs the poem's tone as well as its ultimate threat of revenge: "Herr God, Herr Lucifer / Beware / Beware. / Out of the ash / I rise with my red hair / And I eat men like air."

5. The sadomasochistic dynamic of this scenario will be repeated throughout Plath's work. Michael Balint discusses the existential ramifications of the image of the aerialist and, beyond this, of flight itself. In *Thrills and Regressions* (London: The Hogarth Press and the Institute of Psycho-analysis, 1959), Balint explores what he calls "primitive attitudes" (p. 13) in adults, and posits two radically different types of personality orientations which he names (after the Greek) the "philobatic" and the "ocnophilic." Without embarking on a survey of Balint's argument, suffice it to say that "ocnophilia derives from the Greek, 'to cling to,' 'to shrink,' 'to hesitate,' 'to hang back.' Accordingly the ocnophilic world consists of objects, separated by horrid empty spaces. The ocnophil lives from object to object, cutting his sojourns in the empty spaces as short as possible. Fear is provoked by leaving the objects, and allayed by rejoining them," Balint, p. 32. For the *philobat*, "the whole world is different . . . the philobatic world consists of friendly expanses dotted more or less densely with dangerous and unpredictable objects. One lives in the friendly expanses, carefully avoiding hazardous contacts with potentially dangerous objects," p. 34. The consequences of these divergent, indeed polar-opposite, relations to reality for human personality are Balint's subject. In regard to Plath's images of the aerialist and poems associated with the freedom of flight, Balint's interpretation of

the relation between the philobatic and ocnophilic objects is especially pertinent. Balint writes:

> ... philobatism is symbolically related to erection and potency, although it is difficult to decide whether philobatism should be considered as an early, primitive stage of genitality or, the other way round, as a retrospective, secondary genitalisation in adult age of an originally non-genital function. In any case, this inter-relation explains the other aspect of the objects the philobat clings to, which we call ocnophilic objects. The whip of the lion-tamer, the pole of the tight-rope walker, the sticks of the skier, the baton of the conductor, the sword or rifle of the soldier, the artist's tools, the pilot's joy-stick, are undoubtedly symbols of the erect, potent penis. Having an ocnophilic object with us means also being in possession of a powerful never-flagging penis, magically reinforcing our own potency, our own confidence. (p. 29)

That Plath imagines her aerialist without the pole, which would serve a psychical as well as a physical purpose, in itself points to her sense of unmodified vulnerability. But of perhaps greater interest is Balint's physical symbolization of human conciousness's perceptions of the world. Balint suggests that "philobatic thrills represent in a way the primal scene in symbolic form. A powerful and highly skilled man produces on his own a powerful erection, lifting him far away from security, performing in his lofty state incredible feats of valour and daring, after which, in spite of untold dangers, he returns unhurt to the safe mother earth," Balint, p. 29–30. I find it significant that in Plath's reengenderment of that scene, the earth to which the female performer returns is inhabited by masculine threat and that the tightrope itself offers no empowering locus for erection but an occasion for anxieties associated with physical performance. Balint discusses, although he does not interrogate, the conventional gender associations of such performance. He writes, "It is traditional in the circus for the hero-acrobat while performing high up in the air to be assisted, admired, and finally received back to the ground by an attractive young girl. Acrobatics, therefore, are one special form of shows all of which symbolically represent the primal scene," p. 30. Using the schema of the fun fair's "primative shows of various kinds," Balint goes on to categorize types of display in terms of gender. "One type of showpiece is either beautiful, attractive women, or frightening, odd, and strange females; the other type is powerful, boasting, odd, and strange females; the other type is powerful, boasting, challenging men. Simplified to the bare essentials, practically all stage plays or novels, however highbrow, are still concerned with these three kinds of human ingredients," p. 30.

Instructive for readers of Plath is not Balint's concluding oversimplification, but rather the specific gender divisions that Plath in her scenario restructures at great risk as well as his more generalized observation of the far-ranging symbolic implications of physical performance and the body's position in space. Thus, "Fever 103°," a poem that describes an escape from the mediating risk-taking of "Aerialist," could be understood as Plath's bold attempt to break past the clinging or ocnophilic tendencies that have led to her being hooked and bruised so that she may achieve the freedom of expanse associated with the extreme opposite of human personality types, the philobat. Thus, Balint's metaphorization of spatial relationships can function as one guide to psychoanalytic interpretation of the use of distance, space, and time in literary analysis.

6. Lynda K. Bundtzen, *Plath's Incarnations: Woman and the Creative Process* (Ann Arbor: The University of Michigan Press, 1983), p. 40.

7. Sigmund Freud, "The Ego and the Id," in *The Standard Edition of the Complete Psychological Works of Sigmund Freud,* vol. XIX, ed. James Strachey (London: The Hogarth Press, 1961). The passage in which this phrase occurs is significant, as Jean Laplanche reminds us (see Laplanche's *Life and Death in Psychoanalysis* and my discussion of Laplanche's observations in the following note). What Laplanche and Wollheim fail to mention, however, is the paragraph immediately preceding this passage, wherein Freud emphasizes the dual identity of the particular status of "a person's own

body" as something that is both seen "like any other object, but to the *touch* [it] yields two kinds of sensations, one of which may be equivalent to an internal perception," p. 25. Freud notes that "pain, too, seems to play a part in the process, and the way in which we gain new knowledge of our organs during painful illnesses is perhaps a model of the way by which in general we arrive at the idea of our body," p. 25–26. Freud opens his next paragraph with the sentence "The ego is first and foremost a bodily ego; it is not merely a surface entity, but is itself the projection of a surface," p. 26. The kinesthetic experience of pain would, therefore, provide a new awareness of a hitherto unrecognized part of the ego, itself serving as a "model" and as a means for learning who we are. "The body in pain" (to invoke Elaine Scarry's phrase) might then be a self-knowing body, a possibility important for Plath.

8. Richard Wollheim, "The Bodily Ego," in *Philosophical Essays on Freud,* ed. Richard Wollheim and James Hopkins (Cambridge: Cambridge University Press, 1982), p. 124–38. The quotation appears on p. 136.

9. See Harold Bloom, "Freud's Concepts of Defense and Will," in *Agon* (New York: Oxford University Press, 1982), p. 119–24.

10. Hélène Cixous, for example, in "Le rire de la meduse" (*L'arc,* 1975); repr. *New French Feminisms: An Anthology,* ed. Elaine Marks and Isabelle de Courtivron (New York: Schocken Books, 1981), articulates writing the body as writing through the specificity of an engendered body, an activity Plath certainly performs. What distinguishes Plath's poetics from Cixous's, in my estimation, is that while writing through images that are distinctively corporeal, Plath does not connect this praxis with a revolutionary social project. But Cixous's and Plath's mutual placement of the site of images in the sexualized drama of bodily identification do resemble each other. Cixous and others argue for a communicative system beyond the male-identified system of signification. On this point, French feminists part company with Plath, who remains, even in the face of the deconstruction of her poetic language, thoroughly immersed within the tropological network many feminist theorists at times would reject. Plath's poems, experimental as they are, remain well within traditional notions of experimentation, nor would she choose to write in "white ink." One guesses that she would have preferred black or red (see p. 245–64).

11. Jean Laplanche's brief discussion of the bodily ego, as Freud used the term in *The Ego and the Id,* is especially useful for trying to understand Plath's images of cutaneous sensation and the importance of bodily "surface" in her work (particularly images of aggression where skin is caught by hooks: bruised, or abraded). Commenting upon Jacques Lacan's "attempt to fill in the gap left by Freud's notion of the ego through "his theory of the 'mirror stage,' " Laplanche reminds us that Freud had himself "focused on the situation of specular identification." Referring to Freud's sentence in *The Ego and the Id* that "the ego is first and foremost a body-ego; it is not merely a surface entity, but it is itself the projection of a surface," Laplanche elaborates upon Freud's observation, drawing the reader's attention to a note in the standard edition that received Freud's approval. Here is the note cited by Laplanche: "The ego is ultimately derived from bodily sensations, chiefly from those springing from the surface of the body. It may thus be regarded as a mental projection of the surface of the body, besides, as we have seen above, representing the superficies of the mental apparatus."

Laplanche elaborates upon this observation: "The perceptions which 'partake in the emergence of the ego and in its separation from the id' are, moreover, specified elsewhere: on the one hand, as the visual perception allowing an apprehension of the body as 'a separate object'; on the other hand, as tactile perceptions, the cutaneous surface having a quite particular role by virtue of the fact that the subject can explore his own body through it with another part of his body, the skin being perceived simultaneously from within and from without, and being able to be, so to speak, circumvented. The perception of pain, finally, is mentioned in this context as a last factor, and this will serve us as a pretext for recalling the constant presence, from the very beginning of Freud's thought, of a theory of *pain* that is remarkably precise and quite different from his conception of *unpleasure*. From the point of view of the processes at work, it is characterized above all by the phenomenon of a breaking of barriers: 'In cases where excessively large quantities [of energy] break through the screening contrivances. . . . Thus pain is a *breaking in* or *effraction* and presupposes the existence of a limit, and its function in the constitution of the ego is inconceivable unless the ego, in turn, is defined as a limited entity," p. 81–82. At the close of this paragraph, Laplanche adds the following: "Anxiety, in relation to the limits of the ego, is the precise metaphor of pain in its relation to the limits of the body."

In his subsequent discussion, Laplanche engages the question of the relation between the ego and the "surface," and in this discussion the question of metaphoricity, clearly a linguistic question, arises:

> Freud thus indicates clearly the two meshing derivations of the ego from the "surface": on the one hand, the ego is the surface of the psychical apparatus, gradually differentiated in and from that apparatus, a specialized organ continuous with it; on the other hand, it is the projection or metaphor of the body's surface, a metaphor in which the various perceptual systems have a role to play.

See Jean Laplanche, *Life and Death in Psychoanalysis,* trans. Jeffrey Mehlman (Baltimore: Johns Hopkins University Press, 1976), p. 81–83. At this point, we ourselves must disengage from Laplanche's speculations in order to underline not the ideational but the metaphoric processes. I would venture that it is possible to analogize from the projective or metaphoric relation between ego and body surface to a dynamic relation between the bodily ego and the literary activity of forming images.

12. Suzanne Juhasz, in *Naked and Fiery Forms: Modern American Poetry by Women, A New Tradition* (New York: Harper & Row, 1976), introduces the double bind for women poets but conceptualizes it rather differently than I do here. Juhasz writes:

> Plath is the woman poet of our century who sees the double bind inherent in trying to be both woman and poet with the coldest, most unredeeming clarity: her life and her art embody her attempts to find a solution. She never finds one. The conflict between her woman's body (object, all surfaces, illusion; or else inner space, fertility but also, in the end, illusion) and her poet's mind (vision, reality, and death). As a person who sees division, separation, with her very self, who is conscious of surfaces and interiors everywhere and of the gap between them, she sees the pulse of life as the movement towards disintegration; the stasis of death as the only integration. Her later poetry enacts symbolically the struggle between life and death that is occurring in her consciousness, in her life. Over a period of ten years, her art develops from a glittery poetry of surfaces, in which the poet, observing the external world, orders and controls it through the power of her language to dissect and reassemble, to a poetry of engagement and integration, in which the sole source of reality is her own conciousness, in which objects from the external world are meaningful only as they define that consciousness, in which the outside world has been pulled inside the mind. (p. 59)

I would agree with Juhasz that Plath experiences a conflict which she describes with a "cold and unredeeming clarity"; but my argument emphasizes not a split between woman's body and poet's mind but a conflict between Plath's desire, on the one hand, to draw upon the rhetorical powers of the Romantic imagination and, on the other, her rejection of the identifications that the Romantic tradition would assign her. Against

Juhasz's view of the development of Plath's art from a "glittery poetry of surfaces" to "a poetry of engagement and integration," I would trace the development as an exploration of the possibilities of controlling a rhetoric that is always in danger of turning against the self.

13. Julia Kristeva, "About Chinese Women," in *The Kristeva Reader,* ed. Toril Moi (New York: Columbia University Press, 1986), p. 156–57.

14. For a discussion of the competitive literary aspects of Plath's relationship with Ted Hughes, see Sandra Gilbert's essay, "In Yeats' House: The Death and Resurrection of Sylvia Plath," in *Critical Essays on Sylvia Plath,* ed. Linda W. Wagner (Boston: G. K. Hall & Co., 1984). In this essay, Gilbert addresses the question of poetic influences on Plath and how Plath develops an individuating self-definition in relation to both her male and female precursors.

15. See Bloom on Romantic love and poetic influence in *The Anxiety of Influence* (New York: Oxford University Press, 1973), p. 31.

16. See Julia Kristeva, "Stabat Mater," in *The Kristeva Reader* (1986) for an interpretation of the Catholic cult of the Virgin Mary in terms of the interworking of the erotic and cultural representations of the maternal.

17. See Geoffrey Hartman's discussion of the dream of the Arab passage in *Wordsworth's Poetry: 1787–1814* (New Haven and London: Yale University Press, 1964), p. 225–33. Hartman notes that the three main episodes of Book V are all "marked to an extraordinary degree by motifs of confrontation and engulfment," p. 227. The frame of the dream provides experiential consciousness with a kind of protection. Hartman observes: "The dangers of confrontation and engulfment occur only in the 'sacred' space of the dream: the poet himself stands firmly in nature and narrative. The special character of any dream not an hallucination is that it is separated from life by a cordon sanitaire of the dreamer's consciousness. This cordon, while it prevents total ursurpation, also prevents total integration, so that the dream might be called a *spot* of eternity," p. 227. The dream status thus offers protection from as well as access to threatening materials. This is the very boundary that is crossed by Plath, who, in its stead, describes an absence of boundaries and consequent inaccessibility of experiences outside the self.

18. Interpreting the images of wilderness and flood, Hartman remarks that "a striking feature of the dream is the doubling of (apocalyptic) terror . . .," p. 230. And he goes on to associate the "deluge," "a *wet* chaos (with) the trauma of birth or rebirth," p. 230.

19. Sandor Ferenczi, *Thalassa: A Theory of Genitality* (New York: W. W. Norton, 1968), p. 101.

20. See two earlier works especially pertinent to a feminist psychoanalytic reading of Plath: Lynda K. Bundtzen, *Plath's Incarnations: Woman and the Creative Process* (Ann Arbor: The University of Michigan Press, 1983), and Paula Bennett, *My Life A Loaded Gun: Female Creativity and Feminist Poetics* (Boston: Beacon Press, 1986), chap. 2, p. 95–164. I am indebted to these works for numerous individual insights and for their understanding of Plath's work in terms of feminist poetics.

21. Paula Bennett characterizes Plath's difficulties in both psychosexual and social terms:

Plath's dilemma was of course exacerbated enormously by the fact that her mother had delivered a double message. To satisfy what appear to have been Aurelia Plath's highly conflicted demands, Sylvia on the one hand had to be a good girl, committed to attachment; on the other, she also had to be a writer. The good girl image was supported by society; but the writer was not. . . . As Plath states specifically in her *Journals,* she was able to write seriously only when she stopped writing for her mother and started writing for herself. But in thus insisting on her autonomy, she was also cutting herself off from the safety mechanisms that allowed her to survive. There was, in effect, no way out for her, at least not in that time and place. (p. 281)

22. Bundtzen contextualizes Plath's ambivalence, viewing it as not exclusively the result of an individual pathology but representative of her gender. She argues that Plath's "habitual ambivalence, described by so many commentators as symptomatic of Plath's diseased mind, is inherent in feminine personality. . . . Similarly, the frequent 'boundary confusion and lack of sense of separateness from the world' in Plath's poems have been used by one critic as evidence for her schizophrenic perspective and relationship to the world, while Chodorow's analysis of the daughter's pre-oedipal relationship to her mother suggests that it is a typical characteristic of female psychology." The critic cited is Marjorie Perloff, in her essay "On the Road to Ariel: The Transitional Poetry of Sylvia Plath," in *Sylvia Plath: The Woman and the Work,* ed. Edward Butscher (New York: Dodd, Mead and Co., 1977), p. 51.

23. On biological fertility as a metaphor for literary creativity, Bundtzen writes,

As birth is a woman's special prerogative, so should it be a woman poet's special metaphor for her creativity, and in many of Plath's poems, the action is to take back a fertile body that was originally her own. In Plath's late work, the female body is the vehicle for imaginative transformation and release. She translated social and psychological constraints on women into physical and sexual terms, so that we come to understand not only what it may feel like to live in a woman's body, but also how this affects her inventive freedom and control of the world around her. This theme, too, may well be representative of contemporary women artists. (p. 41–42)

That Plath uses birth metaphorically is certainly true. What I find problematic, however, both in regard to the specific image of the maternal and the position of the female body in Plath's poems is that such an identification or imaginary bridge between the metaphorical and physical reinscribes woman's body and delimits its functions according to cultural codes. It is this very literalization of the body that, in my estimation, precipitates a turning away from language, a movement I trace in this chapter's final pages.

24. Bundtzen, writing of "Medusa," speaks more generally of the breast as it appears in Plath's work.

"The retaliating, devouring, and poisonous breast" is an apt description of the Medusa "Godball" in Plath's poem. There are, in fact, startling similarities in the ambivalence and projection (Melanie) Klein describes and Plath's feelings of persecution by the mother. The opening line of "Medusa"—"Off that landspit of stoney mouthplugs" suggests that the mother's Gorgon stare ("the horror that you saw and what I was you see") has turned the nipples into "stoney mouth-plugs" and made "connectedness to a benevolent and lovable outside force" impossible. (p. 98)

Bundtzen's use of Melanie Klein's work, both here and throughout her book, seems especially pertinent. Indeed, I would suggest that Kleinian psychology will play an increasingly important role in evaluating and analyzing issues associated with female creativity.

25. "Incommunicado," *Collected Poems,* no. 81, p. 100. In this poem, Plath envisions a world that closes itself off, that is aggressively silent. Hers is a marred, gnarled, troubled world that at once allegorizes Plath's experience as it excludes the very consciousness that imagines it into being. Such a perceived rejection is at the heart of the disfiguration which is this chapter's subject.

26. Susan Van Dyne, "More Terrible Than She Ever Was: The Manuscripts of Sylvia Plath's Bee Poems," in *Critical Essays on Sylvia Plath,* p. 154–70.

27. Van Dyne quotes from the first handwritten draft of "Wintering." She notes, "Enclosed material deleted by the poet during her revision of a particular draft." Van Dyne is working from manuscripts in the Sylvia Plath Collection of Smith College. See Van Dyne, p. 169.

28. Paul De Man, "Ludwig Binswanger and the Sublimation of the Self," in *Blindness and Insight* (New York: Oxford University Press, 1971), discusses Binswangerian *Verstiegenheit* in terms of poetic experience. He writes,

> The fragility of poetic transcendence, as compared with the relative safety of direct action, is represented by the anxieties associated with the feelings of height. The comings and goings of the wanderer or the seafarer are voluntary and controlled actions but the possibility of falling, which is forced upon the mountain climber by an outside force, exists only in vertical space. The same is true of experiences that are closely related to falling, such as dizziness or relapses. This is another way of saying that, in the experience of verticality, death is present in a more radical way than in the experiences of the active life. (p. 46)

The fragility described by De Man is a condition to which Plath's poems testify. Experiences associated with the vertical become crucial in the late poems, and this is an issue to which I shall return.

29. Harold Bloom, "Freud's Concepts of Defense and the Poetic Will," in *Agon.*

30. This is the poem from which Kristeva quotes when, in "About Chinese Women," she argues for Plath's desire to move beyond the articulations of speech into inchoate forms of expression. While I agree with Kristeva that Plath is disenchanted with the expressive possibilities of poetic language, I would not agree with her assertion that Plath ". . . took refuge in lights, rhythms, and sounds." Here, Kristeva sacrifices steady observation of Plath's work for polemics.

31. Several critics, most notably Lynda Bundtzen and Sandra Gilbert, have argued eloquently for Plath's final poems as a release from an earlier entrapment by prevailing, male-dominant identities. Bundtzen, for example, understands Plath's development as a poet to be intimately related to her voice's "deliverance from a passive female body through a process of incarnation." The "female body of imagination" Plath "invents and gives voice to" Bundtzen sees as "her particular contribution to the lyric impulse in poetry," p. 43. Gilbert envisions the poems as distinct from and escaping the victimization of their author: "Out of the wax house of *Mademoiselle,* out of the mausoleum of the woman's body, out of the plastic of the past, these poems fly, pure and new as babies. Fly, redeemed—even if their mother was not—into the cauldron of morning" ("A Fine, White Flying Myth: The Life/Work of Sylvia Plath," in *Shakespeare's Sisters* [Bloomington: Indiana University Press, 1979], p. 260). Paula Bennett and Margaret Uroff also emphasize the artistic triumph of the final poems. While not wanting to detract from the poems' achievement, I choose to emphasize the problematic self-questionings raised, in my interpretation, within the poems themselves.

8. "Of Woman Born"

1. In her essay "When We Dead Awaken: Writing as Re-Vision," Adrienne Rich comments on the predicament of patriarchal poetry in this "historical epoch": "To the eye of a feminist, the work of Western male poets now writing reveals a deep, fatalistic pessimism as to the possibilities of change, whether societal or personal, along with a familiar and threadbare use of women (and nature) as redemptive on the one hand, threatening on the other; . . . See "When We Dead Awaken: Writing as Re-Vision," in *On Lies, Secrets, and Silence: Selected Prose 1966–1978* (New York: W. W. Norton & Co., 1979), p. 49.

2. Of Rich's early work, Judith McDaniel notes, "To fill the role of poet, to win the approval of those whom she imitated, Rich had nearly crafted herself out of feeling." Judith McDaniel, "Reconstituting the World: The Poetry and Vision of Adrienne Rich," in *Reading Adrienne Rich: Reviews and Re-Visions, 1951–1981* (Ann Arbor: The University of Michigan Press, 1984), p. 4.

3. Albert Gelpi astutely isolates Rich's early concern with the possibilities and limitations of language: "As the ultimate challenge to her initial assumptions, Adrienne Rich raises the dreaded question for a poet: the very validity and efficacy of language. . . ." "As early as 'Like This Together,' " Gelpi notes, "in 1963 she was worrying that 'our words misunderstand us.' ' For a thorough and insightful reading of Rich's poetic development, see Gelpi, "Adrienne Rich: The Poetics of Change," in *American Poetry Since 1960: Some Critical Perspectives,* ed. Robert B. Shaw (Cheshire: Carcanet, 1973).

4. Virginia Woolf, *The Common Reader: First Series* (New York: A Harvest Book, Harcourt, Brace & World, Inc., 1953), p. 1.

5. For an insightful discussion of women readers' and writers' responses to Milton, specifically to *Paradise Lost,* see Sandra M. Gilbert, "Patriarchal Poetry and Women Readers: Reflections on Milton's Bogey," *PMLA,* vol. 93, no. 3 (May 1978), p. 368–82.

6. Rachel Blau DuPlessis, "The Critique of Consciousness and Myth in Levertov, Rich, and Rukeyser," in *Shakespeare's Sisters: Feminist Essays on Women Poets* (Bloomington and London: Indiana University Press, 1979), p. 295.

7. The poem is entitled "Power." For another treatment of Marie Curie's story within the context of an extended poetic discussion of women and creativity, see William Carlos Williams' *Paterson,* Book 4, II.

8. The phrase "mined with risks" appears in Rich's essay "Vesuvius at Home: The Power of Emily Dickinson," first published in *Parnassus: Poetry in Review* 5, no. 1 (Fall-Winter 1976), p. 57.

9. Susan Stanford Friedman traces the impact of "H. D." on *The Dream of a Common Language.* Friedman emphasizes the importance each poet associates with mother-daughter relationships. She tellingly addresses not only the specific grounds for comparison but also the character of Rich's understanding of influence relations among women. "Rich's stance toward women writers is distinctly compassionate and noncompetitive. It embodies a feminist theory of reading in which the underlying receptivity inevitable in any literary influence overlaps with her desire to build a tangible women's culture," Cooper, p. 172. One might contrast this stance with Rich's initial overdependence upon male modernists and her subsequent break with them.

10. Adrienne Rich, "Splittings," in *The Dream of a Common Language: Poems 1974–1977* (New York: W. W. Norton & Co., 1978), p. 11.

11. Adrienne Rich, "Women and Honor: Some Notes on Lying," in *On Lies, Secrets, and Silence: Selected Prose 1966–1978* (New York: W. W. Norton & Co., Inc., 1979), p. 190.

12. "Women and Honor," p. 191.

13. Consider, for example, the echoes of Robert Lowell's *Notebook: 1967–68* in Rich's *Twenty-One Love Poems.* I would suggest that here Rich draws freely upon Lowell's tone, his form, and the recounting of the dailiness of his life because she claims for herself an alternative centrality in the poetic tradition.

14. See Rich's "When We Dead Awaken: Writing as Re-Vision," in *On Lies, Secrets, and Silence,* p. 35.

15. Rich, "Power and Danger: Works of a Common Woman (1977)," in *On Lies, Secrets, and Silence,* p. 248.

16. See Elizabeth Barrett Browning, *Aurora Leigh, The Poetical Works of Elizabeth Barrett Browning* (Boston: Houghton Mifflin Co., 1974), Book II, 1.106.

17. "Cartographies of Silence," *The Dream of a Common Language,* p. 17.

18. "Cartographies of Silence," p. 18.

19. See Rich, "Shooting Script," sections 1, 8, 13, and 14; repr. Barbara Charlesworth

Gelpi and Albert Gelpi, *Adrienne Rich's Poetry* (New York: W. W. Norton and Company, Inc., 1975), p. 54–57.

20. "Cartographies of Silence," p. 20.

21. "Natural Resources," p. 60. The following two quotations are also from this poem.

22. Although in her discussion of literary influences ("When We Dead Awaken: Writing as Re-Vision," p. 39), Rich does not mention Whitman, he clearly has had an impact on her work. Rich's "The Corpse-Plant" (*Necessities of Life* [W. W. Norton & Co., 1966]) quotes Whitman in its headnote: "How can an obedient man, or a sick man, dare to write poems?" Both the tenor and scope of her recent work remind one of the Whitmanian assertion of an expansive intimacy. The passage cited here is the closing verse paragraph of the 1855 version of "The Sleepers."

23. "Natural Resources," p. 66.

24. Robert Frost's "Directive," with its language of domesticity and spiritual search for origins, may be the poem Rich is addressing, if only indirectly, in "Toward the Solstice." To assess just how far Rich has come from her first volume of poems, one need only compare her self-conscious echoing of Frost, Auden, and other male poets in the earlier work and her dialectical appropriation of the voices of past poets, both male and female, in her most recent work. (For analyses of this progress in Rich's poetry, the development of a clearly delineated feminist stance, see Albert Gelpi's essay "Adrienne Rich: The Poetics of Change" and Wendy Martin, "From Patriarchy to the Female Principle: A Chronological Reading of Adrienne Rich's Poems," in *Adrienne Rich's Poetry*, pp. 130–48, 175–89.

25. "Transcendental Etude," p. 74.

26. "Transcendental Etude," p. 75.

27. "Transcendental Etude," p. 76.

28. For a discussion of Rich's poetry in relation to Emerson, see Gertrude Reif Hughes, "Imagining the Existence of Something Uncreated: Elements of Emerson in Adrienne Rich's *The Dream of a Common Language*," in *Reading Adrienne Rich: Reviews and Re-Visions, 1951–1981*, ed. Jane Roberta Cooper (Ann Arbor: The University of Michigan Press, 1984). Hughes notes, "From beginning to end, *The Dream of a Common Language* recalls Emersonian visions and rhapsodies, because it affirms energies that are potentially limitless (or at least are still to be imagined). At the same time, these poems confirm the misnaming, miscues, and misunderstanding that beset women's energies, impeding women's access to them. Having begun the volume with three poems in which she rechannels those Emersonian ideas of power that are especially congenial to her, Rich ends it with a poem she calls 'Transcendental Etude,' as though to invite comparison with the Emersonian tradition," p. 155.

29. "Transcendental Etude," p. 77.

30. This intersection of the physical and political had long interested Rich. See, for example, "The Blue Ghazals," 4 May 1969: "*The moment when a feeling enters the body* / is political. This touch is political." *The Will to Change: Poems 1968–1970* (New York: W. W. Norton & Co., 1971), p. 24.

31. In *An American Triptych: Anne Bradstreet, Emily Dickinson, Adrienne Rich*, Wendy Martin contextualizes Rich's poetry within a tradition of women poets. She writes, "Finally, Rich has written poetry that suggests alternatives to the city on a hill, the virgin land, and the machine in the garden, metaphors that have been used by writers and literary historians to describe the American experience. As a writer, as an activist, Rich had tried to bring a nurturing ethos to the larger society . . . Adrienne Rich has tried to envision a society in which all women can be at home." *An American Triptych: Anne Bradstreet, Emily Dickinson, Adrienne Rich* (Chapel Hill: The University of North Carolina Press, 1984), p. 234.

32. Helen Vendler's comment on Rich's style acquires renewed importance given the frequent critical objections to the sparse use of figuration in her work. Although writing specifically of *The Will to Change* (1971), Vendler's characterization applies with equal force to Rich's latest work. Vendler writes,

I pause only to say that Rich's "music," so praised by her earlier reviewers and so ignored by most of her later ones, seems to me to reach its height of accomplishment in lines like these, as "hulls," "dull," "crust," "sunk," and "drudge" play one note while "margin" and "barges" play another, both soon to be reinforced by "gulls" and "rubbish" for the first, and "dark" and "harsh" for the second. The unobtrusiveness of these choices, choices perceived as such only when we ask why the lines adhere so to each other, is worth all the prettiness sacrificed in favor of their reticence.

Helen Vendler, "Ghostlier Demarcations, Keener Sounds," in *Parnassus* 2, no. 1 (Fall 1973); repr. *Modern Critical Views: Contemporary Poets,* ed. Harold Bloom (New York: Chelsea House Publishers, 1986). That reticence has come to include an increased use of the conversational and the illusion of transcribing speech. The music, however, continues, in its more reticent forms, unstilled.

INDEX

JOANNE FEIT DIEHL is Henry Hill Pierce Professor of English at Bowdoin College. She is the author of *Dickinson and the Romantic Imagination.*